D1555364

Hemingway and French Writers

For Carlos and Laurel:

Hemingway

and

French Writers

*In remembrance of bulls,
icebergs, and the rising
sun. All best,*

BEN STOLTZFUS

Ben

The Kent State University Press · Kent, Ohio

© 2010 by Ben Stoltzfus
ALL RIGHTS RESERVED
Library of Congress Catalog Card Number 2009026377
ISBN 978-1-60635-039-3
Manufactured in the United States of America

LIBRARY OF CONGRESS CATALOGING-IN-PUBLICATION DATA
Stoltzfus, Ben, 1927–
Hemingway and French writers / Ben Stoltzfus.
     p.   cm.
Includes bibliographical references and index.
ISBN 978-1-60635-039-3 (alk. paper) ∞
1. Hemingway, Ernest, 1899–1961—Friends and associates.
2. Hemingway, Ernest, 1899–1961—Criticism and interpretation.
3. Hemingway, Ernest, 1899–1961—Friends and associates.
4. American literature—French influences.
I. Title.
PS3515 E37Z8823 2009
813'.52—dc22
2009026377

British Library Cataloging-in-Publication data are available.

13 12 11 10 09   5 4 3 2 1

FOR

Judith

Contents

The greatest literary development in France between 1929
and 1939 was the discovery of Faulkner, Dos Passos,
Hemingway, Caldwell, and Steinbeck.
—JEAN-PAUL SARTRE, "American Novelists"

I always try to write on the principle of the iceberg.
There is seven-eighths of it underwater for every part that shows.
—ERNEST HEMINGWAY, *Death in the Afternoon*

Acknowledgments

I am grateful to Susan Beegel, Carl Eby, Raymond Gay-Crosier, Judd Hubert, Erik Nakjavani, Robert Lewis, and Francesca Rochberg for reading portions of the manuscript and for their wise counsel and professional advice. A special thank you goes to Janet Moores for expediting interlibrary loans.

I am also grateful to the following persons at Kent State University Press for all their help: Joyce Harrison, acquiring editor; Joanna Hildebrand Craig, former editor-in-chief; Will Underwood, director; Mary Young, managing editor; Susan L. Cash, marketing manager; Christine Brooks, design and production manager; and Darryl Crosby, assistant design and production manager.

This project has been supported by ongoing grants from the University of California.

I thank Clara Dean and Jerry Dean for their computer skills and their dedication to correcting negligent spelling and typographical errors.

Judith's encouragement is always welcome.

All translations from French into English are mine, except as noted.

We are grateful for permission to reproduce copyright material in modified form from the following sources: the State University of New York Press, *Comparative Literature Studies, North Dakota Quarterly,* and the *Hemingway Review.*

"Ernest Hemingway: *The Sun Also Rises.*" Revised by permission from *Lacan and Literature: Purloined Pretexts* by Ben Stoltzfus, the State University of New York Press. © 1996 State University of New York. All Rights Reserved. "Hemingway, Malraux, and Spain: *For Whom the Bell Tolls* and *L'espoir,*" *Comparative Literature Studies* 36 (1999): 179–94 and "Sartre, Nada, and Hemingway's African Stories," *Comparative Literature*

Studies 42 (2005): 205–28. "Political Commitment in Hemingway and Sartre," *North Dakota Quarterly* 68 (2001): 182–88 and "Hemingway and French Literature: The Paris Years, 1896–1928," *North Dakota Quarterly* 73 (2006): 135–55. "The Stones of Venice, Time, and Remembrance: Calculus and Proust in *Across the River and into the Trees,*" *Hemingway Review* 22 (2003): 19–29.

Introduction

Paris was where the 20th century was.
—Gertrude Stein, *Paris France*

I defy you to wear another hat than the hat of Paris.
—Victor Hugo, quoted in Casanova's
The World Republic of Letters

*I*n the world of letters there exists an international literary space that is relatively independent of the economic and political divisions of the world around it. This "field," to use Pierre Bourdieu's term, posits that world literature is defined by literatures at the "center" that dominate those at the margins. In her book *The World Republic of Letters,* Pascale Casanova demonstrates how, despite this domination, great writers everywhere have detached themselves from historical and geographical forces in order to invent a new literary freedom. Works and authors can thus be situated in relation to each other on the basis of what she calls a "world literary space" (xii). Thus, writers from the periphery can accede to the center if their work rises to the challenge and meets the expectations that are at work in the field.

The historian Fernand Braudel also emphasizes the relative independence of artistic space in relation to political and economic space. He notes that in the eighteenth century, London was the center of the world economy, but that Paris was able to impose its cultural hegemony. Furthermore, says Braudel, France in the late nineteenth and twentieth centuries, although lagging behind the rest of Europe economically, was the acknowledged center of Western painting and literature (68).

xiii

Historically speaking, it was at the beginning of the Renaissance in Italy (Dante, Boccacio, Petrarch), in Spain (Cervantes), in France (Rabelais, Montaigne, and beyond), and in England (Shakespeare and beyond), not to mention the literary heritage of Greece and Rome, that the laws of literature were invented and codified. Due to their age, these "old" literary fields have become autonomous and, by devoting themselves exclusively to literature, as opposed to politics or economics, they feel no need to justify themselves beyond the pursuit of artistic excellence. Accordingly, they possess volume, prestige, and capital, and this freedom gives them an autonomy from national or economic pressures. This is what constitutes international literary space (Casanova 85–86).

Paul Valéry once noted that the older a nation's literature is and the more numerous its canonical texts, the greater is its literary capital. The age of a national literature and its many classics define its wealth ("La liberté" 1081). A "classic" confers legitimacy, and this legitimacy then becomes the coin of the realm. A classic is a work that rises above the competition, and it also escapes from the vagaries of taste and time. It becomes ageless and is declared to be immortal. A classic thus assumes literary legitimacy and is declared to be timeless and invaluable, therefore, *Literature*.

The oldest literary spaces are thus the most endowed, and they exert enormous influence. Because of these pressures, every modern work will inevitably become dated unless it can free itself from the fluctuations of taste and critical opinion. If it rises above the competition and survives the test of time, it too will become a classic. Casanova emphasizes that "*it is necessary to be old in order to have any chance of being modern or of decreeing what is modern*" (89). Having a long national past is the sine qua non for claiming a literary existence in the present. Gertrude Stein was perhaps referring to this ageless modernism when she stated that Hemingway smelled of museums (*Autobiography* 216). While living in Paris, he was not only haunting the museums; he was also reading every classic he could lay his hands on.

In France, the age of its literature, the number of its classics, and the accumulated literary capital were so great that the land of Napoleon exerted dominion over all of Europe, from the eighteenth century to at least 1960 (Hemingway died in 1961). The decolonization that occurred after World War II accelerated the phenomenon of Francophone literature, that is, works written in French by writers from France's former

colonies, thereby shifting interest, even though Paris remains the publishing powerhouse, from the center to the periphery. But before 1960,
the concentration of literary capital in Paris had established it not only in
France but throughout the world as the capital of a republic without bor-
ders or boundaries. Paris became the center of the literary world because
it possessed an exceptional concentration of resources that had been
accumulating over the course of centuries. As a result, the city of light
shone with the greatest literary luminance on earth (Casanova 23–24).

Paris became the intellectual capital of the world, the arbiter of good
taste, and the ongoing source of political democracy. It embodied historical conceptions of freedom: it symbolized the Revolution of 1879, the
overthrow of the monarchy, and the proclamation of the rights of man,
thus projecting an image of tolerance toward foreigners. Paris became
an asylum for political and intellectual refugees. It was an idealized city
where freedom reigned supreme; it was the center not only of the arts,
but also of fashion and luxurious living. Because Paris had become a
universal city, it had the power to confer recognition—a recognition
that affected the course of literary history (Casanova 29). James Joyce,
among others, settled and published in Paris because there he felt free
to experiment and write without censure or constraint from Ireland, its
morals, or its nationalist tradition. Samuel Beckett did likewise, as did
many other writers, including Hemingway, Gertrude Stein, and Edith
Wharton. They all wanted literary freedom and cultural liberalism. As a
result, Paris became *the* center of artistic internationalism.

Today, London and New York vie with Paris for recognition as the publication centers of the world, and it is this magnetism that attracts writers from the periphery. Eugene Ionesco, a Romanian, moved to Paris and
wrote in French in order to assert his legitimacy. Joseph Conrad, of Polish
origin and born in Ukraine, chose to write in English. T. S. Eliot, an American, like Henry James, also moved to London in order to write, as did V. S.
Naipaul, who was born in Trinidad, in the British West Indies, but moved
to England in order to become a writer. Both Eliot and Naipaul won the
Nobel Prize in literature, the highest form of consecration in international
literary space.

Léopold Sédar Senghor, although born in Senegal, studied in Paris and
wrote in French. Aimé Césaire and Edouard Glissant were born in Martin-
ique, studied in Paris, and wrote in French. We thus have the phenomenon

of writers from the periphery adopting French or English in order to claim a place in the field, and writers from the periphery who may not be French or English but are born into one of the dominant languages. There is also Vladimir Nabokov, who first wrote in Russian, then French, and finally in English. His novel *Lolita* was an international blockbuster.

Hemingway fits this pattern: a novice writer from the literary backwater of America moves to Paris; learns how to write; is consecrated by the highest authorities; and, in time, also becomes a Nobel laureate. Consecration in Paris was indispensable for writers from dominated spaces and, at the beginning of the twentieth century, America was still, literarily speaking, compared to France and England, a dominated country. Although America had Walt Whitman, Ralph Waldo Emerson, Henry Thoreau, Herman Melville, Edgar Allan Poe, and Mark Twain, it was a relative newcomer to literary space. To escape America and achieve literary salvation, Henry James chose English nationality. He made the gap between America and Europe the subject of much of his work while noting the literary destitution of America at the end of the nineteenth century. Says Casanova:

> The United States in the 1920s was literarily a dominated country that looked to Paris in order to try to accumulate resources it lacked. Any analysis that fails to take into account the world literary structure of the period and of the place occupied in this structure by Paris and the United States, respectively, will be incapable of explaining Stein's permanent concern to develop a modern American national literature (through the creation of an avant-garde) and her interest in both American history and the literary representation of the American people (of which her gigantic enterprise *The Making of Americans* is no doubt the most outstanding proof). (42)

It was in Paris that Hemingway acquired literary legitimacy in the international arena. Such legitimacy transcends linguistic boundaries and national claims to texts. By appropriating the literary assets of Europe, particularly those of France and Russia, Hemingway succeeded in establishing a transatlantic patrimony. He was accepted, and his works were reviewed, translated, and discussed. In due course, his success as a newcomer to literary space and time allowed him to break into the ranks of the established moderns and earn for himself the right to participate in defining what is modern.

The concept of modernity is frequently and emphatically invoked by writers claiming to embody literary innovation. Charles Baudelaire in the mid-nineteenth century formulated the necessity of being up to date, and Arthur Rimbaud insisted on being modern, even shocking. One hundred years later, Jean-Paul Sartre founded his influential review, *Les Temps Modernes.*

In Paris, Hemingway prepared himself for the challenge of being modern by borrowing books from Sylvia Beach's bookstore, Shakespeare and Company, and reading copiously: Stendhal, Flaubert, Maupassant, Zola, Chekhov, Turgenev, and Tolstoy, among others. But he valued only what he himself could use artistically. He praised *Madame Bovary* but dismissed *L'éducation sentimentale* (*Sentimental Education*). He admired Stendhal's descriptions of the Waterloo battle scenes in *Le rouge et le noir* (*The Red and the Black*) but dismissed most of *La chartreuse de Parme* (*The Charterhouse of Parma*). Of Maupassant he liked *La maison Tellier* (*The House Tellier*) but says little about his other works. Hemingway frequently did figurative battle in the boxing ring of fame with Flaubert, Maupassant, Stendhal, Dostoevsky, Turgenev, and Tolstoy, usually besting them in three rounds, at least in his opinion. He considered Honoré de Balzac a "professional writer," but he did not like Emile Zola, despite the extraordinary influence the father of naturalism has had on writers in underdeveloped countries, that is, those on the margins of literary space.

Paris attracted writers, painters, and musicians, all of whom came in order to gain knowledge and the technical expertise of modernity. Some of them returned to their homelands and rejuvenated their own literatures through the innovations they brought back with them. Having made his reputation at the center of the literary world, Hemingway returned to America and settled in Key West, Florida. His innovations in style helped to accelerate modernity not only in America but throughout the world.

When Hemingway said that "all modern American literature comes from one book by Mark Twain called *Huckleberry Finn*. . . . There was nothing before. There has been nothing as good since" (*Green Hills* 22), he was dismissing all the other nineteenth-century American writers but, nevertheless, making the point that *Huckleberry Finn* introduced a distinctive American oral language, a conversational quality that Hemingway went on to master in his own use of dialogue. He combined Twain's "Americanness," Flaubert's proleptic images, Maupassant's and Chekhov's craft of the short story, Gertrude Stein's aural repetitions, and cablese (a journalist's omission of unnecessary words in a cable to his editor) into a distinctive style noted for its compression, omission, and deceptive simplicity, all of which managed to connote "the dignity of movement of an ice-berg" whose seven-eighths is below the surface and therefore invisible (*Death* 192).

In the *ABC of Reading,* Ezra Pound refers to the power and authority that are granted to a writer when his or her work is recognized. Once someone has gained acceptance by the establishment, he or she acquires value and then, says Pound, credit is conferred (25). Credit is what Valery Larbaud—a writer and acquaintance of Hemingway's in Paris—called "spiritual gold" ("l'or spirituel," in "Paris de France" 15). This spiritual gold shines through *The Sun Also Rises,* the novel in which the word "value" is repeated many times in comic and parodic contexts, and almost everybody, except Robert Cohn, knows the values—be they monetary, oenological, social, amorous, or taurine—particularly Count Mippipopolous, who says that "you must get to know the values" (60). Hemingway is poking fun at wimps, stuffed dogs, and pretentious people, but he is dead serious when it comes to the value of good writing and the credit a writer can accumulate when he is recognized and accepted in the literary marketplace, that is, the literary space where the highest value is placed on excellence.

When Ernest and Hadley Hemingway settled in Paris in 1922, there was already a great interest in American letters, a predisposition that would be of inestimable value to Hemingway's career. His first short story to appear in French was "L'invincible" ("The Undefeated"), published in March 1926 in Adrienne Monnier's *Le Navire d'Argent,* along with translations of Whitman, William Carlos Williams, Robert McAlmon, and E. E. Cummings. *in our time* had already been published in English (1924), but the French took no notice of it, nor did they pay much attention to *The Torrents of Spring,* which was published in May 1926, or, for that matter, *The Sun Also Rises,* published in October of the same year. But all that was about to change. Hemingway had the good fortune and the talent to tap into the French interest in American letters, and interest in his fiction grew exponentially as his short stories and novels were translated, published, and reviewed. For an examination of Hemingway's reception in France, I recommend *Ernest Hemingway in France, 1926–1994: A Comprehensive Bibliography* by Geneviève Hily-Mane.[1]

After the publication of *in our time* and the translation into French of several short stories, Paris decided to consecrate Hemingway. Greater consecration was to follow, but for the moment, at the early stages of his career, this was an important beginning. Translation into another language is essential for international recognition and accession to literary space. After *As I Lay Dying* was translated into French by Maurice Coindreau, one of Faulkner's and Hemingway's preeminent translators, Faulkner was hailed as an important writer, first in Paris, and later in the United States. Hemingway passed through the same stages of translation and acceptance. "Translation," says Casanova, "is the major prize and weapon in international literary competition" (133), because translation, like criticism, establishes value and provides enrichment. Critics, like translators, contribute to the growth of the literary heritage and the expansion of literary space. Paris had the power (still does) to confer recognition and to consecrate emerging writers and that is what happened to Hemingway.

In August 1927, *La Nouvelle Revue Française* published "Cinquante mille dollars" ("Fifty Grand"), and as Max I. Baym notes, this journal played an important role in promoting American writers after World War I (135). In 1928, Gallimard published a collection of Hemingway's stories under the collective title *Cinquante mille dollars* (*Fifty Grand*), and it immediately attracted the attention of many critics who praised its overall excellence. In March 1928, Bernard Faÿ reviewed *Men without Women* in the *Revue Européenne,* saying that Hemingway was the best writer of his generation (Asselineau, "French Reactions" 43). Régis Michaud, in his *Panorama de la littérature américaine contemporaine,* reviewed both *The Sun Also Rises* and *Men without Women,* praising Hemingway's "verbal stenography" (254–55).

In 1932, Hemingway's celebrity in France took a quantum leap when Gallimard published *L'adieu aux armes,* Maurice Coindreau's translation of *A Farewell to Arms* (1929). Coindreau was teaching French at Princeton and he was a gifted translator. Drieu La Rochelle's foreword, in which he compared Hemingway to Maupassant (10), and Denis Marion's review in *La Nouvelle Revue Française* (1933), both praising Hemingway's artistry, also helped. In 1933, Gallimard published *Le soleil se lève aussi,* Coindreau's translation of *The Sun Also Rises,* this time with a foreword by Jean Prévost, in which he compared Hemingway to Stendhal (9). Hemingway now had three books in French translation. In 1933, Philippe Soupault, the surrealist poet, reviewed them all in *Europe,* praising their warmth, naturalness, humanity, and refined art (Asselineau, "French Reactions" 44–46).

In the April and August 1933 issues of the *Revue Anglo-Américaine,* Charles Cestre wrote favorable reviews of *In Our Time* and *The Torrents of Spring,* and in the April–June 1938 issue of *Etudes anglaises,* Jean-Jacques Mayoux praised Scribner's 1937 publication of *To Have and Have Not,* which Marcel Duhamel eventually translated and Gallimard published in 1945 as *En avoir ou pas.* Coindreau's earlier enthusiasm for Hemingway had been waning, and he panned the novel in a 1938 review in *La Nouvelle Revue Française.* The year before, in 1937, Gallimard published *Les vertes collines d'Afrique,* Jeanine Delpech's translation of *Green Hills of Africa* (1935), but the reviews were lukewarm. In 1938, Gallimard published *Mort dans l'après-midi,* René Daumal's excellent translation of *Death in the Afternoon* (1932), but it too was received with general indifference, as was *Dix indiens* (1946), Marcel Duhamel's translation of *Ten Indians and Eleven Other Short Stories.* In June 1946, Duhamel also translated "A Clean, Well-Lighted Place," which was published as "Propre et bien éclairé" in *Solstice.* In the February–March 1949 issue of *Carrefour,* Duhamel translated "The Short Happy Life of Francis Macomber" ("L'heure triomphale de Francis Macomber").

This is a cursory overview of Hemingway's emergence as a writer of note and the reception of his work. Despite some diminishing enthusiasm among the critics, he was attracting a great deal of attention. In 1946, his reputation was greatly enhanced by an essay that Jean-Paul Sartre published in the *Atlantic Monthly,* in which he said that "the greatest literary development in France between 1929 and 1939 was the discovery of Faulkner, Dos Passos, Hemingway, Caldwell, and Steinbeck. . . . At once, for thousands of young intellectuals the American novel took its place together with jazz and the movies, among the best of the importations from the United States" ("American Novelists" 117).

The author of *La nausée* (1938; *Nausea,* 1964) had been reading Hemingway in the 1930s, and he admired what Claude-Edmonde Magny, in *L'âge du roman américain* (see 44–61), calls "the objective technique in the American novel" ("la technique objective dans le roman américain").[2]

Sartre believed that psychological analysis, the hallmark of the French style from Madame de LaFayette to Marcel Proust, could no longer mirror the complexities of the new era or the sense of the absurd generated by the events of World War II. In their book *Transatlantic Migration: The Contemporary American Novel in France*, Thelma M. Smith and Ward L. Miner state that in the wake of the American influence, "it was much more important to express the social interactions rather than indulge in psychological analyses" (41). Smith and Miner chronicle the reception of the American novel in France both before and after World War II, and they detail the reactions of French critics and readers to the so-called objectivity of *le style américain*. Hemingway, in particular, was to have an immense impact on French writers. His use of dialogue, short declarative sentences, and an emphasis on action, instead of inner monologue, appealed to Sartre and Albert Camus, both of whom wanted to express new sensibilities in keeping with the accelerated rhythms of the machine age. In *La force de l'âge* (1960; *The Prime of Life*, 1962), Simone de Beauvoir writes that a great many of the rules that she and Sartre observed in their novels were inspired by Hemingway (145).

In less than twenty years Hemingway had gone from obscurity to celebrity. He had traveled from the periphery of literary space to the center, and there, once consecrated, he was in a position to define by example what would become modern. This is what Casanova calls *littérisation*, that is, the operation by which works from a literarily deprived country come to be regarded by the legitimate authorities as literary (136). As the guru of French existentialism after World War II, Sartre's immense celebrity gave him the power to consecrate and define literary taste, and Hemingway was the beneficiary.

In addition to stylistic changes and an emphasis on social interactions, Hemingway's work, from the beginning, was imbued with a deep sense of loss and the absurd. When Gertrude Stein referred to the author of *The Sun Also Rises* as a member of the "lost generation," she was already alluding to the alienation in these authors' lives and in their works[3]—an alienation that Sartre strove to overcome in his literature of commitment and that Camus defined so eloquently in *L'étranger* (1942; *The Stranger*, 1946) and *Le mythe de Sisyphe* (1942; *The Myth of Sisyphus*, 1955). Coming to grips with the secular implications of death and the absurd is the essential theme in all their works. Jean Bruneau, in "Existentialism and the American Novel," was among the first to point out that existentialism was a French literary movement on which the American novel exercised a strong and acknowledged influence. There was an artistic reciprocity at work, with Hemingway learning the craft of writing from masters both living and dead, and then, having mastered his craft, transferring it to a generation of new writers who would, in turn, hail him as the master of modernity.

In his *Atlantic* essay, Sartre pointed out that Camus' *L'étranger* was influenced by Hemingway's objective style. Indeed, part 1 of Camus' novel shows all the earmarks of the Hemingway technique: short declarative sentences, action, and the absence of introspection. In part 2 of *L'étranger,* after the death of the Arab and Meursault's incarceration, the tone changes and the objective style becomes introspective. Meursault is facing a death sentence, and as he contemplates his human condition and the meaning of life, his thoughts become philosophical. Hemingway's style has changed. What has happened?

Camus believed that *le style américain* was one dimensional because action describes only the outside of consciousness, whereas to capture thought we need to reproduce a character's inner life. In an interview with Jean Desternes in *Combat* about the influence of American novelists, Camus said that this objective style was an easy style. He called it a *technique de facilité:* "The novel, then, ignores all that which up to now has been considered the proper subject-matter of literature, that is to say, broadly speaking, man's inner life. Man is described but is never explained or interpreted. The result is that one can write a novel simply by drawing upon his memory or upon direct observation" (qtd. and trans. by Coindreau, "William Faulkner" 86). At his worst, said Camus, such a novelist is no better than a reporter and such fiction is no more than journalism. It may be a first-rate document, but it has no relation to art.

In a 1947 interview with Jean Desternes in *Combat,* Camus called Hemingway's novel *Pour qui sonne le glas* (1950; *For Whom the Bell Tolls,* 1940) the work of a child compared with André Malraux's *L'espoir* (1937) (2). It is obvious that Camus misunderstood Hemingway's iceberg technique of writing—the technique that Hemingway defines in *Death in the Afternoon* (192). There is Camus, perched on the iceberg, contemplating the flat sea, but had he dived below the surface, he would have discovered the stylistic complexity of the invisible seven-eighths. He thought Hemingway's writing was simplistic because stream of consciousness was missing, whereas in fact Hemingway has infused this consciousness into the narrative descriptions and the action. His proleptic images and time shifts, as in Flaubert's and Proust's fiction, form a network of recurring tropes whose submerged meaning, like the iceberg, is invisible even as it supports the visible portion. The reader must provide the meaning that seems to be absent, and the role of the reader, as we will see in the chapters that follow, becomes all important. In due course Camus adapted the "simplistic" surface of Hemingway's writing to part 1 of *L'étranger,* because in part 1 Meursault is all surface, a man without depth who is leading an absurd existence. For him, conscious life begins only after he is condemned to death, and like Blaise Pascal's "thinking reed," he comes to understand what it means to be a sentient being. Camus is thus an interesting example of an author who misunderstood Hemingway's fiction yet managed to adapt it to his own ends and do so brilliantly.

Over the years, on both sides of the Atlantic, despite the literary dominance of Paris, American and French novelists were enriching each other's works with new styles and new techniques that have been digested, adapted, and transformed. Faulkner's time dislocations would presumably be different if he had not read Proust; the social consciousness of Dos Passos's *USA* trilogy was profoundly influenced by Balzac and Zola, and its form by Guillaume Apollinaire and cubism; a certain epic quality of Jean Giono's *Le chant du monde (The Song of the World)* owes much to *Moby-Dick;* Simone de Beauvoir's *Le sang des autres (The Blood of Others)* reveals her indebtedness to Faulkner; Jean-Paul Sartre's *Le sursis (The Reprieve)* is a deliberate imitation of Dos Passos's "simultaneity," which he in turn absorbed from Jules Romains and Apollinaire. Sartre described these influences in his 1946 essay in the *Atlantic Monthly.* However, it is Félix Ansermoz-Dubois' *L'interprétation française de la littérature américaine d'entre-deux-guerres* (1944), Magny's *L'âge du roman américain* (1948), and Thelma M. Smith and Ward L. Miner's *Transatlantic Migration: The Contemporary American Novel in France* (1955), all three milestone studies in the art of refraction and convergence, that have given impetus to the many comparative essays, articles, and books that have been written and published since then.

Despite the enormous prestige of France's literary space, the French have always been interested in America and its writers. Literary crossbreeding, more specifically the French-American brand of Harry Levin's "transatlantic refraction,"[4] can be traced to Charles Baudelaire's admiration for Edgar Allan Poe and beyond. It was the conviction of Ezra Pound—the Pound who was to take Ernest Hemingway under his wing in Paris in the 1920s—that between 1830 and 1910 virtually all technical growth in the art of writing had taken place in France (Kenner 54). While Pound was emphasizing his indebtedness to Stendhal, Gustave Flaubert, Jules Laforgue, Arthur Rimbaud, and Tristan Corbière, the works of Ralph Waldo Emerson, Henry David Thoreau, Herman Melville, and Nathaniel Hawthorne were being discussed and written about in French intellectual circles.

While French intellectuals were discussing American authors, Henry James was writing essays on Honoré de Balzac, Flaubert, Guy de Maupassant, and Emile Zola. Various critics were stressing Baudelaire's, Stéphane Mallarmé's, and Paul Valéry's attraction to Poe, and they would canonize him by placing a diaeresis over his name: *Poë, poète, poésie* (Levin 214). Indeed, the musicality of Poe's "poetic principle" has shaped the aesthetics of all French symbolist poets: "Music before everything" ("De la musique avant toute chose," 513), said Paul Verlaine in his "Art Poétique" (1882). Poe's life was legendary, and the Parisian setting for his mysteries (a fictional rue Morgue where crimes would be solved by Monsieur C. Auguste Dupin, a Frenchman) would make him an icon of French letters. The debt owed to Zola and French naturalism by Theodore Dreiser, Frank Norris, and American realism did not go unnoticed. The poetry of Walt Whitman was a source of inspiration for Léon Bazalgette, Jules Romains, and the Unanimists. Critics were also studying the effects of French symbolism on the poetry of T. S. Eliot and Wallace Stevens.

But France's interest in America dates back even further. François René de Chateaubriand visited the New World in 1791 and, after his return to France, wrote *Atala* (1801) and *René* (1802), works in which he presented an exotic vision of the American wilderness with its thick forests, tigers, and Native Americans. Chateaubriand's influence on French romanticism was enormous. Three decades later, the hero of Charles-Augustin Sainte-Beuve's semi-autobiographical novel, *Volupté* (1834), spoke of America as the hope of the world, and Sainte-Beuve himself evoked l'Abbé Prévost's vivid descriptions of the American landscape in *Manon Lescaut* (1731),[5] despite the fact that Prévost had never set foot on American soil. For the French, America has always been a dream frontier, what Armand Hoog calls an "elsewhere" (see "The Romantic Spirit"), the elsewhere that Gilbert Chinard has analyzed in detail in *L'Amérique et le rêve exotique dans la littérature française* (16).

One hundred years after the publication of *Volupté*, and some two hundred years after *Manon*, Georges Duhamel excoriated an industrialized America in *Scènes de la vie future* (1930). North America had changed radically during those two hundred years, and Duhamel was not the only one to lament the destruction of nature and the loss of innocence. Hemingway himself decried the clear-cutting of virgin forests in upper Michigan, and when writing about Spain, he compared its culture and unspoiled landscapes to the bespoiled land of America. As France moved closer to those dreaded scenes of future life that were being regulated by mass production and mass consumption, French readers were, nonetheless, showing an interest in the reflection of those mechanized elements in American literature.[6]

Even before the impact of technology, French magazines were publishing Henry James, Jack London, and Ezra Pound. Edith Wharton's novels were being published in French and English simultaneously, and they revealed her indebtedness to Stendhal and Paul Bourget, among others. André Gide said that he was among the first to admire Melville. Gide also recalls a conversation with Flaubert, who once told him that *Walden* was an extraordinary book (M. Baym 136). Although Gide owned a big American car, he, like Duhamel, mistrusted the influence of American technology, as did Giono, the novelist and translator of *Moby-Dick*. Giono's novels are a paean to nature and to men's and women's interrelatedness with the natural rhythms of the world.[7]

Over the years there have been many essays comparing Hemingway with French writers, but there is no full-length study of Hemingway's transatlantic refractions or the literary space they occupy. Perhaps the closest thing to it is Richard Lehan's *A Dangerous Crossing: French Literary Existentialism and the Modern American Novel* (1973). Lehan compares the fiction of Dos Passos, Hemingway, and Faulkner with the works and philosophy of Sartre and Camus. Here my material and his overlap somewhat, but our views and treatment are different and his discussion of Hemingway is relatively brief. John Killinger's *Hemingway and the*

Dead Gods: A Study in Existentialism (1960) also discusses Hemingway's work from an existentialist perspective, comparing it primarily with that of Sartre and Camus. Malcolm Bradbury's *Dangerous Pilgrimages* (1995) devotes one chapter to Hemingway and Fitzgerald in the Paris of the 1920s. Harry Levin's *Refractions: Essays in Comparative Literature* (1966) has a chapter entitled "France-Amérique: The Transatlantic Refraction." This essay compares nineteenth- and twentieth-century French and American connections but says nothing about Hemingway. Michael Reynolds's *Hemingway: The Paris Years* (1989) is a biography. J. Gerald Kennedy's *Imagining Paris: Exile Writing and American Identity* (1993) contains chapters devoted to Gertrude Stein, Hemingway, Henry Miller, and F. Scott Fitzgerald. The chapters focus on the 1920s, whereas my book begins in 1896, the year Alfred Jarry published his provocative *Ubu roi* (*King Ubu*), the play that was to launch the Paris avant-garde of the twentieth century. From there I trace seven decades of literary interaction between Hemingway and French novelists. Kennedy and Jackson Bryer edited *French Connections: Hemingway and Fitzgerald Abroad* (1998). Seven of the essays situate Hemingway in Paris in the 1920s, and one addresses his stay there in 1937–1938. The essays are excellent, but none relates Hemingway to French writers in any significant way.

From time to time the *Hemingway Review* has published articles on Hemingway and Stendhal, Hemingway and Maupassant, and Hemingway and Camus.[8] The *North Dakota Quarterly* has published special issues on Hemingway, perhaps the most noteworthy being *Malraux, Hemingway, and Embattled Spain* 60.2 (1992). The most recent book on Hemingway in Paris is Milton A. Cohen's *Hemingway's Laboratory: The Paris in our time* (2005). It discusses the composition, style, structure, and rhythms of Hemingway's collection of short stories entitled *in our time* (1924). Although they were written in Paris while Hemingway was living there, there is no mention of French writers or the subservience of American letters with respect to France. Many other books have been published on Hemingway in the past several decades, but none deals with French and American refractions.

In addition to these preliminary comments, there is also much to say about recent revisionist criticism of Hemingway. This criticism questions his status as the legendary macho hero, and it seems to have begun with an essay by Aaron Lathan, "A Farewell to Machismo." Gerry Brenner, in

Concealments in Hemingway's Works (1983), refers to Hemingway's "homoerotic wishes" (20). Mark Spilka, in *Hemingway's Quarrel with Androgyny* (1990), alludes to Hemingway's "suppressed femininity" (204). Carl P. Eby, in *Hemingway's Fetishism: Psychoanalysis and the Mirror of Manhood* (1998), speaks of Hemingway's "transvestic impulses" (212). Debra A. Moddelmog, in *Reading Desire: In Pursuit of Ernest Hemingway* (1999), refers to Hemingway's "queer desires" (42). Most recently, Richard Fantina (2003), in "Hemingway's Masochism, Sodomy, and the Dominant Woman," addresses Hemingway's "masochism" (85). This important criticism sheds new light on Hemingway's writing and helps dispel many of the myths surrounding his status as a writer, including the charge that he was superficial.

Some of the chapters in this study have appeared as articles in journals and books, but I have not assembled them here merely to republish. There is an affinity between Hemingway's writings and those of the French authors I compare him with. Indeed, there is a structural necessity to their coupling and the chronological order of the chapters. Together, they are more than the sum of each part, because each one of these writers is an important link in the chain that defines literary space. I discuss Hemingway's major books in the context of French letters in order to focus on the progression from *The Sun Also Rises* (1926) to *The Old Man and the Sea* (1952).

In chapter 1 I look at Hemingway's six years in Paris (1922–1928), where he met French, British, and American writers. It was in the city of light that he read the old masters and absorbed the ferment of innovative art that was to influence his own writing. It is appropriate, therefore, that I compare Hemingway with the major French writers who were his contemporaries, and this comparison begins even earlier with Flaubert, because Flaubert worked with proleptic images and wanted to write poetry as prose. These were also Hemingway's goals, and this is why *Madame Bovary* (1857) adumbrates *A Farewell to Arms* (1929).

In chapter 2 I discuss *A Farewell to Arms* before *The Sun Also Rises* because Flaubert is Hemingway's precursor and the acknowledged father of the modern novel. Also because *A Farewell to Arms* describes events during World War I, whereas *The Sun Also Rises* describes the behavior of the "lost generation" that followed the war. In chapter 3 I incorporate Jacques Lacan's psychoanalytic theories into my discussion of *The Sun*

Also Rises because they elucidate its wordplay, its parody, and the role of the unconscious in orchestrating the novel's love games. Lacan, France's Freud, introduced linguistics into psychoanalysis, and this pushed Lacanian theory to the forefront of literary criticism.

In chapter 4 I discuss Henry de Montherlant, the novelist and bullfighter whose novel *Les bestiaires* (1926; *The Bullfighters*, 1927) probably influenced *Death in the Afternoon* (1932) and *The Dangerous Summer* (1960)—Hemingway's two books on the corrida. In order to fully understand Hemingway's "tauromachia" (*Death* 453), we need to grasp the historical context of the primitive sun god, Mithra, and his influence on bullfighting in Spain. Hemingway never mentions Mithraism, even though the history of the cult provides the missing seven-eighths of the iceberg beneath the surface that we need to intuit when reading *Death in the Afternoon*.

In chapter 5 I discuss Jean-Paul Sartre's nothingness and Hemingway's nada. These concepts imbue *L'être et le néant* (1943; *Being and Nothingness*, 1956) and the two African stories, "The Short Happy Life of Francis Macomber" (1936) and "The Snows of Kilimanjaro" (1936), with reflections and refractions about death, authenticity, and creative freedom.

Sartre declined the Nobel award in literature in 1964, and he could afford to turn it down because he was the very embodiment of literary modernity. He helped define the parameters of literary art, and his power of consecration was immense. He and Camus emerged from World War II as the two dominant writers of the postwar period. Friends at first, Sartre and Camus engaged in one of the fiercest philosophical debates of the 1950s, and it is only now, years after Sartre's death and the collapse of the Soviet Union, that critics have come to acknowledge the legitimacy of Camus' arguments. In chapter 6 I discuss Camus' and Sartre's concepts of rebellion, commitment, and history, which echo ideas that Hemingway was expressing in *To Have and Have Not* (1937) and *The Fifth Column* (1938). These two works represent Hemingway's uneven attempts to engage in a form of writing that is, in the existentialist sense, socially and politically committed. Such commitment prompted both André Malraux and Hemingway to travel to Spain in 1937 in order to support the Republican cause against Franco's Fascist forces. *L'espoir* (1937; *Man's Hope*, 1938) and *For Whom the Bell Tolls* (1940) are their separate responses to the Spanish civil war—two novels that I compare and contrast in chapter 7 while commenting on the rivalry between the two men. Malraux, the novelist, art critic, and minister of culture under Charles de Gaulle's government, was Sartre and Camus' precursor, because in his early fiction he had already explored the ideas of alienation and commitment that were to become the stock-in-trade themes of existentialism. In Camus' Nobel acceptance speech in Stockholm in 1957, he said that Malraux should have won the prize because he was the first to explore ideas that Camus and other members of his generation were to adopt and write about.

The calculus of time and remembrance in *Across the River and into the Trees* (1950) echoes similar themes in Marcel Proust's *A la recherche du temps perdu* (1912–1927; *In Search for Lost Time*). Proust is, arguably, the world's premier novelist, and he should have received two Nobel awards, one for the early volumes of his monumental novel (3,134 pages in the three-volume Pléiade edition) published between 1913 and 1922—the year of his death—and another award for the posthumous ones that appeared between 1922 and 1927. I discuss these convergences in chapter 8.

In his play *Oedipe* (1930; *Oedipus*), André Gide explored the theme of pride—a theme that Hemingway also dramatizes in *The Old Man and the Sea* (1952): pride in what it means to be human, pride in achievement, and pride in essence. As one of the fathers of modernism, Gide helped propel literature from the allusive symbolism of the nineteenth century into the linguistic immediacy of the twentieth. He was a Nobel laureate in 1947. Pride and immediacy are the theme and influence I discuss in chapter 9.

In my conclusion I look at Hemingway's life and achievements in the light of Camus' *Le mythe de Sisyphe* (1942; *Myth of Sisyphus*, 1955). Sisyphus, says Camus, is the parable for twentieth-century man, who, like his Greek counterpart, is condemned to roll a rock toward the summit only to see it roll back down the mountain. But, says Camus, despite the paradoxical nature of achievement and defeat, we must imagine Sisyphus happy. Why happy, when death is the normal and final outcome of all endeavor? This is a replay of the absurd and of Hemingway's winner-take-nothing theme, a theme that Camus develops philosophically and that Hemingway demonstrates artistically. We must also imagine Hemingway happy because despite old age, debility, and death, he, as a writer, reached the pinnacle of success: a Nobel Prize in 1954, worldwide recognition, and sizable royalties. Like Sisyphus in his effort and Flaubert in his craft, Hemingway strives for perfection; struggles to achieve it; and, when all is said and done, shoots himself as though to demonstrate that, in his pride, he is truly a winner with nothing.

Although the purpose of this book is to compare Hemingway with French writers, its subtheme is the craft of writing—Hemingway's writing—which he transforms into poetry and art. From one narrative to another, time and memory also combine to elicit fourth and fifth dimensions—dimensions that emerge from a lifetime of effort, pride in achievement, and the inevitable tragedy of loss. The French novelists with whom I compare Hemingway are all major writers who occupy important literary spaces. They have contributed to the ongoing dominance of Paris as an artistic capital, although now rivaled by London and New York. It is fitting that Hemingway and his New York publisher, Scribner, also assume their rightful place at the center of literary space.

In 1999, Gallimard published *Hemingway: Nouvelles complètes,* seventy-eight French translations of his extant short stories and short story fragments—stories that correspond to *The Complete Short Stories of Ernest Hemingway,* which was published by Scribner in the Finca Vigía Edition of 1987. In addition to the excellent translations by Maurice Coindreau, Jean Dutourd, Jeanine Delpech, Michel Arnaud, Marcel Duhamel, Henri Robillot, Philippe Sollers, and Jeanne-Marie Santraud, among others, the volume also contains critical resources to Hemingway's short stories: Paul Smith's *A Reader's Guide to the Short Stories of Ernest Hemingway* (1989) and the "Comprehensive Checklist of Hemingway Short Fiction, Criticism, Explication, and Commentary, 1975–1989" that appeared in Jackson J. Benson's *New Critical Approaches to the Short Stories of Ernest Hemingway* (1990). A section entitled "Vie et Oeuvre" ("Life and Work") lists all the significant dates and events of Hemingway's life and writings. Still another, "Cinque Critiques" ("Five Critiques"), provides a sampling of early Hemingway criticism by Edmund Wilson, F. Scott Fitzgerald, D. H. Lawrence, Virginia Woolf, and Dorothy Parker, all of them ably translated by the editor himself, Antoine Jacottet. There are additional biographical and bibliographical sections that round out a book of some 1,200 pages.

Gallimard's publication confirms the fact that Hemingway's short stories have been consecrated as classics, and they, like his novels, occupy a permanent and prominent place in international literary space.

One

Hemingway and French Literature

The Paris Years, 1922–1928

Paris, the town best organized for a writer to write in that there is.
—ERNEST HEMINGWAY, *A Moveable Feast*

It is therefore wholly necessary that this man, if he values being illustrious, bring to the capital his bundle of talent, that there he lay it out before the Parisian experts, that he pay for expertise, and that a reputation is then made for him that from the capital is dispatched to the provinces, where it is eagerly accepted.
—RODOLPHE TÖPFFER, unpublished notes, 1834–1836

France informs Ernest Hemingway's life and work, from his first sight of land in 1918 to his last visit in 1960. "France," he said in a piece in the Toronto *Star* in 1923, "is a broad and lovely country. The loveliest country that I know" ("Franco-German Situation"). The city of Paris and the geography of France would mean a great deal to him, and it was Paris's artistic and cultural climate, not only the American and British writers he met there, but also the vibrancy of French literature of that period, that influenced his writing. Paris was, after all, the capital of world literary space.

Much has been written about Hemingway's American and British connections during his apprentice years in Paris, but relatively little has been written about his French contacts and their parallel experiments in the arts—experiments that began in 1896 with Alfred Jarry's publication of *Ubu roi* and André Gide's publication of *Les nourritures terrestres* (*Fruits of the Earth*) in 1897. My purpose is to flesh out the Gallic side of the artistic revolution that was taking place between 1896 and 1928—the year Hemingway left Paris and the year he split with his wife Hadley—and to focus on French writers who were working in new and different styles—styles that would have interested Hemingway, and some of which influenced him. Hemingway and French novelists affected each other in a kind of symbiosis. Stendhal's panoramic battle scene at Waterloo in *La chartreuse de Parme* and the detached, precise irony of Flaubert's writing, particularly *Madame Bovary* and *Trois contes,* taught Hemingway important lessons about the craft of fiction (Oliver, *A to Z* 103, 313).[1] Eventually, influence flowed back into French literature when Sartre, among others, praised him for his direct American style, a style that continued to influence French authors into the 1950s and 1960s, when Alain Robbe-Grillet said that the *nouveau roman* had much to learn from Faulkner and Hemingway.

Hemingway and Hadley Richardson were married on September 3, 1921, and with letters of introduction from Sherwood Anderson (the author of *Winesburg, Ohio,* 1919) to Gertrude Stein; Sylvia Beach, the keeper of the bookstore Shakespeare and Company; and Lewis Galantière, who worked for the International Chamber of Commerce, Mr. and Mrs. Hemingway sailed from New York for Cherbourg on December 8, 1921, on the *Leopoldina.*

Shortly before Christmas, the young couple moved into a Paris apartment, 74 rue du Cardinal Lemoine, near the Panthéon. Two years later, after their son was born, they rented an apartment on 113 rue Notre-Dame-des-Champs, in Montparnasse. It was an attractive street in a nice neighborhood, and a short walk down the avenue de l'Observatoire to the Closerie des Lilas and the Luxembourg Gardens. The apartment was on the second floor and it overlooked the courtyard of a sawmill (Sokoloff 68). For more than six years, Paris was Hemingway's home away from home, because, as Stein said, "Paris was where the twentieth century was" (*Paris France* 11), and, she might have added, the nineteenth and the eighteenth centuries as well. "Paris," said the poet Henri Michaux in a special issue of *Mercure de France,* "is the homeland of those free spirits who have not found a homeland" (52). Paris was a homeland not only for writers but also for translators. According to Valery Larbaud, it was Voltaire who undertook the translation of Shakespeare into French. Indeed, at that time, a great deal of British literature was being disseminated throughout Europe only in French translation (*Ce vice impuni* 31–32). Although Hemingway was only twenty-two when he arrived and, except for his journalism, unpublished, he profited immensely from his new contacts, particularly from Stein and Pound, both of whom adopted him and became his tutors. They taught him how to write and told him what to read, and by the time he left Paris in March 1928, Ernest had become the famous author of *In Our Time* (1925) and *The Sun Also Rises* (1926), a writer on the threshold of consecration.[2]

Paris was an incubator for Hemingway's prodigious talent, and the people he met and the books he read gave him the college education he never had. As George Wickes phrases it, Hemingway "served his literary apprenticeship under the best possible mentors" (5). Pound taught him to use no superfluous words, to avoid abstractions, and to eschew adjectives that did not reveal something (Reynolds, *The Paris Years* 29). In 1935, when Hemingway was writing "The Short Happy Life of Francis Macomber," one of his working titles was "The Short Life of Francis Macomber" (Oldsey, "Beginnings and Endings" 213). The addition of the adjective "happy" makes all the difference and reveals everything about Macomber's cowardice and his twenty-four hours of manhood.

Stein's experimental writing was an eye-opener, and she taught Hemingway the usefulness of repetition and the fact that words such as "tender buttons," whatever their prosaic denotations, could also have connotations, sexual or otherwise. From reading Stein's *Three Lives,* Hemingway learned that the continuous present tense and the repetition of key phrases could create meanings that were larger than the words themselves. He had already used this technique in his Chicago journalism for the *Star,* but at the time it was purely intuitive. In Paris, under Pound's tutelage, he developed a critical self-awareness, and he learned how to repeat what he had gleaned from his mentors (Reynolds, *The Paris Years* 37).[3]

Stein told Hemingway that she wrote *Three Lives* while sitting in front of the portrait of Madame Cézanne, and that her sentences flowed from the red and blue-gray planes of color. Hemingway decided to study the Cézannes at the Musée du Luxembourg and the Louvre—landscapes and bathers, card players, the courtyard at Anvers, and the house of the hanged man. In 1922, while reading Stein's first-draft manuscripts, Hemingway also learned about automatic writing, free association, puns, verbal connections, alliteration, and resonance (Reynolds, *The Paris Years* 38, 40). In the Stein studio at 27 rue de Fleurus, Hemingway also studied the Matisses, Braques, Gris, and Picassos, but it was the Cézannes that would give him essential information about the architecture of art and of writing. In 1932, in *Death in the Afternoon,* he would write that "prose is architecture, not interior decoration, and the Baroque is over" (191).[4] Hemingway once told Valerie Danby-Smith that he always tried "to write as good as the best picture that was ever painted" (qtd. by Danby-Smith 31). Henri Rousseau's primitivism must also have caught his eye, because in a 1945 letter to Mary Welsh, he says that the foliage around Puerto Escondido, Cuba, was as beautiful as a Rousseau jungle piece (*Selected Letters* 598). As he perfected his style, Hemingway was able to see with language, and the visual elements of painting were essential to his craft. As he matured, he mastered the perception of an event that had occurred, and he was able to control the emotion elicited by the event. Whenever he and a particular experience became one, he was able to convey its intensity in words. As an artist he generated the language that would capture the simultaneity and immediacy of description and emotion.

Hemingway's spoken French, if somewhat slangy, was getting better (Llona 165), while his knowledge of written French was excellent. He read all the French and English publications at Shakespeare and Company (Beach 79). He was also reading extensively in nineteenth-century fiction, particularly the Russians: Turgenev, Tolstoy, Dostoevsky, and Chekhov. In her book *Shakespeare and Company* (named after her bookstore), Sylvia Beach has a chapter entitled "My Best Customer," referring to Hemingway's frequent visits and borrowings. At the time, 1922, she was publishing *Ulysses,* and Hemingway was reading James Joyce, T. S. Eliot, D. H. Lawrence, and Henry James (Reynolds, *The Paris Years* 6, 8, 11, 14)—the Henry James that Sartre would later reject, saying that he had nothing new to teach the French about inner monologue and psychological analysis. Compared to Hemingway, wrote Sartre, James was passé ("American Novelists" 117). James's change in citizenship had done little to consecrate him in Paris.

It was at Shakespeare and Company, 12 rue de l'Odéon, that Hemingway met Joyce, after Pound persuaded him to move from Zurich to Paris. Switzerland, like America, was a literary backwater. Another important acquaintance was Ford Madox Ford, the author of *Parade's End*

(1925), who had just moved from England to the city of light. Many Brits were fleeing the Anglo-Saxon conventions of a restrictive English society whose censors would ban *Ulysses* and *Lady Chatterley's Lover*. Ford soon launched the *transatlantic review,* a review that would publish Stein, Pound, Joyce, Ford, and eventually Hemingway's first three Nick Adams stories (Wickes 6–7). Hemingway and Stein were then good friends, and he typed long sections of *The Making of Americans* for the printer, sections that he helped publish in the *transatlantic*. Ford had already made him assistant editor (Cowley 50). Across the street from Beach's bookstore was Adrienne Monnier's La Maison des Amis des Livres, at 7 rue de l'Odéon, and it catered to French authors and buyers. After meeting Hemingway and getting to know him, Monnier predicted that he would be the best-known American expatriate because he cared more for his craft than any of the others (Bryer 212–14).

One of Beach's first patrons was André Gide, and she remembers him as a generous man who was always ready to support the cause of freedom of expression, as was Hemingway, who also filled out several subscription blanks in order to help the publication of *Ulysses* (Beach 51). Sylvia's sister, Cyprian, was a woman of great beauty and a movie star who played the role of Belle-Mirette in the film *Judex*. Louis Aragon, the surrealist poet, was much taken by Cyprian, and he too frequented Shakespeare and Company (Monnier 88). In 1944, when Hemingway "liberated" Paris, his first stop was Beach's bookstore, then Monnier's, where he and his company "took care" of Nazi snipers on the roof. Then he and his men rode off in their Jeeps to "liberate the cellar at the Ritz" (Beach 219–20). Shortly thereafter André Malraux joined Hemingway at the Ritz, where they discussed their respective military roles and their importance in liberating Paris (Baker, *A Life Story* 531–33).

At Shakespeare and Company and La Maison des Amis des Livres, Hemingway met Gide, Paul Valéry, Léon-Paul Fargue, Valery Larbaud, and Jules Romains, as well as surrealists and innovators of all stripes, among them Francis Picabia, a painter whom Hemingway disliked initially, perhaps because he had joined forces with the Dada group in 1918 and was associated with Tristan Tzara, whom Hemingway disliked even more. In his editorial column for Ford's May issue of the 1924 *transatlantic* he wrote: "Dada is dead although Tzara still cuddles its emaciated little corpse to his breast and croons a Rumanian folk-song . . . while he tried to get the dead little lips to take sustenance from his monocle" (qtd.

by Reynolds, *The Paris Years* 183). Picabia participated in sensational performances that scandalized the Parisian public and he loved to astonish in ways that Hemingway would have been attracted to: by way of his ironic sense of humor and the droll means he used to challenge dogma and all manner of received ideas.

Hemingway's early readings in Kipling and O. Henry had not prepared him for the artistic ferment of Paris, but this was about to change (Reynolds, *The Paris Years* 15).[5] Paris was a place of manifestos, extravagant exhibitions, and surrealist outrages that often stopped traffic with questions such as "Do you want to slap a corpse?" The versatile and flamboyant Jean Cocteau said later that France between 1914 and 1924 presented the spectacle of an incredible literary revolution. Cocteau, Serge Diaghilev, Erik Satie, and Picasso invented the ballet *Parade* (1917), soon to be followed by Darius Milhaud's masked spectacle-concert *Le boeuf sur le toit* (1920). Milhaud then wrote a jazz opera, *La création du monde* (1923), which featured a black Adam and Eve. The Ballets russes had a new curtain by Picasso; Man Ray was photographing combs, sieves, and shoe trees; Fernand Léger was beginning his cubist cinema *Ballet mécanique* with music by George Antheil, whose studio was above Shakespeare and Company; and Pound made Villon's poetry into an opera that was performed at the Salle Pleyel (Bradbury 304–5). Hemingway was part of this cultural revolution, the Americanization of Paris, and the reciprocal influence of French cafés, galleries, museums, and bookshops on Americans. In addition to Stein as a salon hostess, there was also the influential and wealthy "Amazon," Natalie Barney, whose "Temple of Love" and formidable lesbian culture were housed at 20 rue Jacob (Bradbury 310).[6]

Most Americans gravitated to the Left Bank and the cafés around Montparnasse, such as the Sélect, the Rotonde, and the Dôme, where they made contacts with other writers, editors, and publishers—kindred souls who could provide support and opportunity (Reynolds, *The Paris Years* 163). The patrons of the Sélect liked racing, gambling, tennis, and boxing. The revolutionaries preferred the Rotonde, while the hardworking painters and writers favored the Dôme (Ross 255). Hemingway scorned the expatriates who frequented these cafés because, he said, no good poetry could be written in places patronized by dilettantes, and Charles Baudelaire, when writing *Les fleurs du mal*, must surely, he said, have been working alone (Baker, *A Life Story* 113). Nonetheless, when Hemingway needed racing or boxing tips he could be found at the Sélect.

In 1922, in addition to Ford, Hemingway met the editors of the *Little Review* and Ernest Walsh, editor of *This Quarter*. These reviews published Hemingway's work when magazines in the United States would not. It was also in Paris, soon after the publication of *The Great Gatsby*, in 1925, that Hemingway says he met F. Scott Fitzgerald at the Dingo Bar, on the rue Delambre *(A Moveable Feast* 147). Fitzgerald's friendship was to prove invaluable because he suggested cuts to the beginning of *The Sun Also Rises* and was helpful in getting it published by Scribner, in 1926.

As the capital of literary space, Paris was an international city with many foreign energies folding into the more radical trends in French culture. But the Paris of the 1920s was no longer the Paris of the belle époque that Stein and Edith Wharton had discovered at the turn of the century. Nonetheless, in 1922, Sydney Schiff hosted a party for Diaghilev and friends from the Ballets russes, and he also invited Picasso, Stravinsky, Joyce, and Proust, the four geniuses they most admired. Joyce and Proust had never met. The former complained of his eyes, and the latter of his stomach, and by the end of the year Proust was dead. He was buried with full military honors and big crowds witnessed the event (Bradbury 314). The "banquet years" that Roger Shattuck chronicles—the years of upper-class leisure and social power—were fading as Paris, after World War I, experienced additional internationalization and an Americanization, processes that Hemingway was to absorb and write about in his fiction as well as in dispatches for the Toronto *Star*. In March 1922, he covered the Economic Conference in Genoa; in September, the Greco-Turkish war; and in November, the Lausanne peace conference (Cowley 50). The franc was falling and Americans were discovering the intellectual, gastronomic, and sexual attractions of Paris—attractions that were beyond the disapproval and censorship of American puritanism. Paris was not only a free-wheeling capital; it was also the mind and heart of France's intelligentsia and the arts. Hemingway thrived in the city that welcomed Josephine Baker in 1925 as the lead dancer in La revue nègre, where she was wowing audiences with her performances (Baker and Chase 3–7). When Charles Lindbergh flew across the Atlantic in 1927 and landed at Le Bourget airport, he was given a hero's welcome.

Archibald MacLeish describes dragging Hemingway to a gathering of writers where Gide, Jules Romains, and others were talking. Romains was a Unanimist poet and Unanimism was one of the many bourgeoning literary movements in the early 1900s. It was the literary manifestation of earlier sociological theories developed by Emile Durkheim (*Les règles de la méthode sociologique,* 1894) and Gustave Le Bon (*Psychologie des foules,* 1895), who were exploring the psychology of groups and the behavior of crowds. They based their theories on the premise of a collective unconscious and the idea of a group soul capable of transcending the individual. In 1910, Romains published his slim Unanimist manifesto, *Manuel de déification,* in which he exhorted the faithful to help create cells of collective awareness. *Le bourg régénéré* (1906) is the narrative of a sleepy town that awakens to its own identity, and *La vie unanime* (1908) is a collection of Unanimist poems. Romains' books had a profound effect on Adrienne Monnier, who was an early fan of his. She even quotes a line from the *Manuel:* "Ton plus grand Dieu de maintenant, c'est peut-être ta plus grande ville" (Monnier 52; "Your biggest God [sic] today is perhaps your biggest city").[7] Despite Monnier's enthusiasm, it is easy to imagine how Gide, the champion of the self and of the individual, might argue against submerging him or her in the anonymity of a collective entity.

In any case, and according to MacLeish, Hemingway was not listening, either because Gide and Romains were speaking too fast for Hemingway to understand their French, or because the argument did not interest him. So Gide, ostensibly irritated, took Hemingway aside and explained how to discipline a cat. You lift the animal up by the scruff of the neck and say, "PHT!" in its face (MacLeish 310). According to MacLeish, neither man looked happy. Hemingway and his son, Bumby, had a cat named Feather Puss (sometimes known as F. Puss), and perhaps this information was useful. None of Hemingway's biographers describes how he disciplined the dozens of cats that roamed the gardens of his Key West house in the 1930s. This incident may have prompted Hemingway to write to Bernard Berenson in 1953, saying that "Gide had that awful lascivious protestant [sic] coldness; like the pastor of the Fourth Presbyterian church who is caught by the janitor interfering with little boys behind the church organ" (*Selected Letters* 809). But there was more to this aside than cats, religion, or sexual predilection.

Gide was a literary force to be reckoned with. At the turn of the century, in 1897, he published *Les nourritures terrestres,* which, in retrospect, was a literary event of seismic proportions because it moved French literature out of symbolism and into the twentieth century. The allusive writing of the symbolists was replaced by a direct narration that named objects and events without cloaking them in tropic vestments. Stéphane Mallarmé's "transparent glacier of flights that have not fled!" ("transparent glacier des vols qui n'ont pas fui!" 123) in "Le vierge, le vivace et le bel aujourd' hui" refers to the sterility of the poet and the poems that have not been born. While the swan in the poem may be a symbol of the poet's impotence, the swan, for Gide and Hemingway, whether it flies or not, was first and foremost a swan. Hemingway was to say later that arbitrary symbols, that is, those stuck in beforehand, were like raisins in a loaf of bread. He preferred bread without raisins. Gide and Hemingway were both interested in the immediacy of experience, and in their writing, they crafted direct links between the signifier and the signified, and their works were uncluttered by esoteric descriptions of mythic animals such as fauns or exotic places such as Cytherea.

In 1909, Gide founded *La Nouvelle Revue Française,* the most influential French literary review of its day. Another Gide landmark was *Corydon* (1924), the first published apologia for homosexuality, published at a time when gay and lesbian relationships were woven into the social fabric of the Left Bank: Stein and Alice B. Toklas, Beach and Monnier, Djuna Barnes and Thelma Wood. When Hemingway met Margaret Anderson, the editor of the *Little Review,* in the company of Georgette LeBlanc, the singer and wife of Maurice Maeterlinck, and the *Little Review*'s coeditor, Jane Heap, he "did not flinch at Jane's masculine clothes, at her hair cut shorter than his own, or at her cigars" (Reynolds, *The Paris Years* 37).

During the 1920s, Sylvia Beach was selling the works of Havelock Ellis (*Psychology of Sex* and *Erotic Symbolism*), Oscar Wilde (*De Profundis* and *Salome*), John Cleland (*Fanny Hill*), and Frank Harris (*My Life and Loves*), among others. When *Lady Chatterly's Lover* was banned in England, Beach sold D. H. Lawrence. According to Michael Reynolds, she "was unashamedly selling erotic books to any who asked for them" (*The Paris Years* 14). In all fairness to Beach, however, she needed the money in order to finance the publication of *Ulysses.* When he was not buying books, not necessarily these books, Hemingway checked out twenty to thirty a year from the lending library, and Hadley used Shakespeare and Company even more frequently than her husband (Reynolds, *The Paris Years* 14).

Sex was everywhere. The year 1923 saw the music-hall performance of Mallarmé's "L'après-midi d'un faune," and that same year Raymond Radiguet, Cocteau's young lover, published *Le diable au corps,* a novel in which a precocious adolescent woos the wife of a soldier with poems by Baudelaire and Verlaine while the husband is away at the front. The poetry of the symbolists and their successors was very much in the air. Hemingway took note of the fact that Verlaine had died in the cheap hotel (39 rue Descartes) where he, Hemingway, was renting a room on the top floor—a room from which "he could see the roofs and chimney pots and all the hills of Paris" ("Snows" 70). Nearby was the place de la Contrescarpe, where the scum from the rue Mouffetard gathered in noisy bistros. Many years earlier the square had been the site of the well-known Café de la Pomme de Pin, frequented by Villon, Rabelais, Racine, and La Fontaine (Sokoloff 46). In a 1931 letter to Archibald MacLeish, Hemingway quoted a line in French from Baudelaire's "L'amour du mensonge," in *Les fleurs du mal:* "Les morts, les pauvres morts ont de grandes douleurs" (*Selected Letters* 338; "The dead, the wretched dead, all have heavy sorrows").

In 1925 Gide published *Les faux-monnayeurs,* a novel that significantly influenced point of view in fiction and the canon of realism. Three years before, in 1922, Paul Valéry published "Le cimetière marin" (*Charmes* 221–40), hailed then and now as one of the most accomplished poems in the French language, or any language.[8] Its tropic density contains the fourth and fifth dimensions that Hemingway endeavored to perfect in his fiction, which, he said, was a fiction more difficult to write than poetry (*Green Hills* 27). This is arguably not true, although the two men, in their different ways, achieved a verbal density and tropic complexity that give language multiple layers of meaning. In 1927, Valéry was elected to the prestigious Académie française, an event that could not have escaped Hemingway's notice. Years later, in 1953, in a letter to Berenson, Hemingway complained that Valéry did not remember him when he "was a very quiet boy whose name nobody knew" (*Selected Letters* 809).

Hemingway's explorations of Paris were not unlike Gide's explorations of north Africa, only in reverse order. Gide was a sickly and bookish young adult when he met Oscar Wilde and discovered sex and the raw appeal of the African desert, whereas Hemingway was in excellent health, loved nature as a boy, and was initiated into sex early on in the north Michigan woods. He was not particularly well read when he arrived in Paris and what he discovered was books.

Gide's brush with death (adolescent consumption and the spitting of blood) and his recovery in north Africa were similar to Hemingway's wounding at Fossalta on the Italian front in 1917, when he almost died. Both encounters served as moral compasses that would guide their daily choices, constantly orienting them toward life and the immediate pleasures of full participation. Gide had his "fruits of the earth," and Hemingway his "moveable feast."[9]

Mallarmé's lament in "Brise Marine" that "the flesh is sad, alas! and I have read all the books" ("La chair est triste, hélas! et j'ai lu tous les livres," 40) echoes Baudelaire's ennui in his "Spleen" poems, an ennui that is countered in *Les nourritures terrestres* by Gide's (or Ménalque's) counsel to Nathanaël to embrace life: "I will teach you fervor" ("Je t'enseignerai la ferveur," 156). *Les nourritures* was a paeon to life that advises Nathanaël to discard the book he is reading and live (248). Hemingway was not discarding books; he was accumulating them. He was also discovering the easygoing sexual mores of Paris although, at the time, happily married to Hadley.

Gide began his literary career under the tutelage of Mallarmé and he had written a symbolist fiction entitled *Le voyage d'Urien,* a symbolic name that recalls William Blake's Urizen.[10] Urien travels to the North Pole in search of the absolute only to find the frozen white wastes of nothing ("du rien," a pun on the name Urien). Having rejected symbolism, Gide was free to pursue his newly discovered earthly delights in a style that was radically different from Mallarmé's allusive poetry—a poetry that veiled his eroticism and concern with creative impotence.

The only influence that Hemingway was shedding was Sherwood Anderson's, and the publication of *The Torrents of Spring* (1926), a parody of Anderson's style, ended their friendship. Unlike Gide's parody, it was not a radical break with the past, although Hemingway was in the process of discovering his own unique voice. Despite many differences, Gide and Hemingway were both forging a style more suited to the temperament of the machine age. It was an efficient style without ornamentation, a style not unlike Cézanne's painterly boxes and cubes, a style that was made for and that had the industrial strength of the new twentieth century.[11]

Meanwhile, Proust was publishing successive volumes of *A la recherche du temps perdu* (1913–1927), in which time and memory emerged as leitmotifs within a vast panoramic view of French culture and society. The philosopher Henri Bergson, reacting against Auguste Comte's positivism, was analyzing the fluid and dynamic nature of consciousness, time, and memory, and emphasizing the primacy of intuition. These influences,

Proust's in particular, are discernible in *Across the River and into the Trees* and significant portions of the unpublished manuscript of *The Garden of Eden*. *in our time,* Hemingway's volume of short stories published in 1924, two years after Proust's death, has the word "time" in the title, as did Proust's novel, *A la recherche du temps perdu,* but Hemingway emphasized the experience of events in the present, whereas Proust probed the effects on the senses of an "involuntary memory" capable of recovering the past. In the window display of Shakespeare and Company, Sylvia Beach placed Hemingway's thin volume with its collage cover of newspaper clippings next to *Du côté de chez Swann* (Reynolds, *The Paris Years* 181).

The collage cover of *in our time* read in part as follows: "More Americans Arrive in Paris. . . . Business Men Want Pleasure Not Study. . . . Drinks Liquor Since Childhood. Passes 104 Mark. . . . Plans to Leave America Forever. . . . Learn French. . . . Smile A While. . . . Common Malady Is Found Serious Among Women Here. . . . Le dollar au secours du franc. . . . \$5 to \$10. . . . Guidance From God. . . . Humor." Centered on the cover were Hemingway's name, the book's title, the name of the publisher (Three Mountains Press), and the year of publication, 1924. Hemingway seems to have chosen clippings designed to offend the sensibilities of his conservative parents and the proper mores of Oak Park, Illinois.

By this time, Hemingway, Sylvia Beach, and Adrienne Monnier were good friends and they could be seen together at the boxing matches and the bicycle races (Beach 80–81). One day at Shakespeare and Company, Sylvia said to Hemingway that Adrienne wanted to have him and Hadley to dinner. "We'd ask Fargue. You like Fargue, don't you? Or Larbaud. You like him. I know you like him" (*A Moveable Feast* 70). Fargue was dazzling in conversation and legendary for being late. When invited to a dinner party, he would arrive in time for dessert (Monnier 89), and on one occasion he arrived two weeks late. In 1935, in a letter to Berenson, Hemingway wrote that "when I was twenty through twenty five in Paris I liked Fargue . . . the best. . . . Valery Larbaud was stupid but kind and pleasant" (*Selected Letters* 809). Valery Larbaud had translated Joyce (*Ulysses* and *Finnegans Wake*) and Walt Whitman, and in 1913 he published the tale of *A. O. Barnabooth,* a fictional character who represented a mixture of influences ranging from Baudelaire and Maurice Barrès to Gide. Larbaud was also a friend of Stein's, and according to her, he meditated while translating *Three Lives* (*Autobiography* 196). Despite Hemingway's opinion of him, Larbaud was anything but stupid, and Hemingway would have done well to listen to him because Larbaud had his finger on the literary pulse of Europe. He was among the first to emphasize the difference between the political map of Europe and its intellectual map, thereby emphasizing literary space and Paris's central role in defining it (*Ce vice impuni* 33–34). He was also among the first to propose an intellectual internationalism that called for a global approach not only to literature, but to literary criticism as well. He wanted to erase the boundaries that defined literary nationalism in favor of a new internationalism in literature and in criticism ("Paris de France" 15).

It was this internationalism that was to launch Hemingway's career: he was living in Paris, his works were being translated, they were receiving critical attention in reviews and forewords, and he was being published on both sides of the Atlantic.

A good friend of Stein's was the painter André Masson. One day, Stein took Hemingway and Hadley to the Masson-Miró studio, where "Hemingway got a close view of the future, for both painters were experimenting with Synthetic Cubism bordering on the surrealism for which both would become famous." Masson was learning from Picasso and Braque and there were also traces of Cézanne in his work. Hemingway bought four small Massons, and later a large Miró, *The Farm* (Reynolds, *The Paris Years* 173). In 1936, in *Green Hills of Africa,* P.O.M. says, "The trees are like André's pictures. . . . Look at that green. It's Masson. Why can't a good painter see this country?" (96).

One of the Massons Hemingway bought was *The Throw of the Dice,* a shallow, flat painting crowded with men's faces. Only one man is watching the die tumble across the canvas—5, 5, 1 (Reynolds, *The Paris Years* 173). In 1897, in the review *Cosmopolis,* Mallarmé published "Un coup de dés jamais n'abolira le hasard" ("A Throw of the Dice Never Will Abolish Chance"), and after his death, in 1914, the poem was republished in a separate edition by Gallimard. In 1961, Masson illustrated a collaborative Mallarmé edition of *Un coup de dés* that reproduces the spatial distribution of sentences on the page following the 1914 Gallimard edition. There is a direct link between the title of Masson's painting (the one Hemingway bought) and Mallarmé's poem. In commenting on the collaboration, Renée Riese Hubert and Judd D. Hubert say that "Mallarmé underplays the outside world in his game of radical substitution," whereas "Masson engineers a stormy and highly chromatic return of the universe" (509). Mallarmé's genius as an innovator was well known and this poem represents his supreme effort to break through the arbitrary nature of poetic creation. Masson's *Coup de dés* is a pictorial nod to Mallarmé's art and, significantly, it appealed to Hemingway because one of his enduring themes was winning and losing. Although his French motto was "Il faut (d'abord) durer" (Baker, *Life Story* 714), he was acutely aware that despite heroic stabs at living, everybody in the end dies. Winner take nothing and to have and have not are what life is all about. Even Santiago, the supreme fisherman of *The Old Man and the Sea*, the man who goes out too far and lands the greatest marlin ever caught, loses it to the sharks. Hemingway's fiction is replete with battlers and gamblers who stake all they have, win, and then lose.

Léon-Paul Fargue, the poet whom Hemingway liked best, had been influenced by symbolism—Verlaine and Laforgue—and he was very close to many avant-garde painters, musicians, and surrealist poets. His poetry blends modernist images of big cities and machines with humor and sensibility. He was also one of the founding fathers of *La Nouvelle Revue Française*. Hemingway profited immensely from these contacts with painters, writers, and musicians; he drank with them in the cafés; and he admired their independence. In *A Moveable Feast* he describes having a beer with Pascin (pseudonym of Julius Pincas), the Bulgarian expatriate painter, whom he also liked. Pascin was sitting at a table at the Dôme with two models, presumably the Ginette and Mireille of the 1929 painting at the Petit Palais. Pascin described them as the good sister and the bad sister, and Hemingway's reminiscence is a clever exchange of witticisms between four friends in 1926. In 1930, Pascin was found hanged in his studio (*A Moveable Feast* 101–4).

Paris in the 1920s was assimilating artistic innovations that had been rejected, ignored, and repressed during the second half of the nineteenth century. Baudelaire's *Fleurs du mal*, which in 1857 had been condemned for offenses to public morality, was finally being published in an unexpurgated edition. Viewers of impressionist and postimpressionist art—the art of Vincent van Gogh, Paul Gaugin, and Claude Monet—now wondered what all the fuss had been about, compared to the visual extravaganzas of the fauves, the first art revolution of the twentieth century to celebrate pure color, or the cubists, who were being criticized and ridiculed for their aberrations, dislocations, and simultaneities. The subject matter and form of Picasso's *Demoiselles d'Avignon* (1907), with its shards of light, jagged figures of prostitutes, and Africanized faces, seemed far more scandalous than Van Gogh's swirling skies, Gaugin's women of Tahiti, or Edouard Manet's *Olympia* (1863). Futurism presaged the unthinkable when in 1909 Filippo Tommaso Marinetti published a manifesto in *Le Figaro* extolling the aggressive beauty of speed and movement while vowing to destroy the museums, libraries, and academies of culture. Compared to the fluid music of Claude Debussy and Maurice Ravel, the primitive violence and irresistible force of Igor Stravinsky's *Sacre du printemps* (1913) was heard as a grating and aggressive aural outrage. During its premiere patrons fought in the aisles, as they had during the premiere of Victor Hugo's *Hernani* in 1830, or when they hurled bottles at the screen during the first viewing of Buñuel and Dali's *Un chien Andalou* in 1928. Parisians had always been passionate about the arts, whether they were defending the status quo or promoting the avant-garde.

On May 17, 1909, at the Châtelet, audiences saw for the first time the dazzling Ballets russes of Serge Diaghilev, an extraordinary troupe of dancers that made classical ballet seem old fashioned. It featured not only Nijinski but also stage settings that were exploding with color. It was for Diaghilev that Stravinsky composed *Le sacre du printemps,* as well as *L'oiseau de feu* (1910) and *Petrouchka* (1911). The invention of the lightbulb, the radio, the telephone, the automobile, and the airplane led Charles Péguy to state in 1913 that "the world has changed less since Jesus Christ than it has in the last thirty years" (qtd. by Shattuck xi). The silent cinema was very popular, with screenings of masterpieces such as René Clair's *Entr'acte* (1924), Carl Dreyer's *La passion de Jeanne d'Arc* (1928), and Buñuel and Dali's *Un chien Andalou.* Ezra Pound referred to Paris as "a laboratory of ideas" (Bradbury 303) where writers and painters could find themselves and express their artistic vision without fear of reprisal or condemnation.

Even before 1900, Alfred Jarry's play *Ubu roi* (1896) was revolutionizing French theater, along with Guillaume Apollinaire's *Les mamelles de Tirésias* (written in 1903) and Cocteau's *Les mariés de la Tour Eiffel* (first performed in 1921), the early beginnings of the "theatre of the absurd" that was to surface in the 1950s and 1960s, and that Antonin Artaud was already legitimizing with an essay entitled "Le théâtre de la cruauté" ("The Theater of Cruelty"), a manifesto first published in *La Nouvelle Revue Française.*

Apollinaire, the most innovative French poet of the twentieth century, published *Alcools* in 1913, the same year as *Le sacre du printemps,*
and *Calligrammes* in 1918 (the year of his death), two volumes in which
the fractured and simultaneous facets of cubism reemerged as literary
tropes. Like Gide, he abandoned symbolism, and instead of pursuing the
Idea of Beauty, he found beauty in street scenes, human drama, and the
anecdotal. He introduced bold color, shock effects, and irregular shapes.
Instead of Mallarmé's high seriousness, he used an offbeat, casual, and
self-mocking humor. In 1916, Tzara founded Dada and organized its first
tumultuous festival. That year, also in reaction to the tragedy of World
War I, Henri Barbusse published *Le feu,*[12] a day-by-day account of life in
the trenches narrated with relentless realism. Jules Romains' *Verdun* also
described life at the front in 1916, as did Henry Malherbe's *La flamme au
poing* (1917). Dada was in large measure a direct response to the beast of
"civilized" horror, the war in which 1,400,000 French soldiers died.

Dada's rebelliousness was followed by surrealism and André Breton's
first surrealist manifesto of 1924, in which he strove to meld art with
Freud's unconscious imagery and free association. Surrealism found
many adherents in art and in literature, and Max Ernst, Salvador Dali,
Philippe Soupault, Paul Eluard, Louis Aragon, and Robert Desnos were
some of its most noted practitioners.[13] In 1923, Hemingway himself made
a stab at automatic writing as a way of priming the creative pump (Reynolds, *The Paris Years* 38–39), but his short sentences, repetition of words,
and intrusive punctuation are closer to Stein's writing than to the flow
and free association of the surrealists. Surrealism was not really suited to
Hemingway's temperament or his need for conscious stylistic control.

In 1922, Hadley met John Dos Passos, whom Hemingway had known
briefly during the war. They called him Dos, they became good friends,
and later he married an old friend of Hadley's, Kate Smith (Sokoloff 56).
In 1923, Hemingway quit his job as a reporter for the *Star* and began writing full time. He and Dos Passos would meet on occasion at the Closerie
des Lilas, a café near 113 rue Notre-Dame-des-Champs, where Hemingway
lived. At the time they were both reading the Old Testament and when
they met they would read choice passages to each other, particularly the
Song of Deborah and Chronicles and Kings. Even then, Dos Passos believed that Hemingway would become the first great American stylist, because his short sentences were based on cablese and the King James Bible
(Dos Passos 141–42).

Overseas newspaper correspondents used cablese in order to omit everything that could be taken for granted, and that is in part how Hemingway learned the art of omission, the kind of omission that he describes in *Death in the Afternoon* (192) and practiced as his iceberg theory of writing. When he was writing at one of the marble-topped tables at the Closerie, Hemingway would order a *café crème,* and with a rabbit's foot and a horse chestnut in his pocket for good luck, he would open a blue French notebook and apply himself. It was there that he wrote much of *The Sun Also Rises* (Ross 256). MacLeish says, in corroboration of Dos Passos, that Hemingway developed "the one intrinsic style our language has produced in this century" (307).

It was at the Closerie that Hemingway saw Blaise Cendrars, "with his broken boxer's face and his pinned-up sleeve, rolling a cigarette with his one good hand. He was a good companion until he drank too much and, at that time when he was lying, he was more interesting than many men telling a story truly" (*A Moveable Feast* 81). Monnier notes that Cendrars lost his right arm in the war and that his loss gave him a certain heroic style (59). Hemingway, like Dos Passos, had read Cendrars and liked his early work. Whether he patterned Harry Morgan's stub of an arm in *To Have and Have Not* after Cendrars' is open to conjecture. But what he says about Cendrars' drinking and writing prefigures the decline in his own life. *Islands in the Stream* has many brilliant passages, but toward the end the book often reads like an action potboiler.

Cendrars' poems and novels epitomized an internationalist spirit of escape and adventure based on speed and motion. His interests in the mechanical aspects of modern life were shared by many other artists of his generation such as Apollinaire, Fargue, Fernand Léger, Maurice Vlaminck, and the futurists. *Prose du Transsibérien et de la petite Jehanne de France* (1913) and *L'or* (1925), among others, influenced Dos Passos. Under his influence and that of Barbusse's *Le feu,* he began writing *Three Soldiers,* in early 1919, about the time he first met Hemingway. In the 1930s, Dos Passos wrote the *USA* trilogy in the same condensed telegraphic style that Cendrars used in *L'or* to tell the story of General Johann August Sutter and the incredible events of the California gold rush.

Like Hemingway's characters in *The Sun Also Rises*—characters shuttling back and forth between Paris and Pamplona—only more so, Cendrars' characters cross one continent after another, their ears deafened by the grind of wheels and the roar of airplane motors. Cendrars' protagonists are anxious and deracinated, like the characters of Hemingway's "lost generation." "Lost generation" was the term that Stein's auto mechanic used to describe the survivors of the war. Stein then pinned it on the expatriates with whom Hemingway was hanging out. Except for his early short stories and *To Have and Have Not*—works that are situated in the United States— Hemingway's novels and essays are situated in France, Spain, Africa, and Cuba, and these two authors, in their writings, share this interest in international locales.

During these years painters and writers were not only influencing each other but collaborating. Of special interest was the work of Robert Delaunay and Apollinaire. Delaunay had assimilated the experiments of the futurists, who had proclaimed the primacy of pure color in pictorial construction, and he believed that when a primary color does not determine its complementary color, it shatters in the atmosphere, producing simultaneously all the colors of the spectrum. Like Picasso and Braque, he strove in his paintings to combine figures and objects into fragmented compositions: "Nothing horizontal or vertical—light deforms everything, breaks everything up." In 1909, Delaunay produced the *Saint-Séverin* series, and in 1910, the *Eiffel Tower*, in which divergent planes are superimposed, the perspectives multiply and swell, and space acquires a new thickness and consistency. Apollinaire called Delaunay's technique "orphic," and he wrote a poem, "Les fenêtres"("The Windows"), that was influenced by Delaunay's painting bearing the same name:

O Paris
From red to green all the yellow fades
Paris Vancouver Hyères Maintenon New-York and
   the Antilles
The window opens like an orange
The beautiful fruit of light. (*Calligrammes* 16)

In "Lundi rue Christine" (*Calligrammes* 31–33), Apollinaire wrote a conversation poem while Cendrars in *Le Transsibérien* brought together Siberia, Montmartre, Fiji, Mexico, New York, Madrid, and Stockholm, among other locations. The forerunner of simultaneity was of course Walt Whitman, but the poetry of Cendrars and Apollinaire assimilated and expanded the technique. Henry Levet's "Cartes postales" (1900) had illustrated the aesthetic possibilities of the simultaneous, the discontinuous, and all manner of synchronized juxtapositions, while Apollinaire's "Venu de Dieuze" (*Calligrammes* 110) blends bits of song with snatches of dialogue in a collage poem that uses many different fonts and sizes. In "Le Panama ou les aventures de mes sept oncles" (1918) Cendrars inserted a blurb from the Denver chamber of commerce (44). His use of advertising—the moneyed slogans of a technological age—underscored the intrusion of a material reality into a person's dreamworld that did violence to intimacy and privacy. In "Zone" (*Alcools* 7–15), Apollinaire compared the flash of neon lights to the raucous cries of jungle parrots, thereby blending the visual-impact blurbs of advertising with an aboriginal primitivism. All these experiments influenced Dos Passos more than they did Hemingway (see Stoltzfus, "John Dos Passos"). Nonetheless, the impact of cubism on Hemingway is enormous and painting and painters are an ongoing presence in his work. His collection of short stories *in our time* inserts a brief paragraph in italics between each fiction. The short shorts are about death in war and death in the bullring and executions—stories and events that occur simultaneously in the United States and in Europe. This procedure adds a layered and disruptive quality to the conventional short story technique and allies it with cubism. Thomas Hudson, the protagonist of *Islands in the Stream* (1970), is a painter (see Brogan).[14]

Another writer of the 1920s was Henry de Montherlant, a former bullfighter who had been wounded in the arena and who had written *Les bestiaires* (1926), a best-selling novel. The 1927 English translation was entitled *The Bullfighters*. The novel was serialized in *Le journal* and the Vélodrome d'hiver held a running of the bulls under floodlights on March 16, 1926, for five thousand spectators. It was publicized as "Tauromachie . . . et Littérature" and Montherlant gave a long talk on the "cult of the bull through the ages" (Sipriot 123). Hemingway always read the Paris newspapers, and he frequented boxing matches, horse races, and bicycle races; with his interest in the annual Pamplona festival—the corrida being central to *The Sun Also Rises*—the double billing at the Vélodrome was an important event, one that would not have escaped his notice, even though, at the time, he was in Schruns, Austria, with Hadley and Bumby, revising *The Sun Also Rises*. Dos Passos notes that Hemingway was contemplating a book about bullfighting and that Picasso was going to illustrate it (154). The seeds for *Death in the Afternoon* (1932)—Hemingway's classic book on the *toreo*—must surely have been planted by the French writer and the Pamplona feria. In due course Hemingway was to share Montherlant's enthusiasm for the corrida as a quasi-religious rite where each encounter, as in Greek tragedy, ended in death. Both men would share this "religion of death" that dramatizes in ritual form the ultimate moment of the human condition (Asselineau, *Ernest Hemingway* 39).[15]

It was in Paris that Hemingway honed his writing, deepened his vision, and perfected one of the dominant styles of modern fiction. Malcolm Bradbury notes that "Hemingway's fiction, more or less from the start, was a clean, well-lighted place, a world of the hard and clearly registered minimum" (317). Compared with that of Joyce and Stein, his writing is deceptively innocent, and it belies the complex elements of concentration, compression, and omission that are embedded in it. For him, writing is a controlled skill, like fishing and bullfighting, and it has a narrative economy and stylistic clarity that make it readable and accessible despite the massive and invisible iceberg below the surface.

During his apprenticeship in Paris, Hemingway was heeding Stein's advice to read Flaubert and he was incorporating the Frenchman's use of repetition and proleptic images into his own writing. In chapter 2 we will see how *Madame Bovary* influenced *A Farewell to Arms*. Both novels generate verbal clusters of interrelated images and events that resonate throughout the text, thereby eliciting the fourth and fifth dimensions of poetry that both Flaubert and Hemingway strove to achieve. Flaubert was already at the center of literary space, and Hemingway's emulation of his "honored master" would propel him into the same rarified space.

Unlike Stein and Joyce, Hemingway intended to make money selling his short stories and novels, and after a relatively short period in Paris in the early 1920s as an unknown writer, his career took off. If he looked back, it was only to reminisce about the good days when Paris was a moveable feast. It was in Paris, the city in which experiment and innovation were tolerated and encouraged, that Hemingway transformed the spirit of the avant-garde into a mainstream modern style—a style that influenced not only French and American writers, but writers around the world.

Two

Madame Bovary and Poetry

A Farewell to Arms

In prose, the slightest comparison can furnish an entire sonnet.
—GUSTAVE FLAUBERT, *Correspondance*

It is much more difficult than poetry. It is a prose
that has never been written.
—ERNEST HEMINGWAY, *Green Hills of Africa*

Gustave Flaubert is arguably the father of the modern novel and *Madame Bovary* is arguably the mother. Without Flaubert's example, Marcel Proust, Henry James, Joseph Conrad, James Joyce, and Virginia Woolf, among others, would not have written the way they do. More recently both Alain Robbe-Grillet and Nathalie Sarraute have acknowledged their indebtedness to the author of *L'éducation sentimentale*. In terms of influence, Martin Turnell also points out that Jules Laforgue's free verse incorporated Flaubert's use of the recurring image and that without Laforgue, T. S. Eliot would not have written *The Waste Land* ("Madame Bovary" 99). Gertrude Stein's writing would also have been different, and inevitably Hemingway's.

Some twenty-five years before the publication of *The Old Man and the Sea,* that is, by the mid-1920s, Hemingway had learned Stein's lessons about word repetition and the continuous present (Flaubert used *l'imparfait,* the continuous past), and he was reading Flaubert, whom, in 1947, he called his "most respected, honored master" (*Selected Letters* 624). Early on, Hemingway was experimenting with word repetition and recurring images and adapting them to his own fiction—that and Ezra Pound's recommendation that he use adjectives advisedly. In *A Farewell to Arms* Hemingway has, in fact, melded the author of *Madame Bovary* into his own innovative writing.

In terms of plot we may describe Emma Bovary as a woman with romantic ideas who married a dull country doctor, had affairs, went into debt, and committed suicide. Plot, however, was not foremost on Flaubert's mind when he was writing the novel. He once told the Goncourts that he was less interested in the story than in the relations between image and structure: "When I am working on a novel, my thought is that I am rendering a coloration, a nuance" (qtd. by Turnell 98). Flaubert was striving to craft *Madame Bovary* into a network of interrelated images, all of which would reflect the coloration he was aiming at. The nuances are so frequent, says Turnell, that there is scarcely a sentence that does not reflect something that has gone before or after (98). Carlos Baker says the same thing about Hemingway's literary practices, adding that once we understand what is going on beneath the surface, we see symbols operating everywhere.

There is also a story line in Hemingway's novels, and that, in part, explains his celebrity, but more than story line, what really matters in Flaubert and Hemingway, and what retains our interest and admiration, is the hidden logic of associated verbal patterns. The novel's structure, word clusters, and interrelated tropes form an ongoing narrative sequence. Although plot exists, narrative complexity becomes all important.

Today, it is generally acknowledged that Flaubert's description of Charles Bovary's hat at the beginning of *Madame Bovary* adumbrates Charles's character while foreshadowing events in the novel:

It was one of those composite headdresses combining a number of different features—part busby, part lancer's cap, part pillbox, part otter-skin cap, part cotton nightcap, in short, one of those shoddy objects whose dumb ugliness has depths of expression like the face of an idiot. Ovoid in shape, its upper end was stiffened with whalebone and rose from a base formed by three bulging, circular protuberances. Above these was a pattern consisting of alternating loz-

enges of rabbit fur and velvet separated from one another by strips
of scarlet material. Higher still was some kind of bag ending in a
polygon of cardboard covered with a complicated design in braid,
ending in a long and excessively thin cord from which hung a small
cross of gold thread in place of a tassel. Everything was new; the
peak glistened. (4)

Victor Brombert notes that the hat is a strange combination of shako,
bearskin, billycock hat, and nightcap, the layers, tiers, and superstructure
of which sum up Charles's lack of intelligence (*The Novels* 41). Turnell
says that this dunce cap symbolizes the whole novel because its circular
layers display aristocratic, middle-class, and proletarian trappings (100).
Flaubert begins the novel with Charles's hat and ends it with Charles's
death, and in between he introduces the reader to a wide range of imbe-
ciles, from l'Abbé Bournisien, the priest, to Homais, the town pharma-
cist. It is Charles, however, who faces the greatest life challenges in his
marriage to Emma and as a country doctor. To say that fate caused his
misfortune, as he does, is to be singularly obtuse, and the extraordinary
hat sums it all up.

The hat's three circular protuberances correspond to the three main
parts of the novel: Emma's marriage to Charles in part 1, her seduction
by Rodolphe in part 2, and her seduction by Léon in part 3. The corre-
sponding events are the visit to La Vaubyessard, the comices agricoles,
and Emma's meeting with Léon in the Rouen Cathedral. Each event is
surrounded by complex and interrelated images of phantasy and irony.
The memory of the ball at La Vaubyessard governs all of Emma's day-
dreams. The comices agricoles scene, during which Rodolphe courts
Emma while prize cattle low and official speeches are heard, is one of
high comedy and irony. Emma's visit with Léon to the Rouen Cathedral anticipates her fall. While the beadle exhorts them to look at the
"Last Judgment" and at the sinners condemned to hellfire, we smile at
the ironic foreshadowing, the forthcoming seduction.

Hemingway's oft-quoted opening paragraph in *A Farewell to Arms,*
like Charles's hat, also prefigures events that will lead to Catherine Bark-
ley's death.

In the late summer of that year we lived in a house in a village that
looked across the river and the plain to the mountains. In the bed

of the river there were pebbles and boulders, dry and white in the sun, and the water was clear and swiftly moving and blue in the channels. Troops went by the house and down the road and the dust they raised powdered the leaves of the trees. The trunks of the trees too were dusty and the leaves fell early that year and we saw the troops marching along the road and the dust rising and leaves, stirred by the breeze, falling and the soldiers marching and afterward the road bare and white except for the leaves.

Detailed as this paragraph is, we need the entire first two pages of chapter 1 to fully grasp the import of the events that will follow. The opening paragraph of book 1 resembles the opening paragraph of book 5 in both tone and content: "In the late summer of that year we lived in a house in a village that looked across the river and the plain to the mountains" (book 1). "That fall . . . we lived in a brown wooden house in the pine trees on the side of the mountain. . . . We could see the lake and the mountains across the lake. . . . A road went up the mountains" (book 5). In between book 1 and book 5, the opening paragraphs of chapter 21 and chapter 25 use the same language, the same time of year, and similar landscapes. It is late summer or September or fall, and the trees are bare and the road is either dusty or muddy and the fields are brown and sometimes it is raining and the mountains are always there. There are trucks and soldiers on the road.

In book 5, the pronoun "we" refers to Catherine and Frederic Henry, whereas in book 1 the pronoun seems to refer to the troops, but it does not exclude Catherine, because Henry is writing the story after her death and he carries her memory with him. That is why the soldiers on the road "marched as though they were six months gone with child" (4). Catherine's pregnancy and death are still very much with him and that is why the packs of clips and cartridges bulging under the soldiers' capes remind Henry of pregnant women. Indeed, the first two pages of book 1, with the house, the road, the trees, the plain, the mountains, the soldiers, the war, and the rain, like Charles's hat, adumbrate the entire novel, foreshadowing all the events that will follow. Baker says that the river, the plain, and the mountain are the novel's central symbols, and critics generally see the first chapter as an imagistic microcosm of the novel. The words "we" and "now" emphasize the ongoing presence of memory, the writing process, and the nuances of Henry's narration.

Madame Bovary also begins with the pronoun "we." Flaubert describes Charles as a fifteen-year-old student who wears the hat of clumsiness and diffidence—a hat that defines him from the moment he enters the classroom—and this dunce hat is greeted with a roar of laughter from Charles's classmates. The pronoun is a generalized "we," but it soon slides into a selective omniscient third-person narrative. The "we" also serves as a point of transition from Charles to Emma because we first see her through his eyes. In due course, his medical incompetence and general stupidity guide our vision, and it is appropriate that the "we" of Flaubert's overture serve as a transition into Emma's consciousness and eventually to the other characters in the novel.

Although the "we" with which *A Farewell to Arms* begins is Henry's voice, the pronoun belongs to a broader narrative perspective. It is his voice, to be sure, but it is also the voice of his two selves—the dutiful soldier and the disillusioned deserter—as well as the collective "we" of Henry and Catherine together. It is a brilliant opening and, like Flaubert's opening, it also encompasses the reader because both texts solicit our attention and collaboration. We have to figure out what is going on at the various narrative levels in order to understand how each text comes together.

A Farewell to Arms is composed of five "books" and forty-one chapters. Books 1 through 4 take place in Italy during World War I, while book 5 is set in Switzerland. Book 1 opens in a small Italian village in the late summer. Book 2 opens in Milan on the way to the American hospital where Henry will convalesce after he has been wounded at the front. "We got into Milan early in the morning" (81). This "we" echoes the "we" in the first sentence of book 1. It denotes Henry's two selves and the people on the train and those in the ambulance, but it also connotes Catherine, who, when Henry writes, is always with him. Book 3 opens with "now in the fall the trees were all bare and the roads were muddy" (163). The first paragraph incorporates the bare trees, the dead leaves, the fields, the mountains, and the rain of chapter 1. The word "now" signifies the ongoing present. In book 3 Henry is almost executed by the battle police, but he escapes and deserts. His two selves, the "we" of books 1, 2, and 3, will now be sundered, and book 4 opens, appropriately, with "I dropped off the train in Milan" (237). In book 5, Henry and Catherine have fled Italy and are now in Switzerland, where "that fall the snow came very late. We lived in a brown wooden house in the pine trees" (289). The pronoun "we," the house, and the mountain all echo opening passages from the preceding books. The symmetry, as in *Madame Bovary,* is now complete.

Chapter 1 contains everything: the late summer, the house in the village, the river, the plain, the mountains, the road, the troops, the mules, the dust, the leaves, the guns, the trucks, and later the cars, the rain, the mud, the cholera, and seven thousand dead in the army. Each noun is an incipient image that Hemingway amplifies like a Japanese paper pellet that, when placed in a bowl of water, magically unfolds to become a house, a street, a tree, and a town. The amplification of nouns (the road, the mountain, the troops, and so forth) begins with the overture in chapter 1—the two pages that adumbrate all future events. Hemingway carefully constructs sequences that expand connecting images around an initial seminal noun.

Flaubert's tropes are more complex and both Proust and Albert Thibaudet criticized him for their ponderous immobility. Nonetheless, Flaubert was a great creator of images and, as Douglas W. Alden points out (66), their sometimes frozen quality opposed Proust's supple and fluid use of metaphor (see also Proust, "A propos"). But, as Turnell points out, the intrinsic quality of Flaubert's metaphors "is less important than the relations between them" (99). Hemingway's correspondences are much less obvious. His nouns and adjectives, with the reader's help, do all the work, and it is the repetition of a word, a scene, or a conversation whose trace lingers in our memory that triggers our recognition and the acknowledgment of artifice, as opposed to reportage.

For example, mules are mentioned in chapter 1 along with the mud, the soldiers, and the river. The dominant image is the incessant rain that later on bogs the trucks down in the fields during the retreat of the Italian army. The battle police are shooting deserters, and after his arrest, in order to escape, Henry dives into the swollen Tagliamento River. Later, it will still be raining in Stresa and again in Switzerland when Catherine dies. Rain is the novel's leitmotif and the mules seem like an afterthought. Nonetheless, as both Lawrence Beemer and H. R. Stoneback point out, they are an important narrative detail that relates to the Saint Anthony medal that Catherine gives Henry in chapter 8, where Hemingway invokes the image of the mule three times in one paragraph (Beemer 5). Saint Anthony's patronage covers travel by water, expectant mothers, and loss. Thus, the medal foreshadows the lovers' successful escape into Switzerland, Catherine's pregnancy, the loss of her child, and her eventual death. As Beemer points out, Saint Anthony is also the patron saint of domesticated animals (5–6) and, as Stoneback notes, mules play an important role in the story of Saint Anthony: the mules are "an allusion to Saint Anthony's best known miracle, involving the mule that knelt before the Blessed Sacrament" ("Lovers' Sonnets" 50).

Flaubert's tropes and Hemingway's nouns surface periodically to remind the reader of their ongoing presence. Also, Flaubert's descriptions of good weather, as in Hemingway, correspond to moments of happiness, whereas bad weather, wind, and rain are symptomatic of bad times ahead. From her window Emma watches the dark clouds gather and roll ominously toward Rouen. These are premonitory clouds and they are part of a system of correspondences that Flaubert sets in motion. Hemingway's dark clouds rolling in toward the mountains bring the rain, bad weather, and defeat. They are also the clouds of death.

In *Madame Bovary,* the rain falls and becomes the water imagery that accompanies Emma's ennui and the entropy of all things around her. In a moment of great distress, the earth becomes a sea and the furrows of a field are waves (290). The crowd coming through the three portals of the Rouen Cathedral is like a river flowing under the three arches of a bridge (277). The reflection of the full moon on the river resembles an undulating serpent covered with luminous scales (185). These phenomena are Emma's point of view and Flaubert depicts her as drowning in her sensual corruption (179). This extreme sensuality is part of her damnation and it insinuates itself into her affair with Léon. "She would undress brutally, tearing off the thin lace of her corset which hissed around her hips like a gliding grass snake" (262). The *s* sounds in both English and French convey the hissing of the serpent, and when combined with the infernal imagery of the panels of the Rouen Cathedral, they anticipate Emma's fall. After she swallows the arsenic her death throes are indeed hellish, and in moments before she expires, "she glues her lips onto the body of the Man-God in one of the biggest love kisses she has ever given" (301). After she dies, a "black liquid" issues from her mouth. There is a lot of oozing and melting in *Madame Bovary,* and we hear the endless dripping of water. Liquids flow from the eyes of the Blind Man, more black liquid oozes from the blisters on Hippolyte's leg, and even the walls of Emma's house sweat. In *A Farewell to Arms,* the clouds, the rain, the drizzle, and the mud provide comparable although not flamboyant images. In the winter in Switzerland the snow is hard and the lovers are happy, but when it melts and turns to water, everything goes downhill from there. The landscape is enveloped in a drizzle of death.

When Henry first meets Catherine, she is a little crazy but her craziness is the grief of losing her fiancé. She soon recovers and she devotes the rest of her short, happy life to Henry. Henry is introduced to us as a patriot, he does his duty as a soldier, and he even shoots a deserter. But after his near-death experience at the hands of the battle police, he sheds his illusions and focuses his attentions on Catherine and their love together. Both Catherine and Henry are transformed by love, and love becomes their religion. When they conclude that the world and the system are determined to kill them, they concentrate on happiness, not duty.

Despite their efforts, Catherine dies, but not because of a flaw in her character. She dies because she has too narrow a pelvis for normal childbirth and because of medical incompetence—conditions beyond her control. Emma, however, wants reality to fit her dreams. Everything she does is an attempt to transform the world about her, to make her dreams come true. Her feelings and emotions are authentic enough, but it is the discrepancy between desire and the brutality of the world that does her in. She commits suicide. Her act may be an act of desperation, but Flaubert orchestrates the events that lead to her death, which is the result of both social determinism and character flaws. If only Emma had read fewer romantic novels, if only Charles had been more intelligent, if only l'Abbé Bournisien had been more sensitive to Emma's lament and less formulaic in dispensing advice, if only her creditors had been more generous and less demanding, if only Rodolphe had been less callow and Homais less self-serving, the conspiracy of people and of events might not have been lethal.

Henry and Catherine, by contrast, have few inner failings, at least none that count. They are done in by outside forces that Hemingway records carefully: Henry is wounded by the explosion of an enemy shell, the enemy kills Catherine's fiancé, Rinaldi gets syphilis, Aymo is shot, and Henry is arrested by the battle police. Nothing that happens to them is really their fault, except for one thing. If Henry and Catherine had not made love, she would still be alive. But that is like asking the earth to stop revolving around the sun. People make love and the sun also rises.

Emma's first love for Léon remains repressed, like Catherine's love for the soldier who died. Catherine says that had she known he would die, she would have given herself to him physically, and it is this loss that prepares her for Henry's advances. In like manner, as Brombert points out, Emma's successful defense against Léon fills her with the sadness of her "sacrifice," increases her resentment toward Charles, and makes her a ready victim for Rodolphe's aggressive advances (*The Novels* 68).

Flaubert's proleptic descriptions function as recurring tropes and as objective correlatives. So far, we have discussed bad weather and the water imagery, but there are so many others that it would be cumbersome to list them all. A few examples will serve to further define Flaubert's working methods. For example, when Charles begins to court Emma, his horse shies violently at the gate of the Bertaux farmhouse. Turnell notes that this is a premonition of what is to come and a warning against a disastrous marriage (101). The horse is an evocative symbol of the unconscious and of its life force.

Frequently, Flaubert's description of a landscape, an object, an event, or a situation corresponds to a character's subjective state of mind. For example, the flat fields surrounding the Bertaux farm stretch endlessly, fading into the gloom of the sky, and they represent the ennui that surrounds Emma. Charles, the doctor, will presumably save her from this endless boredom, and indeed her father's broken leg serves as a pretext for their courtship. During one of Charles's visits to the farm, the three are having a drink, and Flaubert describes Emma throwing her head back in order to catch the remaining drops of liqueur in the bottom of the glass. He zooms in on the tip of her tongue and this proleptic lick of pleasure prefigures a future disenchanted Emma trying to savor the last drops of happiness from an empty and boring life.

Flaubert's butterflies are another original touch and they too signal tropic shifts in time and mood. After Emma pricks her finger on the wire of her wilted and discarded wedding bouquet, she tosses it into the fire. As the flames consume it, the ashes fly up the chimney and settle on the countryside like black butterflies (64). During the agricultural fair the wind lifts the big bonnets of the peasant women and flutters them like the wings of white butterflies (140). This is before Emma's affair with

Rodolphe. Much later, while Léon is seducing her inside a carriage, the conveyance wanders from one end of Rouen to the other and out into the countryside. All we see of the love scene between Emma and Léon is a cab with the blinds drawn, alternately trotting quietly and galloping furiously as the changes of speed, the mounting crescendi, and the torn letter detail the nature of Emma's erotic experience (Brombert, *The Novels* 69). At one point a naked hand emerges under the little yellow curtains and throws pieces of paper (Emma's Dear Léon letter), which disperse "in the wind and settle further on, like white butterflies on a flowering field of red clover" (228). Ironically, the black butterflies of Emma's marriage have become the white butterflies of adultery, and the white bonnets of the peasant women were premonitory flappings.

There is also Flaubert's brilliant counterpoint at the agricultural fair, during which he contrasts Rodolphe's language of seduction with the speeches honoring the farmers who are receiving awards for their prize animals. The dignitaries speak of manure and a race of swine while Rodolphe speaks of love. Manure and swine undercut Rodolphe's appearance of sincerity and lace it with ironic contrast (138–40). He is of the race of swine and his words are bullshit. Nonetheless, Emma succumbs to his advances and later, in her adulterous ardor and exasperation with Charles, even before Rodolphe dumps her, she slams the door of her living room in anger. The barometer falls off the wall and breaks, and we know that bad weather will dog Emma, as indeed it does (174).

Emma's subsequent affair with Léon fails, her extravagant purchases and debts overwhelm her, her credit is beyond repair, and her illusions of romantic happiness are broken. Desperate, she swallows mouthfuls of arsenic from Homais' pharmacy and dies slowly in excruciating pain. The world has broken Emma. Although her expectations may have been unrealistic, we sympathize with her desire for love and an elegance with which to counter the boredom of provincial life, "and the web of ennui that the silent spider was spinning in all the shaded corners of her heart" ("et l'ennui, araignée silencieuse, filait sa toile dans l'ombre, à tous les coins de son cœur," 42). Emma wants more than life can offer, and with her dreams of success she tries to rise above a prosaic existence and the unwanted attentions of a doltish husband. Emma is also trapped by circumstance, gender, and male duplicity. In *A Farewell to Arms* the world grinds down the lovers, and Emma, too, feels its weight. Flaubert's rain falls on her, even as Hemingway's rain falls on Catherine and Henry.

The fabric of proleptic tropes may well correspond to the fourth dimension and the poetry toward which Flaubert aspired. Hemingway's nouns and narrative tissues capture similar dimensions. The descriptions in prose of both writers, from a writerly point of view, generally cover the same kind of ground: landscapes, events, situations. Where Hemingway differs from Flaubert, and this may be the fifth dimension he strives to achieve, is in applying these techniques to dialogue.

Flaubert uses prolepsis and objective correlatives to good effect, and their metamorphoses throughout *Madame Bovary* produce a cutting irony and the subversion of received ideas. Hemingway also uses objective correlatives, and his irony undermines the hollow platitudes of authority and ideology. When Hemingway writes dialogue, and despite Pound's advice, his adjectives and adverbs multiply in order to define character while also emphasizing verbal play. Catherine's frequent use of the word "lovely" not only defines her character but also, through repetition, elicits comparisons that jump back and forth in time from one situation to another. The repetition is like a musical theme or color in painting that highlights certain relationships. Hemingway orchestrates the repetition and resonance of words and images and this musicality affects the structure of the novel. He has adapted sound to dialogue, and his wordplay generates meanings and associations that transcend the prosaic denotation of words. Connotation and paranomasia engender the fourth and fifth dimensions and the poetry to which he alludes. Sound and color—Flaubert's coloration and nuance—have become essential to prose poetry. In advising Hemingway, both Pound and Stein believed that modern writing, like modern painting and music, required a basic restructuring of its elements in order to defamiliarize everyday occurrences. The tension and tautness of this new form would then convey the necessary freshness and intensity of lived experience—the lived experience that is such an important element in Hemingway's writing.

However, in addition to dialogue, Hemingway also uses the word "lovely" in a number of descriptive passages. For example, in chapter 2, he describes the wine as "clear red, tannic and lovely" (7), thus giving it both color and taste. But "lovely" is vague, harder to define, and the word stands out because it belongs to a different descriptive order. In chapter 3, and for the second time, Hemingway again uses the word "lovely," this time to describe the stock of Henry's Austrian sniper's rifle: it is a "lovely dark walnut" (11). Why is the dark walnut, like the wine, lovely? We know that Hemingway liked good wine and hunting, but this is perhaps no reason for a meticulous craftsman like him to casually inject the word into a novel about somebody else. We don't encounter "lovely" again until chapter 6, when Henry says that Catherine "looked very lovely" (29). Like the wine and the stock of the rifle, she too is no doubt desirable and perhaps this is sufficient, but in chapter 8, the mountains above the snow line are "white and lovely in the sun" (45). The white of the snow is appropriate, but although "lovely" may be pleasing visually, it is not objectively descriptive. It is subjective and therefore helps to define who Henry is. Hemingway is using binocular vision, that is, the simultaneous presentation of two points of view, the subjective and the objective. The description of white snow in the sun is objective and can be verified by anyone, whereas "lovely in the sun" is subjective and may or may not correspond to everybody's view of what snow on the mountains represents.

The next time the word "lovely" appears is in chapter 9. Passini has been mortally wounded and he is screaming in pain: "Oh purest lovely Mary shoot me" (55). In his agony he implores the Virgin to intercede on his behalf, to soothe the pain, and indeed he soon dies. In chapter 10, Rinaldi describes Catherine as a "lovely cool goddess" (66), thereby connecting Catherine, the virgin, to the mother of God, the supreme Virgin. A pattern is beginning to emerge. In chapter 11, the priest describes the chestnut woods of the Abruzzi in the fall as "lovely" (77). The Abruzzi is unspoiled and in the mountains, and the word "woods" echoes the "wood" of the rifle stock.

In chapter 15, Dr. Valentini calls Catherine "a lovely girl" (99). Soon thereafter Catherine appropriates the word and she uses it constantly. Her night with Henry is "lovely," he has "a lovely temperature," and even Henry begins to use the word: "You've got a lovely everything" (102–3). A lovely Catherine, a lovely night, and a lovely everything, and the connotations are clear. In no time the words "proud" and "love" attach themselves to "lovely" and henceforth, the wordplay is unstoppable. Catherine is now lovely because she does what Henry wants. She is also "a darling" and she is "good," although in this context her goodness is purely sexual and her implied obedience is ironic (106). The adjectives "lovely," "good," and "obedient" slide imperceptibly into the adjectives "nice" and "fine." Fergy is a "fine girl" and "damned nice," Henry and Catherine have a "fine time" together, and Henry's damaged leg is "fine" (109–10). As meaning slides back and forth, the cumulative energy of the adjective generates comedy, ambiguity, irony, and play. Clearly, Hemingway is having a good and lovely time. Henry sums it up by saying, "We had a lovely time that summer" (112).

We, in turn, can sum it up as the progressive slidings of pleasure—the title of Alain Robbe-Grillet's film script (*Glissements progressifs du plaisir*) in which verbal and visual play assume a life of their own—a life that is independent of the story line. Such a horizontal sliding back and forth from one event in the text to another is a function of time and memory and it becomes a fourth dimension. The fifth dimension is vertical and one of depth, in which all the intermeshing elements begin to resonate as the reader remembers and, in turn, plays with the text's horizontal and vertical musicality. All the themes and all the chords vibrate together and when that happens the reader can legitimately say that the work is a masterpiece.

Flaubert achieves this musical effect in *Madame Bovary* with the ongoing past tense (*l'imparfait*), which Proust describes as Flaubert's one great innovation. The *ay* sound of the imperfect, which in French ends in "ait" and "aient," generates both sound and rhythm and becomes Flaubert's distinctive style. His prose rings with his favorite verb tense, which James Wood compares to "a bell tolling the very sound of provincial boredom in *Madame Bovary*" (11). In comparing Flaubert and Hemingway, Wood says that Hemingway's lean, pared-down style resembles a "highly controlled richness" (10). When Flaubert describes Charles's reaction to Emma's pregnancy, he says: "L'idée d'avoir engendré le délectait," which means that he was delighted at the idea of having engendered. The sound effects are probably more important than the meaning, because if we say the French out loud we get four *ay* sounds in three words: "l'idée," "engendré," and "délectait" (Wood 11). Stein may well have learned the lessons of repetition and the fourth dimension from Flaubert and passed them on to Hemingway. In any case, and this is Hemingway's originality, repetition in dialogue sometimes generates miniature poems in which sound is everything and it is the sound that also, eventually, generates meaning.

Meanwhile, the associations in *A Farewell to Arms* have been multiplying. Catherine's hair is "lovely" and, although the lovers are not married, she is a "lovely wife" (114–15). She says that Henry is her religion: "You see

I'm happy, darling, and we have a lovely time. . . . We're happy and we love each other. Do let's just please be happy. You are happy, aren't you? . . . Can I do anything to please you? Would you like me to take down my hair? Do you want to play?" (116). Although Catherine's insistence on happiness has a disquieting effect, the repetition of "lovely" and "happy" culminates in the verb "to play." Coming to bed in order to play makes sense textually, but the verb also emphasizes the fact, indirectly, that Hemingway is also playing. He is playing with language while moving the story forward.

The wordplay through chapter 18, incorporating wine, beauty, love, and war, is relatively simple and straightforward. With chapter 19, the connotations and the irony darken. The Italian army is bogged down in the rain, Catherine is afraid of the rain, and she sometimes sees herself dead in it (126). Rain is the objective correlative that accompanies the lovers to the very end and, after Catherine dies, Henry, had he known the Verlaine poem, could have said: "My heart is breaking / And in the city it is raining" ("Il pleure dans mon cœur / Comme il pleut sur la ville," 256).

Despite a lovely summer, in the fall before Catherine dies, Henry says that "the summer was gone" (133) and the war is going badly, and he acknowledges the fact that the Allies are cooked. He repeats the word "cooked" some thirteen times in a context of playful irony (133–34), but despite a "lovely day" at the races, and a stiff upper lip, the trap is closing. It is not only the biological trap that haunts the lovers, but the war itself, and the bureaucracy of incompetence that accompanies it. Indeed, the incompetence of Charles and the determinism of *Madame Bovary* also haunt *A Farewell to Arms*. Henry says that "if anything comes between us we're gone and then they have us" (130). Gone, that is, like the summer. Subsequently, he almost dies when the Austrian shell explodes in the trenches, he barely escapes execution by the battle police who have arrested him for alleged desertion, in Stresa he and Catherine are only two steps ahead of the authorities bent on arresting them, and in the hospital in Switzerland medical incompetence is the final straw that does them in. Catherine is finally broken and bravery is not sufficient to resist the forces that will destroy happiness. It is appropriate that the words "happy" and "lovely" ring throughout the novel like funeral bells.

The lovers put up a stiff fight, but the world breaks them even as Hemingway blends reality and illusion into a narrative in which brave words are but temporary bulwarks against adversity. In a cheap hotel room by the railroad station, a room that Catherine calls their "fine house," the lovers play at happiness and they put on a good show (155). Despite feeling like a whore, Catherine says that the room is "lovely," "splendid," and "fine," and Henry calls her a "lovely girl." She is no longer "crazy," despite having lost her fiancé at the Battle of the Somme, and the wine is still "grand." Catherine says she is now happy and married to Henry, an ironic untruth that buttresses their pretense and delays the tragic end of their five acts together (154).

Hemingway peppers his text with key words such as "love," "lovely," "grand," "fine," "splendid," "brave," and "good," and they serve as antidotes to the collective madness that envelops them. These words are the cocoons that protect their individuality and they insulate them from the cruelty of the world—two people in love against "them" and the ideology of received ideas: duty, obedience, and patriotism. After he deserts, Henry says that "abstract words such as glory, honor, courage, or hallow were obscene beside the concrete names of villages, the numbers of roads, the names of rivers, and numbers of regiments and the dates" (185). The realm of received ideas is also Homais' domain and he revels in it. When Charles dies, Homais beats off three new doctors who might have opened practice in Yonville. "The authorities support him and public opinion protects him." He receives "la croix d'honneur" (324).

After Henry's "separate peace" (243) he opts for love because duty has failed or, rather, the system to which he had pledged allegiance has failed, and he has no reason to return to a burning building from which he has just escaped (232). Hemingway's critique of encratic language, that is, received ideas and the empty slogans of ideology, remind us of Flaubert's hatred of the bourgeoisie and the self-satisfaction of Monsieur Homais. Throughout *Madame Bovary* Flaubert's cutting irony is directed at the arrogance of doxa and the values of a social system that privileges appearance over substance.

Despite fundamental differences between the two works, repetition, prolepsis, and poetic resonance exist in both. Hemingway can, with good reason, say that Flaubert is his most respected and honored master. Hemingway even borrows the image of the statue that is the climax of Catherine's death scene, and from which he derives the title—a trope that adumbrates the novel.

In death, Catherine, like a statue, can no longer embrace and Henry must say farewell to her arms as he had said farewell to military arms.

The title derives in part from George Peele's poem "A Farewell to Arms." Bernard Oldsey notes that contrary to the idealization of love and honor in Peele's poem, Hemingway's title and novel give ironic emphasis to the fact that "there is very little glory or honor on the field of battle, and that human love dies in the flesh" (*Hemingway's Hidden Craft* 34). Oldsey says that Hemingway rejected thirty-three other working titles before choosing *A Farewell to Arms*. Despite Hemingway's preference, however, Michael Reynolds opts for one of the rejected titles, *A Separate Peace,* because the word "piece," a homonym for the word "peace," "would have been a sardonic statement about the love affair" (*Hemingway's First War* 64). "A piece of ass," however, lacks the caring connotation of "arms," and its pejorative meaning radically alters the reading of the novel.

Because Hemingway claimed he never forgot anything he read, we must assume that he remembered Flaubert's description of Emma immobilized and lying flat on the bed "like a white waxen statue" ("blanche comme une statue de cire," 194). When Emma dies, Charles is standing at the foot of her bed and he too is "as pale as a statue" ("pâle comme une statue," 300).

Flaubert's subtitle for *Madame Bovary* was *Mœurs de province—Provincial Customs*—and it points to the paradox of trying to write realistic prose and poetry simultaneously. The accuracy of every detail in Flaubert's novel has been documented, and it is indeed a true portrait of country life in Normandy in the mid-nineteenth century. Paul Valéry, who was suspicious of the novel generally, mocked the contradictions of a genre that purported to describe the trivia of everyday existence in a style that wanted to be beautiful.[1] He once said that he could never bring himself to write a sentence such as "the Marquise went out at five" ("la Marquise sortit à cinq heures"). Yet somehow Flaubert manages to pull it off, and he communicates the boredom of Emma's life with Charles in a style that entrances most readers. Perhaps it is in the repetition of the *ay* sound, or the rhythm of the sentences, or the tropes themselves and the gradual construction of the novel paragraph by paragraph and segment by segment. Whatever it is, it is also in the fabric and the linguistic weave that holds everything together, that is, the repetition of recurring images that activates what has preceded and what will follow. Historically, Flaubert's writing marks the transition between romanticism and realism, not only stylistically but also emotionally. His classical style is the manifestation of what Gide calls "a controlled romanticism" ("l'œuvre classique ne sera forte et belle qu'en raison de son romantisme dompté," *Incidences* 40). In trying to tame Emma's romantic temperament ("Madame Bovary, c'est moi"), Flaubert was using the cold hard facts of objective prose while linking them together into tropic clusters.

Hemingway's figurative clusters also activate what has preceded and what will follow. His nouns and the repetition of words and sounds become thematic generators that propel the novel forward, but also backward, as words such as "lovely," "fine," "grand," "happy," and "brave" become the mnemonic traces of preceding passages. Toward the end of the novel, the earlier optimism of these words slides into desperation as Catherine keeps repeating, "I have a lovely life, . . . I have a fine time" (298), and "The nights are grand" (299), and "You're sweet. And I'm not crazy now, I'm just very, very, very happy" (300). Her statements anticipate the coming of the rain and her impending death: "I'm not going to die, . . . I won't die, . . . it's silly to die" (319). Catherine's fear of dying in the rain will be fulfilled and we sense that there is an artistic link between rain and death. Not a necessary link, but one that exists in Catherine's mind and one that Hemingway manages to persuade the reader is real.

Both Emma and Catherine die, but the contrast between the two women couldn't be more striking. Although pregnant, unmarried, and technically a sinner, by the cultural standards of 1917, Catherine remains virginal in her innocence and fidelity, whereas Emma's affairs and unbridled sensuality, by the standards of the 1850s, were indeed scandalous. The realism of Hemingway's novel, like Flaubert's, is a realism that coexists with the resonance of repetition and the figurative language of poetry. They are not mutually exclusive, as Valéry would have us believe. In Hemingway's fiction and in Flaubert's, the two are mutually dependent and we could not have one without the other. If Baudelaire could grow "flowers of evil," then surely Flaubert can grow flowers of ennui, and Hemingway, in his fashion, the flowers of irony and innocence.

Flaubert can justifiably say that prose has many third and fourth dimensions, and that the slightest comparison can furnish an entire sonnet (*Correspondance* 446). In like manner, Hemingway can say that prose is more difficult to write than poetry and that prose can provide a fourth and fifth dimension (*Green Hills* 26–27). When Hemingway was learning how to write, *Madame Bovary* was already a classic. The lessons he learned from his respected and honored master served him well, and *A*

Farewell to Arms can now also qualify as a classic in the tight and competitive race for excellence. It is one of the novels that has helped to place Hemingway at the center of literary space.

The tropic weave in *A Farewell to Arms* was already manifest in *The Sun Also Rises*. Indeed, Hemingway had been exploring the effects of verbal play in his first novel, a novel that is not only about expatriates in Paris and Pamplona, but also about the creative vagaries of the unconscious. Lacanian theory reveals the strings governing the puppet-like behavior of Jake Barnes and Brett Ashley—their goings and comings—the strings of their attachment—that always, inevitably, bring them back together.

We move next to Paris and the scene of language where Hemingway's playful irony foregrounds acts of comedy and tragedy.

Three

Jacques Lacan Reads _The Sun Also Rises_

The unconscious is structured like a language.
—JACQUES LACAN, _Ecrits_

"Isn't it pretty to think so?"
—ERNEST HEMINGWAY, _The Sun Also Rises_

_A_ll readers of _The Sun Also Rises_ agree that Jake Barnes is impotent—
an impotence that leaves desire intact—but that, despite desire, he cannot
fulfill himself sexually.[1] Although the novel itself is vague about the exact
nature of Jake's injury, in an interview with George Plimpton, Hemingway insisted that Jake "was capable of all normal feelings as a _man_ but
incapable of consummating them," that the "wound was physical and not
psychological and that he was not emasculated" (Plimpton).[2]

This impotence has raised many questions and prompted many interpretations. Perhaps, in Susan Sontag's words, we need to go "against
interpretation" and look for something else (3–14). Perhaps we need to
focus on language, words, and traces of meaning, not on the plot. Perhaps the real hero or heroine, in the postmodern sense, is the writing
itself, not the characters. Hemingway's craft of omission and the need
for audience complicity certainly point in this direction. If _the_ overriding metaphor in _The Sun Also Rises_ is impotence, then we need to look
at how it manifests itself in the writing. Because postcards, telegrams,
letters, and newspaper dispatches, in addition to the characters' riding

(sounds like "writing") in taxis and trains, may be symptoms of desire and of the repressed, we need to ask what these symptoms represent. If writing and riding are similar and, because of their homonymy, textually related, then, in the context of Freud's *Beyond the Pleasure Principle,* the novel's love games and train trips and the characters' goings and comings assume special (spatial) significance. Messages are being dispatched and destinations are reached but they say more than a realistic reading of the text can reveal.

Perhaps we need to look beyond realism toward the play of meaning within the text. Instead of focusing on linear discourse, we need to see what a simultaneous discourse can reveal, a simultaneity that results from the privileged overview of rereading when special moments and significant things come into focus to form a spatial oneness that may, at first, go unnoticed. It will be similar to a vertical discourse whose chords resonate like music. Because the discourse of the Other, that is, the discourse of the unconscious, is always embedded in the text, we need to track its metaphoric and metonymic images and the phonemic echoes that trigger responses in the reader's mind. Reynolds has begun to unravel the meaning of these repetitions that resonate in "our mental matrix," but the metafictional implications of such dissemination need closer scrutiny (see Reynolds, *Novel of the Twenties* 40).[3] It is certainly true, as Reynolds points out, that "unconsciously the reader picks up these repetitions" and it is also important to understand the cumulative value of words such as "hell," "nice," and "value," and actions such as bathing and paying the bill (39). In this connection, John Atherton says that it is the narrator's "total recall"—and, I would add, the reader's recall as well—that "restores to words their capacity to play *between* situations" (215). Lacan calls it a "resonance in the communicating networks of discourse" (*Ecrits* 55; "résonance dans des réseaux communicants de discours," *Ecrits I* 143). Indeed, Nina Schwartz, John Atherton, Robert B. Jones, Elizabeth D. Vaughn, and others believe that *The Sun Also Rises,* despite its realism, exhibits postmodern characteristics. This postmodernism is determined not only by Flaubert's repetitions, but also by Lacan's psychoanalytical theories. It may be useful, therefore, to delineate his insights in order to see how they apply to Hemingway's writing.

When Lacan stated that the unconscious is structured like a language, he opened a royal road between literature and the unconscious, one for which Freud had already cleared the way with, among other essays, his psychoanalytic reading of E. T. A. Hoffman's "Sandman." Also, although Freud's analysis of dreams drew attention to linguistic structures, he was unfamiliar with Ferdinand de Saussure's seminal work in linguistics, which was to have such a profound influence, despite their subsequent modifications, on the oeuvre of Claude Lévi-Strauss, Lacan, Roland Barthes, Jacques Derrida, Michel Foucault, and many others. Therefore, in bringing together literature and psychoanalysis, we need to incorporate Freud's *Interpretation of Dreams,* Saussure's *Course in General Linguistics (Cours de linguistique générale)*, and Lacan's *Ecrits* as the triad from which a psychoanalytic theory of reading can be developed.

After a fiction tells its story, there is also the story of telling, a procedure that foregrounds language and the enchantment of the text. The reader's accomplices in this endeavor are the tropic, symbolic, and homonymic traces that are embedded in its tissues. Words in literary texts, like the images in Freud's dreams, are constantly being displaced, condensed, deformed, and dramatized. Indeed, rhetorical language is a second sign system that functions in collusion with character, plot, and suspense but is also independent of them. Moreover, the literariness of the text, in Roman Jakobson's sense, gives us freer access to the voice of the Other, which, in Lacanian terminology, is the voice of the unconscious.

Whenever we focus on the literariness of a text, we are less interested in its message than in how meaning is circulating through it. In essence, the reader produces meaning, and thus the creative role of the audience is indispensable. Without active readers, a trope is inert. It is a lifeless combinatory mass waiting for someone to animate it, to give it form, to make it sing, to reveal its latent mysteries. The indeterminacy of certain texts suggests that the reader must step in to give plausible explanations for redundancies, gaps, and contradictions. Textual aporia may well mean that something has been repressed and that the magnetic field of this black hole needs to be explored and its energy brought into play.

However, as Ellie Ragland-Sullivan points out, the aim of Lacanian poetics is not to psychoanalyze a text but to "study the paralinguistic points of join between visible language and invisible effect" (382), that is, the points at which the conscious mind connects with the unconscious. The reader is invited to collaborate in the creation of a text parallel to the one the writer has scripted, and in doing so the reader forms his or her own tropic network using the holes, traces, words, repetitions, sentences, structures, paragraphs, and figural motifs. Underlying all this is the voice of the unconscious caught in the folds of the text, which the reader unfolds so that its body can be heard and seen and touched and felt almost intuitively in what Barthes describes as orgasmic bliss (*jouissance*) (*Plaisir du texte* 105). The pretext for happiness is the game of writing, the play of reading, and the sweep of similitude that gives the reader a leading role in rewriting the text. In reading a trope the reader has to figure out the semantic transposition from a sign that is present to one that is absent. For example, in Verlaine's poem "Chanson d'automne" ("Autumn Song") he evokes the "long sobs of the violins" ("Les sanglots longs des violons," 105), sobs that refer to the autumn wind, and which the reader infers. Although the autumn wind is implied, it is never stated. It is thus the absent referent, which the "long sobs of the violins" signify. The images in dreams and in the unconscious work the same way. One image has displaced another, and the riddle of the unconscious is to find the missing referent. Somewhere between, around, over, and under these pulsive forces the points of join between visible language and invisible effect come into play. The reader works through the different levels of the written and unwritten text (Freud's *durcharbeiten*) in order to weave his or her network of associations. Tropes and traces are the flesh and blood of this figurative body and its tissues.

The warp and woof of this weave are metaphor and metonymy, and they occupy an intermediary zone between the plot of the macrotext and the particles of the microtext. As tropes, they inscribe their mnemonic traces on the reader's mind and it is these tracings embedded in the text and in the reader that invite rereadings so that a polyphony can be heard, "for it to become clear that all discourse is aligned along the several staves of a score" (*Ecrits* 154; "pour que s'y fasse entendre une polyphonie et que tout discours s'avère s'aligner sur les plusieurs portées d'une partition," *Ecrits I* 260–61). Lacan's musical analogy is an apt one because tropic traces coexist in the reader's mind and it is their simultaneity that allows him or her to move backward and forward along a horizontal axis. The scoring of a text resonates with connotations and contexts that Lacan says are suspended vertically (*Ecrits* 154), but I would say also horizontally, because it is the simultaneity of these horizontal units that gives the text its musical presence and vertical reality. All this is analogous to a pianist striking chords with both hands so that the vibrations of each note will be heard in unison. This is also the poetry of prose that both Flaubert and Hemingway wanted to write and that I described in the preceding chapter, the main difference being that repetitions in *The Sun Also Rises* unveil unconscious behavior patterns, whereas in *A Farewell to Arms* they define prose as conscious poetry.

Repetitions as pulsive forces inscribe their passage on the mind. Derrida calls it a *frayage,* whereas Freud's metaphor for such inscriptions is the magical writing pad. Although the pad's inscriptions may be erased, they do, nonetheless, leave a mark—a trace that can be seen when the pad is examined at a certain angle and under certain lighting conditions (Freud, *Beyond* 25). In writing, such traces leave conscious and unconscious trails. They may be hidden or disguised or barely noticeable, but their presence can be felt, and it is the reader who apprehends and organizes them into meaningful units. These units of meaning circulate within a text, energizing the activity of writing and reading. They reinforce the tropes and the voice of the Other; they disrupt realism and representation; they form gaps; and in collusion with the floating signifiers, they bar the way to the signified. In so doing, they call attention to the creative process and to writing as an activity, opposing mimesis—mimesis being the artist's attempt to reproduce reality. Metafiction is less interested in telling a story than in the story of telling. It focuses on how a work of art is put together, not on whether it mirrors the world.

Traces take on meaning through their differential opposition to and in combination with other traces. Lacan's readiness to play with sounds is legendary: the word "lettre" becomes "l'être" (being), "language" becomes "lalangue," "linguistics" evolves into a pejorative "linguisterie," and everything ends up as "litière" (litter = letter). There is also the ostrich, from which Lacan develops *la politique de l'autruiche,* a word enriched by the denomination of one letter and the familiar head-in-the-sand proverb (see "Seminar" 32; "Le séminaire" 24).

We as readers, if we value our creative roles, will play the writing game, nimbly dancing over, around, and within the interstices of the letter where the Other resides. The writer writes because he or she has to and in order to be recognized (read). The reader, in turn, derives pleasure from the text and he or she plays with the materiality of words. In order to experience the bliss to which Barthes refers in *Le plaisir du texte,* the body of the text must be pressed into action so that desire—the desire embedded in the writing and in the reader—may be heard and felt. The creative reader resonates with what is unconscious in the writer's communication.

Traces and dissemination confirm the fact that no signifier ever refers only to itself. Moreover, because language is a system of signs distinguished from one another only by their mutual opposition, no element in a discourse can function as a sign without referring to another element that is absent. The dispersion of meaning throughout the text, the fragmentation of the "letter" (signifier) into *semes* that inseminate the narrative with multiple meanings—a narrative whose center is everywhere and nowhere—is a dispersion that has a material reality, which, when reassembled, can constitute a whole. Never mind that Osiris's mythical phallus is still missing. In *The Sun Also Rises* we can reassemble the phallus—Jake's phallus—from fragments that are scattered throughout the text. Like Isis in search of the missing organ, Brett Ashley is also on the go, questing after substitutes for Jake's missing part and his impotence. The signifier may be unstable and its dispersion inevitable, but the parts can be reassembled.

In realist writing the reader sometimes mistakenly believes that the words in the text are people, objects, and events in the real world. A Hemingway story, for example, may provide enough descriptive detail to convey the illusion that X, Y, and Z are flesh-and-blood characters in an historical setting. Clearly, his descriptions of Paris streets, the Basque landscape, and the Pamplona fiesta evoke a vivid and accurate sense of place. In postmodern texts, however, meaning derives not only from such detail but also from a network of interconnecting signs. This network emphasizes words, images, and connotations that function independently of the codes for people, chronology, and causality. The play of different voices occurs as a spatial unfolding of language that speaks independently of any one character. In essence, the reader produces meaning from an elaborate web of associations that contribute to the thickening of the plot. Joseph Frank, in "Spatial Form in Modern Literature," refers to it as a pattern of internal references that can be apprehended as a unity (383). Although he has the language of poetry in mind, the principle applies also to fiction whenever the structural complexities of the text foreground what Jakobson calls its "literariness." Frederic Joseph Svoboda also points out that Hemingway wanted to write a prose that would "work on his readers with the subtlety normally associated with such a genre as poetry" (112).

Murray Krieger reminds us that words have a dual power, that in addition to newspaper language (Jake, like Hemingway, is a newspaper man who is writing a novel), words can work with and against each other. A poem, in contrast to newspaper language, remakes language as a web, a tissue of interrelationships that foregrounds the weaving process. The reader must therefore be attentive to the force that words generate among each other because "they function both as intelligible, transparent carriers of meaning, . . . and, simultaneously, as dense, sensible entities on their own" (11). These verbal manipulations—a form of language play—perform another function while obstructing our conventional use of newspaper language. When words are transparent we focus on the story; when they are opaque we fix on the verbal surfaces in order to apprehend them as separate entities instead of pointers to objects, people, or events in the "real" world. Whenever this happens, fictional discourse swerves away from the story toward a system of internal relationships whose parts are sustained by "mutual justification instead of by reference to outside realities" (Krieger 13). However, if we are looking for meaning or reference, these networks may also help to unveil the unconscious (with its reference to death, desire, and impotence), or they may be seen as mimetic signs of impersonal, random, and entropic events—the cosmic "Game" that Kostas Axelos refers to (15).

A theoretical text (such as this one) has to mediate between the rigors of philosophical or psychoanalytic discourse and the practical work of criticism. In addition to the obvious patterns of *The Sun Also Rises*'s plot and its characters, there are floating signifiers denoting and connoting sex, money, value, hell, and death disseminated throughout the text. For example, there is a passage that involves Jake, Brett, Count Mippipopolous, and a Greek artist named Zizi. The word *zizi* in French is a boy's penis. The "pippi" sound in Mippipopolous that occurs when its two phonemes are read backward has juvenile scatological traces. The count's allusion to "big doings" in London and Brett's cryptic statement, "Enormous," are comical, in part, because the connotation contrasts the size of a boy's *zizi* with an adult's (28). This is also the context of Jake's "accident," which occurred on the Italian "joke front" and is supposed to be "funny" (31), but which, in reality, despite the wit and the irony, makes him one of the wounded, like all the other expatriates who suffer in one way or another, either physically or emotionally. The word "joke" resembles the word "Jake" whenever we substitute the vowel *o* for the vowel *a*. The impotence inscribed on Jake's body at the Italian "joke front" has become a "hell of a joke." The conversation in chapter 7 between the count, Brett, and Jake foregrounds the connection: "joke" is used as a verb nine times and is linked directly to Jake with statements such as, "You don't joke him" and "I wouldn't joke him" (58). In no time at all "Jake" and "joke" become interchangeable, and the floating signifiers and vocalic traces define the text's resonating network. The joke and the irony derive from the fact that Jake's *zizi* is neither small nor big, but absent. The "joke front" is also a pun on Jake's front—the front part of his anatomy—his missing penis, a penis that is neither seen nor described in the mirror scene, as Jake prepares for bed one evening in his Paris apartment. This part of *The Sun Also Rises* reads as though Hemingway was consciously incorporating Freud's theories concerning jokes and their relation to the unconscious.

Phallic absence, which fits in so well with Freud's theory of the primal castration, regulates the structure of the novel. In one sense Jake's creativity overrides his impotence (he is writing the novel we are reading), but in another, this impotence, both directly and indirectly, affects everyone in the cast, from Brett Ashley to Robert Cohn to Romero, the bullfighter. Brett's promiscuity is, in large measure, a reaction to Jake's inability to make love, but Jake's relationship with Brett and her relationship with him are a dramatization of the *Fort!/Da!* game that little Ernst (Freud's grandson) plays in Freud's *Beyond the Pleasure Principle* (15–16). Ernst's game of tossing the spool across the crib (*Fort* = gone) and retrieving it (*Da* = here), which Freud interprets as the game of retrieval of the absent mother, is like Jake's game with Brett. Jake is Ernst (in more ways than one) and Brett is the mother-spool. She may go away temporarily, but she always comes back or he goes to her, as though they had each other on a string. Her infidelities may be painful but they are tolerated, and the nature of their relationship—a connection with strings attached (postcards, wires, and telegrams)—is that she does return. As with Ernst's spool, which is tossed across the crib, Brett's destination is inevitably someone's bed.

Within the context of the symbolic bed and the absent *zizi*, there is an undercurrent of Freud's primal scene and of the repressed, and it derives in part from the cumulative effect of words and phrases such as "Saint Pères," "royalty," "father," "boy," "little friend Zizi," "hard," "mummy,"

"Mumms," "Veuve Cliquot" (referring to the widow Clicquot, whose widowhood on the bottle's label identifies the champagne—Hemingway misspells "Clicquot" and "Mumm"), "love," "desire," "money," and "values" (63). Together, these words create a network of interconnecting signs—a spatial (special) unfolding that connotes the primal scene (Laius, Jocasta, Oedipus) while contributing to the work's literariness.

Money, in contrast with impotence (no penis), has power and potency, and it buys things, sex, and pleasure. Money, in addition to impotence, is one of the pervasive themes of the novel. Indeed, the frame of reference shifts quickly from the boy's *zizi* to the adult world of "big doings" where the actors play out their "stuffed" lives on the stage of monetary exchange. Count Mippipopolous knows the "values," he has lots of money, and he gladly pays for all his pleasures. In a material economy everything has value and this value supplements Freud's psychic economy of impotence and the need for love. In time ("time," like the sun that rises, is another word that resonates throughout the text), the less experienced actors pay for everything they do and get and, sometimes, as Brett and Jake do, comment respectively on that fact: "Don't we pay for all the things we do, though?" (26) and "the bill always came" (148). Jake not only counts his money, adding it up in his checkbook; he also pays the bills that inevitably come due. There is both realism and resonance in the bills that are due, but in order to produce meaning (the writerly and resonant level), the reader moves from realism (the readerly level) to linguistic interplay—an essential element of metafiction and of postmodern critical strategy.

This shift is a relatively recent phenomenon in Hemingway criticism. Not so long ago (1950), critics such as W. M. Frohock, in "Violence and Discipline," said that "it might be impossible for anyone opening the book now to find anything much, other than irrelevant digression, in the pages about the self-made Greek Count" (286). Within the past decade, however, critics such as James Hinkle have been emphasizing the fact that "playing with multiple meanings inherent in words is a pervasive feature of Hemingway's writing" (77). Atherton points out that comic operations on language open up the signifier to a form of free play, that Bill Gorton's repetition of words and phrases such as "wonderful," "never be daunted," and "utilize" lose their denotation through ludic insistence (213–14). Verbal play, like irony, also contributes to the novel's disguises.

It conceals the devastating effects of Jake's wound with wit and humor, it hides the empty lives of the expatriates with merriment, and it masks the *Fort!/Da!* game of repetition compulsion with postcards, telegrams, and trips to San Sebastian.

Jake's impotence is, in fact, responsible for everything that happens, and it is his war wound, his symbolic impotence, that both generates and regulates the machinery of the novel. Jake is the narrator of events and it is his discourse that keeps things moving. What also keeps things moving is the expatriate's pursuit of pleasure.

They bring their moveable feast from Paris to Pamplona, where the fiesta literally explodes in their faces. Brett (Circe) reduces men to swine; Jake becomes a pimp; a churlish Cohn fights with Jake, Mike, and Romero; and, except for Cohn, they all get drunk. They behave in ways that are decidedly not "nice," and Brett, who cannot resist what she wants, leaves for Madrid with Romero. The expatriates' behavior in Paris was perhaps dissolute, but in Pamplona, by Montoya's standards, it is degraded. At first Montoya forgives Jake his friends because he is *aficionado,* but after the pimping episode, he is no better than they are. Jake, like the steers, is both physically and morally deballed. He is doubly impotent. He cannot stop his friends' slide into disgrace or his own. But why would Jake dishonor himself by sending Brett off with Romero? Are not love and honor supposed to be more important to a man than life itself? Cohn fights in order to protect his idea of a chivalric code, and Romero's code, whenever the occasion demands it, is to face death in the bullring. Has Jake no sense of honor? Is he not aware of the values? Why, since he knows Spain so well and loves the corrida so much, should he defile his honor and alienate Montoya?

The answer is perhaps not self-evident. Jake's behavior, like that of the other expatriates, is subject to the pleasure principle. His love for Brett overrides the reality principle. If he now seems indifferent to Spanish honor, it is because his impotence and love for Brett have changed the rules of the game. Or have they? This will not have been the first time Brett has gone off with another man. There was Cohn before Romero, and before Cohn there were others. It's as though Jake and Brett, together, were playing the *Fort!/Da!* ritual—the game of going away and coming back. Jake fixes Brett up with a man, and she goes away with him, but her departure, in essence, ensures her return.

The desire that Jake experiences (perverse as it may seem) assimilates the reality principle. The symbolic pleasure of the game is the new reality principle, and he subordinates everything to it. Indeed, Jake's relationship with Brett illustrates Derrida's contention that the pleasure principle is stronger than the death drive, or rather, if repetition compulsion is a symptom of the death instinct, then the pleasure principle remains dominant—dominant because it incorporates the reality principle (*Post Card* 286). Instead of returning to Paris after the fiesta, like the others, Jake goes to Biarritz and then on to San Sebastian. Why? In part because he knows Brett has gone off without money, but also because we are witnessing the climax of the *Fort!/Da!* game that the two have been playing.

The pleasure principle, like Ernst's string and spool, reels the characters in, connecting them with letters, wires, postcards, newspaper dispatches, and words. If writing is a deferral that reenacts the primal loss, be it breast or mother, then this retrieval inscribes pain and pleasure as the new reality principle. Hemingway adumbrates the process with his Paris sidewalk description of jumping frogs and boxer toys being manipulated by strings (35). And when Brett, who is so infatuated with Romero that she can't stand it anymore, says that she's "a goner" (183–84), the reader knows that she is voicing the *Fort!* and that she will soon be back, *Da!* Strings, wires, and writing are the metaphoric ties for this compulsive and repetitive behavior activated by the pleasure principle.

Sending Brett away represents Jake's unconscious strategy to retain control over their relationship. In the *Fort!/Da!* game little Ernst sends his mother away symbolically in order to experience the pleasure of bringing her back—the *Da!* of retrieval. Loss and retrieval are a form of control that Brett also practices whenever she sends Jake away. Thus Jake's ritual of repetition compulsion—the substitute men with whom he sends her away—is his effort to maintain mastery over the situation.

The city of San Sebastian, like Ernst's crib, regulates and binds the goings and comings of both Jake and Brett. Topologically, San Sebastian is a nodal point between Paris and Pamplona, a point toward which all the characters gravitate. For several years Jake has passed through the city on his way to the bullfights. Brett and Cohn have an affair in San Sebastian and Brett sends Jake a postcard of the Concha, and *concha* in Spanish is a slang word for "vagina," in other words "cunt." She and Mike Campbell, her fiancé, stop off there on their way to Pamplona. Instead of going fishing with Jake and Gorton, Cohn returns to San Sebastian in order to be with Brett. After the fiesta, Jake stays in San Sebastian waiting for a message from Brett. When her two telegrams asking him to come to Madrid because she's in trouble arrive, he says: "Well, that meant San Sebastian all shot to hell" (239).

Sebastian, as an historical figure and favorite youth of Emperor Diocletian, was martyred because he had embraced Christianity. Diocletian ordered that he be shot with arrows, but he survived and in time, after his sanctification, became a frequent subject for religious paintings. For example, in Andrea Mantegna's work (about 1455–1460) fifteen arrows pierce Sebastian's head, body, and legs. He is depicted standing, naked (except for a loincloth), enduring his misfortune. His wounds are visible and his suffering is tangible. It is appropriate, therefore, that San Sebastian, the city, act as a magnet for the novel's expatriates. Like him, they too were martyred, this time by World War I, and their suffering epitomizes a loss with which they are trying to cope.

In a postwar context of arrow wounds (Mippipopolous), Oedipal scars, suffering, and impotence, Jake's comment about San Sebastian being "all shot to hell" has an irony that not only connotes Sebastian's martyrdom but also echoes the ninety times or so that Hemingway uses the world "hell" and the thirty-five times he uses the words "damn" and "damnation." A *man shot* resonates paronomastically with the one-armed soldier Jake sees in the park in San Sebastian. In French, a man with one arm is a *manchot* (man shot), another wounded specimen of the war. Jake knows French, as Hemingway did, so the verbal play and slippage of meaning from Sebastian to shot to one arm is easy to follow. Jake speaks and understands French and he reads French newspapers, even the letters to the editor.

In due course Brett's telegram arrives. Jake dispatches his own telegram of reassurance and catches the Sud Express for Madrid. The telegram (wire) is like the string on Ernst's spool. It is the symbolic link between presence and absence. Also, when Brett's telegram arrives, Jake, fittingly, is in San Sebastian, the city named after the wounded martyr. In essence Brett's telegram says, "Come and get me," and Jake's says, "I'm coming, the wire connects us." The telegrams are an act of retrieval using the connecting wire of words and language. The wire, by synecdoche, links the telegram (a short version of a longer message) with writing, with the writing of *The*

Sun Also Rises. Hemingway's novel is another act of retrieval and deferral, because language, as Roland Barthes so aptly phrases it, gives the writer an incestuous relationship with his or her mother tongue (*By Roland Barthes* 119). If writing is a compulsion, and most writers admit that it is, then this constant return to language is part of the ritual.

The telegram is written, but we hear each of the two characters speaking. Their utterances of commitment to each other may be spoken (at a distance) but they record the inscription of the *Fort!/Da!* that binds (wires) one to the other. The telegram illustrates Derrida's *différance,* but like writing (when wiring), it is also a deferral of death—a deferral that manifests itself because we see that the pleasure principle has triumphed over the reality principle. This is what Derrida seems to mean when he says that the repetition compulsion can converge with the pleasure principle in order to form an intimate partnership (*Post Card* 343).

What is repeated in Jake's and Brett's departures is not some secret fantasy of Hemingway's, but the symbolic displacement of a signifier, in this case a person, through the insistence of the signifying chain. Each person's departure and return is not one of sameness but of difference, a differential interrelationship in which what returns is an other (see Felman, "On Reading Poetry"). Brett goes to San Sebastian and returns to Jake in Paris, whereas after she goes to Madrid, Jake returns to San Sebastian and then goes to her. The structural significance of the repetition compulsion is determined by this difference and the sequential reenactment of it.

Two other intimate partnerships are worth noting: the relationship between Jake and Brett, of course, but also the dissemination of words and their traces throughout the text—the patterns that structure its spatial form. It is the partnership of kindred traces whose genealogy generates a family of surplus resemblances that gives the reader essential supplemental information with which to organize the shifting marks of the signifiers. By transgressing the canon of realism and foregrounding dissemination and the unconscious, the reader achieves levels of insight that would otherwise go unnoticed. These strategies apply with renewed pertinence to the final scene of the novel, whose symbolic wiring with everything that has preceded it makes it so unusual.

The ending of *The Sun Also Rises* has generated as many contradictory interpretations as the novel itself. In general critics are divided between those who think that it is upbeat and those who think it is not, between those who say that Jake and Brett have a future together and those who say they don't. At the risk of repeating an ending that is already too familiar, let us take a look at the last lines, which read as follows:

> "Oh, Jake," Brett said, "we could have had such a damned good time together."
> Ahead was a mounted policeman in khaki directing traffic. He raised his baton. The car slowed suddenly pressing Brett against me.
> "Yes," I said. "Isn't it pretty to think so?"
> The End

Jake has just retrieved Brett from the Hotel Montana. They have taken a taxi to the Palace Hotel for drinks (martinis), have arranged for berths on the Sud Express back to Paris, and have lunched at Botin's, where Jake drinks more than three bottles of *rioja alta*. After lunch they take a taxi ride around Madrid. The above exchange occurs as the taxi turns onto the Gran Via and Jake puts his arm around Brett.

If we focus on the words "mounted" and "taxi," Jake's conversation with Gorton concerning stuffed animals and the taxidermist who *mounts* them comes to mind. Although elements of *The Sun Also Rises* function primarily on the level of Lacan's unstable signifier, words such as "hell," "taxi," "taxidermist," "stuffed dogs," and "dead" leave mnemonic traces whose meaning emerges only when the reader follows the marks left by their passage. A taxi may have one destination at a time but the intersecting tracks of words and phonemes create the resonating network.

The word "hell" appears approximately ninety times and the words "damn" and "damnation" appear some thirty-five times. The word "hell" may appear on a page anywhere from one to five times (190). The words "damn" and "damned" are less frequent, although on page 143, for example, "damn" appears five times. Sometimes the words "damn" and "hell" appear on the same page, where they are used casually, descriptively, in anger, as insults, and as expletives. Together, they build a network of associations, a topology that defines the psychological landscape of the lost generation. These are repetitions that remind us of passages in *A Farewell to Arms,* where the words "lovely," "fine," "good," "happy," "brave," and "die" define the ironic landscape of Catherine's and Henry's love affair.

In addition to the words "hell" and "damn," the sound of the word "taxi" has its own deferred and disseminated meanings. Whether in Paris

or Madrid, taxis are the expatriates' vehicles of choice. It is in the comical
and yet ironic context of destination, values, and hell that the pyrotechnics of Gorton's verbal play manifests itself. The traces and the slippages
of meaning within different passages generate clusters of meaning that
reverberate throughout the novel. "Here's a taxidermist's," says Gorton.
"Want to buy anything? Nice stuffed dog? . . . Simple exchange of values.
You give them money. They give you a stuffed dog" (72). The "exchange
of values" revives the conversation with Count Mippipopolous concerning money and values and the unconscious economy eliciting the need
for love. Moreover, words such as "taxidermist" and "stuffed race-horses"
connote a semblance of an outer life that is devoid of inner substance,
particularly when we learn and remember (in view of his drunken behavior in Pamplona) that Campbell, Brett's fiancé, is "in the stud-book
and everything," meaning one of the blue bloods (75–76). If, in the context of Gorton's humor, Mike is a stud for stuffed racehorses, then the
connection between the wounded, the walking dead, and their taxis produces a species that we might call a "taxiderm." The walking dead are
all also so "nice," and they know their values, particularly money. The
word "taxidermist" appears on pages 72 and 75, and by the end of page
75, in a context of dead and stuffed animals, it has been coupled with the
word "taxi" four times. Thus, whenever one or more characters gets into
a taxi, the mnemonic effects of the word "taxidermist" accompany their
displacements. Together, the words "taxi," "taxidermist," and "hell" spin a
web of connotations to which the reader responds and from which he or
she produces meaning. We are not surprised to learn from Gorton that
the "road to hell [is] paved with unbought stuffed dogs" (73).

The novel's ending contains the embedded traces of feelings, conversation, and meanings that transcend the immediacy of descriptive realism.
It is the layered simultaneities that make the spatial form of the novel so
complex. The apparent surplus of dissemination is not just something
left over, but material that is essential to a full reading of the text.

What makes the ending so rich (best value for your money) is the
symbolic act of the policeman's raised baton, which, judging from the
suddenly slowing taxi, means "Stop." In any case, he is the one direct-
ing traffic. The policeman's gesture, both literally and figuratively, is the
Law, the civil law to be sure, but also Lacan's Law of the phallus and all
the psychoanalytical meanings ascribed to it: the name of the father (*le
nom/non du père*), the incest taboo, repression, castration, and death.

The raised baton (the phallus) is also the prohibition ("Do not proceed") inscribed by the father onto the child when the Law separates the infant and its mother. This prohibition is responsible for the feelings of death and castration experienced by the child. It is a symbolic event—one that never really happened—but, according to Lacan, it is the origin of language because the mark of this inscription and its *frayage,* says Derrida, leave such a profound impression on the mind (*L'écriture* 315–17). The *Fort!/Da!* game is a symbolic reenactment of impotence and desire and it is this symbolic level that the policeman's baton addresses.

The words of the book's ending denote an event that takes place at a street intersection in Madrid, but they connote the dual inscription of Hemingway's intentional and unintentional tracings. Insofar as wordplay facilitates the unveiling of unconscious discourse, we should look at some of the connotations of the word "not" contained in the sign of the raised baton. It signifies "Do not proceed!"—the same interdiction that Oedipus experiences when Laius (the father) blocks his way. But the word "not" is also a homonym for "knot." Such homonymic play is an important element in Lacan's strategy, because for him, "the unconscious castration complex has the function of a knot" (*Ecrits* 281). From the point of view of the Law, says Lacan, "castration should be the punishment for incest" (*Ecrits* 282). The raised baton provides the missing element—the phallus—to the game Jake and Brett have been playing. It puts into perspective symbolic castration (Jake's impotence) and gives it its necessary meaning. Without Jake's wound, this novel would not have been written. Its symbolic language exists in the form of a knot (not)—a knot to be untangled and a prohibition to be understood. The letters, postcards, and telegrams and the writing of the novel are its symbolic untangling. The reader's role is to unravel and connect all the lines.

On another level, however, the raised baton is not a prohibition but a warning. If Jake and Brett are hell bent in a taxi that is driving over a well-intentioned pavement of unbought stuffed animals (Gorton's admonition), then they have indeed reached a dead end—the "stop" of the policeman's raised baton. Brett's "damned good time" is full of irony and Jake's "pretty to think so" is appropriately doubtful. Moreover, the words "The End" are inscribed at the end of the novel, thus reinforcing the dead end of an impotent relationship that has reached the "end of the line" (239).

Finally, the raised baton and the slowing taxi have two simultaneous and contradictory meanings. The text's realism and the symbolic connotations of the baton signal for both Derrida and Maurice Blanchot an *arrêt de mort,* which can mean both a death sentence and the suspension of death (Derrida, *Post Card* 285–86). It comes from the French word *arrêter,* meaning "to stop," and like Derrida's use of the word *pharmakon* in *La dissémination,* it has two meanings (146–53). In the same sense that *pharmakon* was both remedy and poison, the raised baton signifies both life and death. It is within the power of the Law to administer both, and the ending of the novel serves either possibility.

The baton is the Law that defines "the end of the line" and the beginning of the game, because both death and desire are inscribed in the policeman's gesture. The reader's unconscious resonates with the text's unconscious, but the ending reads the reader as often as the reader reads it, hence the frequency of contradictory exegeses.[4] Together, Brett and Jake play the game of *Fort!/Da!* just as little Ernst did, and as Freud did in writing *Beyond the Pleasure Principle* (see Derrida, *Post Card* 257–409). The reader's unconscious responds to the symptom of compulsion repetition. The Symbolic in the text activates the Symbolic in the reader and they resonate together as the baton, like the clapper of a bell, tolls the letter of the unconscious on both sides of the divide.

In conclusion, San Sebastian is the *point de capiton,* the nodal point that gathers together the different strands of the novel. The memory of San Sebastian (the man) is a metaphor for the wounded generation that has survived the shooting of World War I, but only as traumatized survivors of the conflict. San Sebastian, the city, is the symbolic crib from which and through which Jake and Brett, little Ernst's Siamese twins, reenact their game of loss and retrieval. *La concha,* Brett's *concha,* and the mother's repressed *concha* are the object of desire. It is worth keeping in mind that Hemingway, according to Reynolds, "knew his Freudian theory" (*Novel of the Twenties* 24). Moreover, *Beyond the Pleasure Principle* was published in Vienna in 1920. The first English translation appeared in 1922, and the Boni and Liveright edition appeared in 1924. In 1925, Boni and Liveright published *In Our Time,* and in 1926, Scribner published *The Sun Also Rises.* There is thus every reason to believe that Hemingway, when writing *The Sun Also Rises,* had read *Beyond the Pleasure Principle.* Not only do the characters, verbal traces, and linguistic connotations dramatize the pleasure principle and its beyond, but it's as though Hemingway had taken to heart Freud's speculative admonition to his grandson (little Ernst) that he play with trains and not with spools.

Indeed, Hemingway's taxis, his trains to San Sebastian, and the Sud Express to Madrid ("the end of the line") are part of the game that Freud wished his grandson would play.

However, in the final analysis, whether Hemingway had read Freud or not is irrelevant because, as Barthes maintains, "the author is dead" ("Death" 167–72). Also, reader-response theoreticians quite correctly privilege the reader at the expense of the author and his or her intention, and, insofar as every text manifests desire, it is inevitable that all writing, in one form or another, stage the pleasure principle as a reenactment of Freud's *Fort!/Da!* episode. Writing manifests desire and deferral, simultaneously. If modernism stages deferral as difference, then postmodernism embeds the traces of desire within this *différance*. Writing, riding in taxis and trains, wires, telegrams, postcards, fishing lines, railroad lines, the end of the line: the lines of the novel are all strings that bind absence to presence, loss to retrieval—ties that link desire with life and the postponement of death.

San Sebastian thus functions as the symbolic knot of Jake's missing organ, and his impotence organizes the writing game, the novel, the wires, the string of words, and the *son* (Jake), who cannot have an erection except and insofar as the *sun* also rises. This ascent traces the arrows' trajectories linking "pippi," "zizi," "big doings, "enormous," money, and the economy of value with the scars of repressed feelings whose spoken content and inscribed message weave the unconscious into the manifest texture of Hemingway's first major novel. The reader, in responding to these trajectories, regenerates the pleasure principle in a postmodern context.

This reading of *The Sun Also Rises* is one that Lacan himself might have written. Indeed, he could have analyzed all of Hemingway's writings. More to the point, however, is the way Lacan's theories facilitate postmodern readings of Hemingway's works. In this context, many contributors to Miriam B. Mandel's *Companion to Hemingway's* Death in the Afternoon have written exemplary essays that situate Hemingway as a precursor of postmodernism.

The coupling of two central figures, that is, the application of Lacan's theories to Hemingway's fiction, enriches both writers, thus giving their centrality in literary space even greater resonance and weight. Lacan's theories highlight Hemingway's craft and it is essential that the reader play a pivotal role in generating meaning. Meaning derives from rhetorical devices (both conscious and unconscious) embedded in the text: tropes, prolepsis, repetitions, verbal clusters, and key words such as "hell," "money," "value"—all of which contribute to the pleasure of the text while also confirming Hemingway's prodigious talent. Lacan's own allusive style of writing has given him not only great status as one of the world's foremost theoreticians but also that of a writer whose texts have been analyzed for their poetic value.

The Sun Also Rises and *A Farewell to Arms* are two novels in which repetition, verbal play, and tropic resonance generate a prose that connotes poetry. For Hemingway, in due course, the art of writing folds into the art of the corrida. Bullfighting, which he discovered in Pamplona, the bullfighting that is such an important component of *Sun,* became a lifetime passion, metamorphosing into *Death in the Afternoon* and *The Dangerous Summer,* works in which Hemingway infuses the corrida with his enthusiasm for art and writing. Indeed, the spectacle of bull and matador locked in mortal combat becomes a metaphor not only for life and death but for an art form that, although ephemeral, is perceived as sculpture in motion.

In the next chapter I compare Hemingway and Henry de Montherlant, who was both a writer and a matador. Not only is Montherlant one of France's foremost novelists and playwrights; he was also an expert on the corrida, its rituals, and its Mithraic history. Proof of consecration by Paris is not only his election to the Académie française, but also the street along the quai d'Orsay that bears his name. All of this makes a comparison between the two men very interesting, as we shall see.

Four

Death in the Afternoon and

The Dangerous Summer

Bulls, Art, Mithras, and Montherlant

It is impossible to believe the emotional and spiritual intensity and pure, classic beauty that can be produced by a man, an animal and a piece of scarlet serge draped over a stick.

—ERNEST HEMINGWAY, *Death in the Afternoon*

The fight had ceased to be a struggle; it was a religious act like an incantation, wrought in chaste gestures, lovelier than those of love itself, subduing men as well as bulls, and bringing tears to the eyes.

—HENRY DE MONTHERLANT, *Les bestiaires*

$\mathcal{H}$emingway and Montherlant both loved Spain, they knew the country well, and they incorporated its people and their love of bullfighting into their writing. In addition to their knowledge of the corrida and their careers as famous writers, the lives of Hemingway and Montherlant parallel each other in ways that are astonishingly similar.

Hemingway was born in Oak Park, Illinois, in 1899. Montherlant was born in Paris, France, in 1895. Both men are distinguished twentieth-century novelists, although Montherlant is perhaps better known as a dramatist for plays such as *La reine morte* and *Le maître de Santiago,* among others. Hemingway's play, *The Fifth Column,* is worth noting, but he is not primarily a playwright.

Both men loved the outdoors. Hemingway fished and hunted in the north woods of Michigan and he remained an active sportsman all his life, with safaris to Africa and marlin fishing off Key West and Cuba. Montherlant was an ardent soccer player and a sprinter. He once ran the one hundred meters in eleven and four-fifths seconds. In his teens he went to Seville, Spain, to learn bullfighting and he became a matador. Montherlant's interest in sports led him to write and publish *Les olympiques* (1924), a paean to the Paris Olympics of that same year. The book was reprinted in many subsequent editions, and in 1938, he wrote a new preface in which he applauded achievement in all sports. He equated physical strength with moral strength, and "genius," he said, "was first and foremost to have good muscles," because they would give you the necessary endurance for the long haul (Garet 33). In a similar note of praise for endurance and survival, and in order to get his work done, Hemingway lived by the maxim "il faut (d'abord) durer" (Baker, *A Life Story* 714).

Unlike Hemingway, who was not a team player, Montherlant loved group sports because there he found the same fraternity and solidarity among men that he had experienced during World War I. Hemingway also loved the camaraderie of men: on the Italian front during World War I, then during the time he spent as a war correspondent during World War II, and also in his travels and, over the years, in various drinking bouts on several continents.

In 1918, Hemingway went as a Red Cross ambulance driver to Italy, where he distributed candy, cigarettes, and magazines to the Italian troops in the trenches. On July 8, an Austrian shell exploded and he was severely wounded at Fossalta di Piave. The man next to him was killed. Hemingway recuperated for three months at a military hospital in Milan and was operated on twelve times, and many pieces of shrapnel were removed from his right leg. He was decorated by the Italian government for his courage in carrying a wounded Italian soldier to safety on his shoulders (see Baker, *A Life Story* 62–63).

Montherlant was mobilized in 1917, and in 1918 he went to the front as a volunteer in the infantry—the twentieth regiment, which had the reputation of being the toughest and most glorious in all of France. He was wounded by the explosion of a German shell and was hospitalized at Saint-Dié and at

Bernay, where seven pieces of shrapnel were removed from his back (Perruchot 19–20). After the armistice he too was decorated for valor (Garet 23).

In 1924, Motherlant published *Chant funèbre pour les morts de Verdun,* which the French critic Jean-Louis Garet refers to as Montherlant's "farewell to arms" (53). It represented a break from patriotism and service to country—the subject matter of his early works—and marked the beginning of his prolonged exile from France, with sojourns in Morocco and Tunisia. In 1933, he also said farewell to mendacity, to Catholicism, and to the arena where he had been a bullfighter (Garet 68).

From 1922 to 1928, Hemingway was an American expatriate living in Paris, working for the Toronto *Star,* and learning how to write, whereas Montherlant, by 1924, at the age of twenty-nine, had already published four books and was famous in Parisian literary circles. He was being hailed as the new Maurice Barrès, a defender of Catholicism and the French conservative Right. With time Montherlant would move politically to the Left.

In the 1930s, both men had their African periods, Hemingway with his safaris to Kenya, and Montherlant with extended sojourns in Morocco and Tunisia. *Green Hills of Africa,* "The Short Happy Life of Francis Macomber," "The Snows of Kilimanjaro," *True at First Light,* and *Under Kilimanjaro* are, generally speaking, apolitical, whereas Montherlant's novel *La rose de sable* is both a love story and an account of the French military and political presence in Morocco.

In 1935, Montherlant participated in the International Congress of Antifascist Writers; he opposed Franco; and, like Hemingway, he admired André Malraux's *L'espoir,* the novel about the Spanish civil war. In *Le chaos et la nuit,* Celestino Marcilla, the protagonist of Montherlant's novel, blames Franco for ruining Spain, and he blames France for its refusal to aid the Republican cause. Hemingway also favored the Republican cause and he went to Spain in 1937 as a war correspondent. In the United States he raised funds and spoke against Fascism. In 1938, Montherlant opposed Germany's hegemony, and he called Chamberlain the Marx brother of peace (Garet 115). *Le chaos et la nuit* is Montherlant's civil war novel as much as *For Whom the Bell Tolls* is Hemingway's.

Although he began as a Catholic, Montherlant left the church and became an atheist. Nonetheless, like Hemingway, he always admired the social edifice of Catholicism, its ceremonial beauty, and its cultural heritage (Garet 195). Hemingway's relation to the church is more ambiguous insofar as he never broke with it and his behavior and writings are open to interpretation.

In 1954, Hemingway won the Nobel Prize because his writing had left an indelible stamp on world literature. Although Montherlant was elected to the prestigious Académie française, he is not an innovator and he stays within the traditional literary mold. He is a great stylist, a poet in prose, and his writing is a felicitous melding of art and emotion. His narrative pacing is exquisite and it pulls the reader effortlessly into its diegetic tissues, that is, its narrative structure.

Toward the end of their lives both Hemingway and Montherlant were suffering from declining health. Hemingway had survived two airplane crashes in Africa, but a severe concussion and a back injury were giving him trouble. By 1960, his health was deteriorating badly. He was suffering from depression and paranoia, and in 1961, he was hospitalized twice and given shock treatment at the Mayo Clinic in Rochester, Minnesota. By 1968, Montherlant had fallen thirteen times and lost the sight in his left eye. In early February 1972, after two more falls, he went to a clinic to recover and remained there until March. He was slowly going blind. Both men's dwindling physical and mental capacities were, it seems, the causes of their suicides.

Hemingway shot himself in the mouth with a double-barreled shotgun early in the morning on July 2, 1961, in Ketchum, Idaho. His gravesite is in Ketchum. Montherlant shot himself in the mouth with a revolver on September 21, 1972, after taking a cyanide capsule. He died in his apartment in Paris on the quai Voltaire. His body was cremated, and, eight months later, in April 1973, his ashes were dispersed at the Forum in Rome and over the Tiber.

The ending of *Le chaos et la nuit* can serve as an epitaph for both men. Celestino Marcilla, having fought against Franco during the Spanish civil war, and living in exile in Paris ever since, travels to Madrid to settle his late sister's estate. It is 1959 and Celestino has grave misgivings about returning to Spain. After the legal formalities and the funeral, he goes to one final corrida but leaves early because he is disgusted with the decadence of modern bullfighting. He returns to his hotel room and dies there like a fighting bull, perhaps assassinated by Franco's henchmen. When the police arrive, blood is flowing into the hallway from under the closed door of his room. The policemen examine the body and count four wounds between the neck and the shoulder blades, four thin slits as though from a knife or a sword, from which blood is still flowing between the overturned chairs (1047).

Both Hemingway and Montherlant died like fighters from self-inflicted wounds, and the wounds, like those on Celestino's neck, were the symbolic wounds of life and the arena, because for both men the corrida was symbolic of man's passion. The thematic mood of *Le chaos et la nuit* is close to the existentialism of Jean-Paul Sartre's *L'être et le néant* because the chaos of being, ultimately and inevitably, becomes the nighttime of nothingness. Garet summarizes what he calls "le montherlantisme" as follows: everything equals everything else and there is no truth or error, only successive illusions (189). Hemingway's very personal obsession with death and the tragedy of life was with him to the end. We should not forget that *Death in the Afternoon* contains "The Natural History of the Dead," a story about the fragmentation of people, events, and the world. Nonetheless, for both men, pessimism is tempered by the idea of life as "a moveable feast," the ongoing dignity of effort, and always grace under pressure.

While Hemingway was living and working in Paris, he visited Spain frequently and he came to love the country as much as he did France, if not more. At the end of 1923, he wrote to his friend James Gamble, saying that Spain was "the very best country of all" (*Selected Letters* 107). He also wrote to William D. Horne, an American Red Cross ambulance driver who, like Hemingway, had been in Italy in 1918 and who was his Chicago roommate in 1920–1921, saying that the best times he had had since the war were at the Pamplona feria. He described the corrida as "the most beautiful thing" he had ever seen (*Selected Letters* 87–88).

In 1925, Hemingway wrote to Max Perkins, his editor, saying that he wanted to write a book on bullfighting and illustrate it with good photographs (*Selected Letters* 156). That proposed book eventually became *Death in the Afternoon.* Meanwhile, he went to Pamplona a third time and transformed the experiences there with his friends into *The Sun Also Rises*—the novel that incorporates the fiesta of San Fermín and the climactic moment of Pedro Romero's faena with the second bull.[1]

In his three major books on bullfighting—*The Sun Also Rises, Death in the Afternoon,* and *The Dangerous Summer*—Hemingway describes the corrida as tragedy and the *toreo* as art.[2] However, overriding his love for Spain and enthusiasm for the corrida was first and foremost his dedication to writing. That he was able to meld all three into his art—Spain, the corrida, and writing—is an example of his creative genius. Hemingway assimilated the discipline and spectacle of bullfighting, even as he forged a language that would mirror the rich cultural heritage of Spain and its deep roots in a mythical Mithraic past.[3]

Death in the Afternoon, as many commentators have noted, is not only about bullfighting. Nancy Bredendick points out that its subject matter is death—the death of bulls, horses, and human beings—and that Hemingway "explores the philosophical, emotional, and artistic implications of death" (209). Edward F. Stanton notes that *Death in the Afternoon* evolved into a book on Spain, Spaniards, Spanish life, and the whole culture (93). Miriam B. Mandel and Amy Vondrak both emphasize the book's postmodern diversity. In addition to being a travelogue and a manual on bullfighting, it incorporates different genres such as journalism, the short story, drama, parody, humor, biography, autobiography, lexicography, history, criticism, scientific description, folklore, translation, and prose poetry (Mandel 258).

Even if *Death in the Afternoon* is a kaleidoscope of genres, or perhaps because it is, it is essentially and unavoidably about writing. Peter Messent says that "writing and bullfighting are linked in symbiotic connection throughout the book" (123). Hilary K. Justice says that "Hemingway's metacritical project . . . resides in the complex analogy between the art and business of bullfighting and the art and business of writing" (239). Beatriz Penas Ibáñez says that Hemingway's interest in bullfighting is subordinated to his interest in literature ("Very Sad" 143). Bredendick says that *Death in the Afternoon* is a book "about writing a book" (234), the ultimate in self-reflexive art. "Its taurine dicta," she says, "are congruent with dicta on the art of writing" (206). *Death in the Afternoon* is, after all, the book in which Hemingway develops his iceberg theory of writing. Stanton notes that the work itself is like an iceberg whose tip looks like a manual on bullfighting but "whose submerged body contains the deeper levels of life, death sacrifice, and renewal" (117). It is the submerged portion of the iceberg that also sustains Hemingway's theory and practice of prose poetry, providing the coloration and nuance that Flaubert was after, as well as the unconscious (hence invisible) realm of writing that Lacanian theory reveals and which I analyzed in the preceding chapter on *The Sun Also Rises.*

Despite Hemingway's emphasis on writing, his corollary purpose in writing *Death in the Afternoon* was to give the corrida its just due as an art form. A poem and a painting survive in time, and music can be revived whenever we replay a Beethoven quartet, but a great faena, says Hemingway, is as fleeting as a dream. Dream or not, *Death in the Afternoon* is, among other things, an apologia for the cult of death and the pleasure of killing, gestures that are, generally speaking, alien to Anglo-Saxon audiences. Furthermore, Hemingway shifts the observer's attention from the blood and gore of the event to the matador's performance and the spectacle. Not that Hemingway eschews the violence. Bulls bleed, horses are gutted, they spill their entrails, and matadors are sometimes killed. Nor does Hemingway hide the obvious: the ultimate death of the bull. However, in building toward this climax, he emphasizes the beauty and artistry of the performance.

Although Hemingway believes that bullfighting is an art, he sees it as an impermanent art. It is impermanent, he says, because, unlike most other arts, the artistry is in the performance. When it ends, nothing remains except a few dead bulls, a horse or two, and perhaps an injured matador. Unlike a great sculpture or a great novel, artifacts that we can point to repeatedly and say, "Yes, this is art," the bullfight is ephemeral. Its art, like that of the dance, is in the visual moment, and when it ends, it is over. It remains as a mnemonic trace. Hemingway's goal was to lend permanence to the traces of memory; to restore their intensity; and, insofar as writing can lend permanence to such things, to give the corrida its just due as an art form.

Hemingway envies the permanence of sculpture and he strives to give his writing about the bullfight a sculptural hardness. But not all sculpture is equal. In *Death in the Afternoon* he says that he knows of "no modern sculpture, except Brancusi's, that is in any way the equal of the sculpture of modern bullfighting" (99). In *The Dangerous Summer* Hemingway also compares bullfighting to music, poetry, painting, mathematics, and writing. Here, for example, is an account of Ordóñez's performance: "with the muleta [he] *sculptured* his passes gently and slowly making the whole long faena a *poem*" (170). And "it was the closeness and the slowness that *carved* the figure and made each pass seem *permanent*" (171). And "then Antonio was doing it all to music and keeping it as pure as *mathematics* and as warm, as exciting and as stirring as *love*" (130, my

emphasis throughout). But, if Antonio's performance is a poem, as stirring as love, as precise as mathematics, and as moving as music, it is due
to his superior artistry, his courage while facing death, and his ability
to communicate these sensations to the observer. If prose can become
poetry, why not also a great faena?

Thus Hemingway compares the *toreo* to the works of Velasquez, Goya,
Cervantes, and Lope de Vega (*Death* 73). He also describes the three acts
of the corrida as though he were at the theater (96, 98), and when he refers
to the event as tragedy, we think of drama and Shakespeare. Finally, when
Hemingway says that the goring of the horses is comedy—"the death of
the horse tends to be comic while that of the bull is tragic" (6)—we become aware of all the actors on the program, and the sun, the sand, the
blood, and the shadows, in addition to the bull, the horses, the matador,
the picador, the banderillero, the *puntillero,* the peon, and the president
also play their roles. Furthermore, and tellingly, "Charri, a rotund, hard-
drinking Basque who was devoted to Antonio and followed all the fights,
had the old Shakespearean role of the Fool" (*Dangerous Summer* 119).

Hemingway believes that bullfighting is an art and, conversely, he incorporates the aesthetics of bullfighting into his writing. Not only does
he think of bullfighting as an art, but he equates the skill of a great matador with the skill of a great writer. In equating the two, he stresses their
ability, discipline, courage, honor, honesty, rhythm, pacing, movement,
action, drama, comedy, tragedy, emotion, and ecstasy. In due course he
illustrates each one of these categories and we come to understand how
they function in bullfighting and in art. Skill, rhythm, and courage in
dominating the bull combine to generate the emotion in the matador
and in the observer, and it is this emotion that Hemingway equates with
the effect produced by a great work of art. Maera "gave emotion always
and, finally, as he steadily improved his style, he was an artist" (*Death*
79). This artistry is the "real thing," says Hemingway, and it is "the sequence of motion and fact" that makes the emotion (2).

Stanton points out that if Hemingway learned from Cézanne how to
write about the country, he learned from the *toreo* how to make writing a performative art (*Hemingway and Spain* 29–30). He says that
Hemingway's "prose of ecstasy"—a prose that has "emotional and spiritual intensity"—has the "pure classic beauty" of a brilliant faena (*Death*
206–7). Death unites man and bull in the "aesthetic and artistic climax

of the fight" (*Death* 247), and this moment of tragedy in the arena and on the page produces the ecstasy that is both emotional and spiritual. Not only that, but the emotional appeal of a great faena "is the feeling of immortality that the bullfighter feels," which is also the emotion "that he gives to the spectators" (*Death* 213). In *The Sun Also Rises* Hemingway describes Romero's performance as giving "real emotion, because he kept the absolute purity of line in his movements . . . through the maximum of exposure" (168). Inferior matadors, unlike Romero, use tricks in order to exaggerate the danger: they twist themselves like corkscrews, they raise their elbows, and they lean against the flanks of the bull after the horns have passed (*Sun* 167–68). Tricks or not, every bullfighter exposes himself to death. The difference between the good ones and the bad ones is in the degree of exposure, the manifest skill, and the eventual reprieve from death. These are the qualities that provide the emotion for the matador and the observer. No wonder that Hemingway describes Antonio's purity of style and timing as Bach-like.

Although *The Dangerous Summer* stresses the rivalry between Miguel Dominguín and Antonio Ordóñez, Hemingway, in this sequel to *Death in the Afternoon,* again equates bullfighting with writing while emphasizing both as art. The writer, he says, is free to break the rules of syntax and grammar for artistic effect, but if he fakes in order to cover up his incompetence or lack of knowledge, he mystifies where there is no mystery. He has failed to master his craft and he substitutes overwritten journalism or a false epic quality in lieu of good writing (*Death* 54). Having talked about the fakery of bullfighters—about matadors who do not keep the absolute purity of line but simulate the appearance of danger in order to fake the emotional appeal (*Sun* 168)—Hemingway praises the artist who "writes clearly" because "any one can see if he fakes" in order to cover a "lack of knowledge" or ability (*Death* 54). Ordóñez, in his purity of line and absence of fakery, was clearly an artist, as the following passage from *The Dangerous Summer* makes clear:

> He took the bull with the muleta so suavely, so simply, and so smoothly that every pass seemed to be *sculptured.* He made all the classic passes and then seemed to try to *refine* them and make them *purer* in line and more dangerous and he *purposely* shortened his

naturales by bringing his elbow in to bring the bull by him closer than it seemed any bull could be passed. It was a big bull, entire, brave and strong and with good horns and Antonio made the most complete and *classic faena* with him that I had ever seen. (94, my emphasis)

It was on May 30, 1959, during this fight in Aranjuez, that Ordóñez was gored.[4] Hemingway, who knew him well, was on hand for his recovery and convalescence. During one of their many conversations on various topics, they talked about the craft of writing and fighting and the fact that some days were better than others and that during the good days you could do certain things without forcing it. "It's wonderful when you really write," says Ordóñez. "There's nothing better." Hemingway's aside to the reader—an aside full of meaning—tells us that Antonio "was very pleased, always, to call the faena writing" (*Dangerous Summer* 102–3).

Not only are artists happy when the juices are flowing, but they also alter reality in order to make it conform to their inner vision of things. Hemingway did it, he says, in order to paint a truer portrait of the world, and it is a process that necessarily incorporates the observer. The artist's role, says Hemingway, is to communicate the emotion of lived experience, and he must do it simply and without fakery and to the best of his ability. To fulfill his vision, the artist does not simply mirror reality; he invents it, and when he invents correctly he produces a work of art. Hemingway applies all this to one of Ordóñez's fights, during which he invents the bull, much as an artist invents his work.

On this occasion Ordóñez has drawn a worthless animal that is hesitant with the horses and does not charge frankly. At one point in the different sequences, he picks the bull up with the cape, delicately and suavely, fixes him, teaches him, and encourages him by letting him pass closer and closer. Antonio *fabricates* him into a fighting bull and you see it happen. In his enjoyment and knowledge of the bull he seems to be working in the bull's head until the bull understands what is wanted of him. All of this is done in slow motion as in a picture or a dream and, after he places the sword, Antonio guides the bull's death as he had guided his one performance in his short life (*Dangerous Summer* 71–72). When it is over Antonio says:

"Contento Ernesto with the first one?"

"You know," I said. "Everybody knew. You had to make him. You had to invent him." (*Dangerous Summer* 73)

In his writing and in conversation Hemingway frequently calls attention to the artist as a person who invents, as someone who transforms the ordinary into the sublime, and, in the process, he invents the reader by getting inside his or her mind, and he fabricates the emotion to which the reader will respond.

In bullfighting, a superior performance is both art and tragedy because it ends in the death of the bull and because it reenacts in ritual form the mystery of life and death. The matador performs a work of art and he plays with death, bringing it closer and closer with each veronica (the pass with the cape), which, if he is an artist, shows his domination of the bull. These are moments of immortality that the matador proves to himself and to the observer, and at the moment of truth "he proves it with the sword" (*Death* 213). "Killing cleanly and in a way which gives you aesthetic pleasure and pride has always been one of the greatest enjoyments of a part of the human race" (*Death* 232).

So, the matador, like the writer, is an artist; the faena is comparable to writing; and the *toreo* is tragedy. But in Spain the death of the bull goes beyond art and tragedy, incorporating myth, religion, ritual, and the cult of the bull throughout history. What we read in Hemingway on this subject is the tip of the iceberg. To experience the seven-eighths below the surface, we need to go to the works of Montherlant, particularly *Les bestiaires* (1926) and *Le chaos et la nuit* (1963). Hemingway owned the original French edition of *Les bestiaires* (Paris: Grasset), and he borrowed the 1927 English translation (*The Bullfighters*) from Sylvia Beach's Shakespeare and Company (Mandel 113).

Les bestiaires recounts the initiation into bullfighting of a young matador, Alban de Bricoule. While learning the *toreo,* he falls in love with Soledad, the daughter of a rancher who raises bulls. They meet and she promises her favors to him if he will fight a very dangerous animal. Despite his youth and inexperience, Alban's pride goads him to overcome his fear and he confronts the bull, but having killed it, he rejects Soledad, because he objects to her capricious frivolity that would have him risk his life in order to submit to her sexuality. The real subject matter of the novel, however, in addition to the love story, is the corrida, which is presented in all its vitality as ritual and sacrifice—a ritual inherited from the cult of Mithras.[5]

In order to write about Mithraism, Montherlant borrowed heavily from the two volumes by the Belgian scholar Franz Cumont entitled *Textes et monuments figurés relatifs aux mystères de Mithra*. Mithras, or Mithra, as he was called by the Persians, is the Roman name for the Indo-Iranian god Mitra. He is the god of light between heaven and earth and he is also associated with the sun. According to Noel Swerdlow, a leading Mithraic scholar at the University of Chicago, Mithraism is the ancient Roman mystery cult that began during the early Roman Empire and flourished from the second through the fourth centuries of the Common Era. Although the exact origins of cult practices remain controversial, the earliest datable evidence comes from the hills surrounding the valleys of the Rhine and Danube rivers, where, in little grottoes, soldiers of the Roman frontier legions were initiated into the rites of Mithras. Relics of Mithraic rituals litter central and southeastern Europe, central Italy, and Rome itself, and they consist of inscriptions, mosaics, frescoes, statues, and bas-reliefs. The most celebrated are the reliefs of Mithras slaying the bull, and the best-known examples of the tauroctony are the reliefs from Heddernheim and Osterburken. They depict Mithras astride the bull with his left knee on its back and his right leg along the animal's hind leg and pulling its head up by the snout with his left hand while he plunges a sword into the bull's shoulder with his right hand. The youthful Mithras wears a tunic, a Phrygian cap, and a billowing cape. He is sometimes depicted looking over his shoulder at a bird, possibly a raven. The bust of a male sun is in the upper left, and a female moon in the upper right. A scorpion grasps the bull's genitals and a dog leaps toward the wound. A snake slithers on the ground and shafts of wheat spring from the bull's tail (Swerdlow 48).

In tracing the history of Mithraism, Mithraic scholars such as Roger Beck and David Ulansey argue strongly for its astrological origins. Still others, notably Ernst Renan, see a close link between Mithraism and Christianity. Swerdlow, however, in a review article, "On the Cosmical Mysteries of Mithras," dismisses Mithraism's astrological origins and its links with Christianity (48–63).

Even though Mithraism had a wide following from the middle of the second century to the late fourth century of the Common Era, the belief that Mithraism was the prime competitor of Christianity is, according to Alison Griffith, blatantly false. Furthermore, Mithraism was only one of several cults imported from the eastern empire, and the major competitor to Christianity, says Griffith, was the combined group of imported cults and Roman cults subsumed under the term "paganism" (4). In the final analysis, Mithraism failed as a religion because it was polytheistic and excluded women, and like other mystery cults, its central figure was mythical, not historical. Swerdlow maintains that Mithraism had more in common with Freemasonry, Dungeons and Dragons, and the Loyal Order of Moose than with Christianity, which, at the time, was attracting converts in the major cities of the empire (48).

Although Christianity prevailed in the West, a vestigial Mithraism survives in Spain and the south of France, where the cult of the bull, the sun, and blood sacrifice remains alive to this day. As Hemingway's books on the corrida demonstrate, he was drawn to the ritual because of its emphasis on death and killing, but it is Montherlant, not Hemingway, who incorporates Mithraism into his writing. Hemingway may well be alluding to the cult when he says that "the sun is very important. The theory, practice and spectacle of bullfighting have all been built on the assumption of the presence of the Sun" (*Death* 15). But the sun will always be present and it will also rise over the Iberian peninsula, with or without Mithraism. Mithraism is never mentioned in Hemingway's descriptions of the *toreo*, whereas Montherlant alludes to it frequently and directly. Furthermore, as a former matador and scholar of the cult, he gives the reader an insider's appreciation of both.

In 1909, at the age of thirteen, Montherlant saw his first corrida in Bayonne, France. In language adumbrating Hemingway's letter to Horne in 1923, Montherlant wrote to J.-N. Faure-Biguet, a schoolboy chum, saying that bullfighting was one of the most moving things he had ever seen (*Les bestiaires* 247). The following year he went to Spain, where he began his apprenticeship as a *novillero*, that is, as a matador of young bulls. In 1911, he was killing *novillos* in a private arena in Burgos, and his name was appearing for the first time in French and Spanish newspapers. In 1930, a Pronvençal journalist, Marius André, printed a song he had heard in a café in Seville honoring Montherlant. It appeared in *L'Action française:*

Un Francés en la plaza
Toreaba un novillo.
Hizo tan bien la faena
Que el bicho se maravillo. (*Les bestiaires* 8)

A Frenchman in the arena
Fought a *novillo*
So skilled was his faena
That the creature was bewitched.

It is essential that a matador be able to control the bull, or, in the parlance of bullfighting, dominate the animal. Both Hemingway and Montherlant describe this skill, but Hemingway does so as an observer, whereas Montherlant's point of view is that of a matador and a writer. Not only did he himself practice the art, but in December 1925, he was gored in the chest. Fortunately the wound was superficial and he recovered quickly.

If we compare the two writers, contrasting point of view and narrative style, Montherlant uses inner monologue to good effect because his hero, Alban, identifies with Mithras and he comments frequently on the mythology of Mithraism, whereas Hemingway does not, nor does he use stream of consciousness. Although his descriptions are frequently poetic, as are Montherlant's, they are descriptive, not introspective.

Montherlant wrote *Les bestiaires* in Paris in the summer of 1925, the same year that Hemingway was writing *The Sun Also Rises,* and both novels were published in 1926. It is interesting to note that *The Dangerous Summer,* although not a novel, resembles *Les bestiaires* more closely than *The Sun Also Rises* or *Death in the Afternoon.* In *Les bestiaires* and *The Dangerous Summer* both writers are describing numerous bullfights over a period of time, and the lyricism of the former spills over into the latter, thirty-three years later. Also, when we compare extant photographs of Montherlant with Belmonte in 1925, they remind us of Hemingway's photographs with Dominguín and Ordóñez in 1959.

Montherlant's narrative and Alban's narrative overlap as the author re-creates the past in the present. An evocative description of the novice bullfighter depicts him on his horse, looking at the blue sky, the expanse of buttercups in the fields, and the dazzling black of the bulls. At this moment Alban compares himself to the Acheans, who tamed their horses, and he thinks of himself as a link in a chain of events dating back to Homer (*Les bestiaires* 74, 52). Alban feels that the cult of Mithras is still alive in him, and, in his mind's eye, he sees a youth dressed in diaphanous robes with Ganymede's cap on his head. He sees Mithras doing battle with the Sun and, from the depths of the struggle, he senses an emergent love. Like Mithras before him, Alban forms an alliance of friendship with the Sun and he feels fortified. Then, with the help of his dog, Alban imagines hunting the Sacred Bull, vanquishing it, and dragging it back to his lair, where he receives an order from the Sun, through the voice of the crow, to kill the animal. Alban now understands the love that has to kill in order to fulfill itself (71).

According to the legend, Mithras kills the Bull and from the blood comes wine; from the marrow, wheat and all vegetables; and from his sperm, every beast useful to man. This one bloody act engenders all good things on earth, and the Bull's horn is a symbol of plenty. Alban believes that in due course, at the end of time, Mithras will come again to sacrifice the Sacred Bull and that the sacrifice will not engender life on earth as it did before, but the resurrection of the body and the soul accompanied by eternal punishment or reward (71). Alban thinks of redemption and he evokes the cults of Mithras and Cybele and the sacrifices of the Bull throughout the ages, sacrifices that produced two ideas of mystical generation: the generation of love through strife and the generation of abundant life through the act of killing. The Apocalypse refers to sinners "washed in the blood of the Lamb," and in St. John we learn that "the blood of Christ doth purify us." As *Les bestiaires* melds Mithraism and Catholicism Alban is overcome with religious feelings, which, he says, thousands of years before his era made the men of Thessaly, Crete, Egypt, Persia, and Asia Minor bow down before the Bull (72–73). While contemplating the taurine landscape, Alban feels stirring within him the same zeal that swept the Roman legions off their feet. He remembers that Mithras was born from a rock and he thinks of the stones in the Rhône Valley, the Roman roads, and the amphitheaters of southern France.

In keeping with Mithraic doctrine, Alban loves the bulls too much not to kill them, and he feels that he must possess them in order to be free. Such possession is but a variation of primitive sacrifices when people adored the animals they hunted and killed. Was not the bull Apis the most perfect example of the godhead in animal form? And was he not in due course drowned by the priests in a fountain dedicated to the Sun (70–71)? Alban is reminded of Mithras's contract with the Sun, and Montherlant notes that Frenchmen of the Midi, like Spaniards, still adore the bull and associate the animal with the sun (12). Alban believes that he is a solar child and that he, like Mithras, was born in sacred blood, and that Mithraism and Christianity are connected and that the bullfight is the visible manifestation of this union. In linking Mithraism to Christianity, Montherlant draws heavily on the theories of Renan and Cumont, and all three were unaware of archeological evidence and Mithraic scholarship done since 1960. Cumont's works were published in the 1890s, and *Les bestiaires* in 1926.

This mythology is arguably still alive today in the minds of bullfighters and aficionados. It is perhaps difficult to generate much enthusiasm for the corrida as a bloody spectacle without an appreciation of the cult of Mithras and the mythology that accompanies it. I'm surprised that in arguing so eloquently for the beauty, tragedy, and art of the corrida, Hemingway did not incorporate the Mithraic cult into his writings, but perhaps he couldn't without violating his own iceberg theory of writing.

In Montherlant's novel Mithras is everywhere, and in great detail. One evening, Alban borrows a book on the art of bullfighting from his mentor—a book in which one chapter, entitled "Bullfights and the Church," catches his eye. Montherlant's purpose here is to educate Alban and the reader, and we do indeed learn that in the teachings of Mazdaism the bull was the first living thing created; that the Indra of the Veda was the divine bull, like Marduk, Neneb, and Anu in Babylon, or Horus in Egypt; that Heliopolis was a center of worship for the Bull of Râ; that the bull was celebrated by bullfights six thousand years ago, in Crete, the cradle of civilization in pre-Hellenic times; that in Greece, Jupiter assumed the form of a bull in order to seduce Europa; that Pasiphaë fell in love with a white bull and thus became the mother of the Minotaur; that Dionysus of the mysteries was portrayed in the form of a bull; that during the spring festivals, the women of Elea sang a famous hymn: "Come hither, divine Labor, borne upon your ox-hoofs! Come hither, divine Bull, Bull, showering blessings upon us!"; that in Boeotia there was probably a cult of Poseidon in the form of a bull, the "Bellower"; that in Thessaly, bull catching resembled the Spanish corrida or the bull games of the Camargue; that at Eleusis, young men fought with bulls; that in the Tauria of Ephesus, they identified with the god, calling themselves bulls. Alban learns that there are countless representations of bulls throughout Spain, which are associated, according to Diodorus Siculus, with the voyage of Hercules, who built Seville and presented cows to a native princeling; they bear witness to the living and sacred nature of bulls in Spain ever since (164–65).

Also, Alban learns that Seville was loyal to Julius Caesar and that Caesar introduced bullfighting to Rome, where it remained popular until the end of the Renaissance; that the sacrifices of bulls and the cult of Mithras, the Bull Slayer, soon followed; that the emperor Julian, as a devotee of Mithras, celebrated his mysteries in Constantinople; that Christianity and Mithraism, because of their similarities, had struggled bitterly for supremacy. Alban remembers a passage in a book by the French historian Ernst Renan in which he says that had Christianity failed as a religion, the world would belong to Mithras; that the Mithraic clergy had accused the Christians of plagiarism because they substituted the blood of the Lamb for the blood of the Bull (166–67).

Alban learns that Pope Pius V had issued many decrees concerning the *agitatio taurorum* and had even excommunicated toreros. The ban was withdrawn by Gregory XIII and reimposed by Sixtus V, but the Academical Council of the University of Salamanca refused to obey it, saying that Spaniards had bullfighting in their blood, that to interdict the practice would do them great harm. So, Clement VIII, in a supplementary decree, recognized bullfighting as a school for courage and an important part of Spanish tradition. He lifted the ban of excommunication, except for clergymen who had performed in the ring. Henceforth, survival of Mithraism and its union with the Catholic Church in Spain were ensured, and bullfighting, the symbol of this treaty, has lasted until this day. Until recently, no canonization, no transference of relics to a new church, could take place without a bullfight honoring the occasion. Again, Montherlant is drawing heavily on the theories of Cumont and Renan and is unaware of recent scholarship that downplays the struggle for supremacy between Mithraism and Christianity. Ironically, the *toreo* illustrates the melding of the two, not their opposition.

Bishops often organized bullfights at their own expense, the dignitaries of the church attended, and the dean of the chapter of Burgos even wrote and published a book on the *toreo*. Two hundred bulls were killed when Saint Teresa was canonized, in order to commemorate the two hundred convents she had founded. For the canonization of Saint Ignatius of Loyola, the Jesuits asked the Seville chapter to put on a "dazzling" *toreo* right after the religious ceremony. The canonizations of the Jesuit saints Aloysius of Gonzaga and Stanislas Kostka were also honored with bullfights. The pope himself celebrated the Jubilee of 1500 in Rome, on Saint Peter's Square, with a huge bullfight. In Calderon's time, when a young priest said his first Mass, it was celebrated with a bullfight. Under Ferdinand VII, it was not unusual for a young girl on the eve of taking the veil to go to a *toreo* and make a few passes with a young bull. At the festival preceding the election of a convent abbess, the nuns organized mini-fights and played bullocks with the cape. The representation of *suertes* was carved on the choirs and the transepts of cathedrals, notably the cathedrals of Plasencia and Cordova (*Les bestiaires* 167–68).

On one occasion, so that bad weather would not spoil the afternoon fights in Salamanca, three hundred masses were said to honor the souls in purgatory. A brotherhood in Cacerès, formed to honor the Virgin, admitted no one who could not work the bulls on horseback. And Roa, having escaped the plague, pledged to pay for four bulls to be sacrificed every year, "for the love of God." There are many additional examples concerning the coexistence of Mithraism and Catholicism in Spain and the festivals reveal the persistence of ancient beliefs in the sacredness of the bull—beliefs that persisted into the nineteenth and twentieth centuries (*Les bestiaires* 169–70).

Montherlant multiplies these examples in order to demonstrate the pervasive historical influence of Mithraism on Spanish culture. Hemingway, like the Spanish, identified with the killing of bulls as a source of ritual pleasure and he understood the profound spiritual connotations of tragedy. It is odd, therefore, that he does not write about Mithraism and the corrida, as Montherlant does; nor does he mention the Frenchman, despite the fact that he had read his book and owned a copy of it. One reason, perhaps, for not acknowledging this influence is that Montherlant's writing explores themes that Hemingway will develop in *Death in the Afternoon* and *The Dangerous Summer,* namely, the bullfight as tragedy, as art, as poetry, as music, as emotion, as love, as dream, as slow-motion film, and as the economy of mastery. All this and more is already present in Montherlant. Writers are frequently reluctant to acknowledge debt, and this may explain Hemingway's silence.

Here, for the sake of comparison, are some examples from *Les bestiaires.* Alban is in the arena, and because he "knew what [the bull] was going to do he could dominate this beast." And "a man can really conquer only what he loves, and conquerors are tremendous lovers. Even as a poet in the throes of inspiration, or a composer improvising, Alban *shaped* the bull" (222, original emphasis). The key concepts are domination, love, poetry, music, and the shaping of the bull, concepts that Hemingway also uses in *Death in the Afternoon* and *The Dangerous Summer.* Here is another example from *Les bestiaires:*

> As in all art, mastery in the end produced simplicity. The ritual passes were made soberly and with great dignity, appearing as easy as *actions in a dream,* endowed with the superhuman grandeur and freedom of *slow-motion films.* It became manifest to all that in the center of the arena a sovereign power was at work, with a detachment verging on disdain: the sovereignty of the man was obvious to all. It was no longer a combat; it was a religious incantation, wrought in chaste gestures, lovelier than those of *love* itself, *subduing crude spectators* as well as the bull, and *bringing tears to the eyes.* (222, my emphasis)

Once again, the familiar Hemingway themes are present. Not only does the matador dominate the bull, not only are his actions as easy as in a dream, or as grand as those of a slow-motion film, but the fight becomes a religious act that brings tears to the eyes of the spectators. Every emotional element is present, including the essential link between the matador and his audience, as well as the writer and the reader. This is already the so-called prose of ecstasy, and it is 1925, seven years before the publication of *Death in the Afternoon.*

Because Montherlant is writing from the point of view of an experienced fighter, his style develops a voluptuous and sensuous rhythm that transforms the struggle between man and beast into an act of love—an act in which the death of the bull is also an orgasmic climax:

Henceforward there was not a series of passes, but one continuous pass, one tragic comingling of two beings confounded in one, one single brutal and continuous embrace. . . . That body was made for his body, and each movement of the man was attuned to every movement of the beast; man and beast locked together within the evolving spaces of their displacements; and the withheld laughter, the eyelids lowered at the culminating point of the exquisite sensation, the passion animating the gestures—it is the god and his priest constructing their impending communion, enclosing it in a nuptial dance. (216–17)

This description not only communicates Montherlant's personal experience; it also reveals his admiration for Juan Belmonte, who sometimes, when training, fought bulls naked. In the Pléiade edition of the *Album Montherlant* there is a pen-and-ink drawing by Montherlant of a naked Belmonte fighting a bull (Sipriot 117). Belmonte had developed a fighting style to accommodate a chronic illness that prevented him from moving his legs, and for which he substituted arm movements. These changes brought him much closer to the bull than usual, so close in fact that each pass left froth and slaver on the man. Belmonte himself acknowledged this closeness as highly erotic (Sipriot 116–17).

Montherlant's description is both erotic and religious, and he combines the two into a moving and voluptuous Mithraic ritual that extols the bull's regenerative blood as an act of worship and love. In the following passage, in which Alban has already dedicated the bull to "the unvanquished Sun" (*Les bestiaires* 219), "he saw the path of sunlight between his hand and the withers shining in their golden blood; and he saw the sword as a longer beam from the sun which smote the very body of Mithras. . . . The purifying lifeblood flowed like water from the double wound" (223). Montherlant has incorporated poetry, drama, eroticism, and Mithraism into *Les bestiaires,* and he communicates the layered dimensions of this background to the reader. The fight and voluptuousness, says Montherlant, are like brother and sister. Mithras wields the sword of the Ram, the sign of Mars, and he rides the Bull, the sign of Venus (83).

In both *Death in the Afternoon* and *The Dangerous Summer* Hemingway equates bullfighting with art. But the missing dimension in both books is Mithraism, and we are indebted to Montherlant for descriptions that communicate the *toreo* not only as art, but also as a religious spectacle, regenerative act, and sensual experience. The invisible seven-eighths of the iceberg in Hemingway's three works about bullfighting is foregrounded and highly visible in Montherlant's *Les bestiaires.*

The existential tragedy of the bullring continues to resonate in Montherlant's title *Le chaos et la nuit,* connoting the chaos of being and the night of nothingness, the ontological dimensions of Sartre's *L'être et le néant.* There is an echo within the rhythm and sound of the two titles that adumbrates their meaning and their similarities. It is appropriate, I think, to keep Montherlant in mind as we move into a comparison between Hemingway and Sartre, because such convergences confirm and reinforce the dignity and tragedy of the human condition.

The tragedy of life and death is a dominant Hemingway theme, be it in the bullring, on the battlefield, or in daily life, and this is one of the reasons why Sartre incorporates Hemingway's writing into his thinking. Death is a leitmotif for the philosopher and the novelist, but because death is so prominent in their oeuvres, inevitably it forces the subject back toward life and the vicissitudes of living. In the next chapter, in addition to death, we will also look at the congruence of ideas about identity, authenticity, and the freedom to choose as manifest in Sartre's *L'être et le néant* and Hemingway's two short stories "The Short Happy Life of Francis Macomber" and "The Snows of Kilimanjaro." The two stories display all the omissions, compressions, and complexities of Hemingway's craft while melding them with ideas that dovetail with the philosophy of existentialism.

Five

Sartre, Nada, and the "African Stories"

Cowards die many times before their deaths;
The valiant never taste of death but once.
—SHAKESPEARE, *Julius Caesar, II*

They are free, and human life
begins on the far side of despair.
—JEAN-PAUL SARTRE, *Les mouches*

$\mathscr{D}$eath is the leitmotif that haunts Hemingway's oeuvre, and titles such as *Death in the Afternoon* and "A Natural History of the Dead" are symptomatic of artistic, epistemological, and ontological affinities with the author of *L'être et le néant* (1943; *Being and Nothingness*). Nowhere is this nada—the void, emptiness, meaninglessness—more insistent than in the two African stories that Hemingway wrote in 1936: "The Short Happy Life of Francis Macomber" and "The Snows of Kilimanjaro."[1]

In 1969, Scribner published a critical edition of these two stories entitled *Hemingway's African Stories,* an edition that does not include five other works whose topic is Africa. *Green Hills of Africa* is a 259-page autobiographical narrative in which "none of the characters or incidents . . . is imaginary" (foreword). *The Garden of Eden* also has an African story embedded in the narrative; Scribner's published version is a novel (247 pages), and the unpublished manuscript is over 1,000 pages. *True at First Light* (319 pages) is characterized as a "fictional memoir" and is an abridged edition of *Under Kilimanjaro* (456 pages). Like *Green Hills of Africa,* the narrative for both of these is, for the most part, based on actual events. Three early excerpts about Hemingway's East African safari (1953–1954) were edited by Ray Cave and published as "African Journal" in *Sports Illustrated* (1971–1972).

This chapter deals with the subject of death in Hemingway's two short fictions of 1936 and the nada that both he and Sartre allude to.

"THE SHORT HAPPY LIFE OF FRANCIS MACOMBER"

Although "The Short Happy Life of Francis Macomber" mirrors the void and the shame in Macomber's life, it is also a story about a man who discovers freedom and courage. It is about a man who fills meaninglessness with a newly found essence. Macomber is on safari in Africa and he is afraid of lions. He panics while shooting a large male, but the very fear that makes him run away from danger teaches him, in less than twenty-four hours, how to face a charging buffalo with all the bravery of a seasoned hunter. How could this happen? How could such a profound change occur in so short a time, and, more important, how did Macomber find happiness?

Hemingway measures Macomber's short life in hours. This is not his biological age (Macomber is thirty-five), but his psychological age, the narrative of his brief passage from boyhood to manhood. Macomber's dramatic emergence into adulthood manifests itself as eagerness, anticipation, and euphoria. "Instead of fear he had a feeling of definite elation" (31). His fear disappears and is replaced by the self-assurance and strength of a man who can stand his ground when confronting the buffalo or his wife. "Yesterday he's scared sick," thinks Wilson, "and today he's a ruddy fire eater" (31). Overnight, the husband forges a new identity and, although he dies (his wife, Margot, shoots him in the head—a Freudian slip of the finger), he dies happy, knowing that he is a winner.[2] Although this is a variant on Hemingway's theme of the undefeated, it is, nonetheless, a quintessential example of Sartre's existential hero. Why existential? Because Macomber's accelerated self-realization and fulfillment illustrate Sartre's ideas about choice, freedom, and authenticity.

However, before we compare Sartre's ideas on human behavior with Macomber's dramatic transformation from coward to hero, it will be useful to take a brief look at the story's larger context, namely, the relationship between Francis Macomber and his wife, Margot; Francis's death—was it deliberate or accidental?—and the critics' divergent views of this event. We also need to evaluate Macomber's early cowardice as a form of subservience to his wife. In this regard feminist and revisionist criticism shed light on the sexual dynamics of this relationship and the shifting points of view within the narrative. As we compare Sartre and Hemingway, it will be important to contrast Macomber's impotence and cowardice with his newly found authenticity and courage.

"The Short Happy Life of Francis Macomber" (1936) is often viewed as one of Hemingway's finest stories, and he himself considered it one of his best. The plethora of critical readings also demonstrates how characteristic it is of Hemingway's style and preoccupations. Indeed, the hunt as a rite of initiation into manhood is a typical example of Hemingway's macho posturing that feminists loved to hate when, in the early 1970s, they began to scrutinize the cultural meaning of American literature. But in doing so, they discovered new sensibilities in his writing, an openness to the woman's point of view, and to a heretofore neglected androgyny in both male and female characters. Feminist criticism uncovered conflicts of sexual identity that belie the image of the unflinching code hero, and we now recognize the importance in many of his best stories of the woman's point of view and how good Hemingway is in communicating it. Despite these revisions, "The Short Happy Life" continues to present a binary view of man and woman in a culturally conditioned context of gender warfare. Bernard Oldsey notes that most of these issues raise social and moral questions about Robert Wilson's reliability as a code hero, Macomber's switch from cowardice to courage, and his wife's motives in shooting her husband. Hemingway himself crafted Margot as a self-serving bitch (Oldsey, "Beginnings and Endings" 226), but Hemingway's intentions are not necessarily reliable evidence. Inevitably, connotations of words and their meanings transcend authorial control and open the text, any text, to multiple, even contradictory, interpretations.

In "Vicious Binaries: Gender and Authorial Paranoia in Dreiser's 'Second Choice,' Howells' 'Editha,' and Hemingway's 'The Short Happy Life of Francis Macomber,'" Susan K. Harris argues that Margot is so enraged by the culturally defined roles of the active male and passive female that she kills the man who has both oppressed her socially and failed her physically

(73). Culture defines her role as a subservient woman, yet she manages to dominate a husband whom she sees as inadequate. Because Macomber has not been able to manage his emasculating wife, he comes to the story with cowardly attributes, and this is indeed how Hemingway has structured their relationship. Bolting like a rabbit from the charge of the lion is Hemingway's dramatization of a latent condition that, as in a dream, becomes manifest. The lion's charge is the revelation of a truth that has been dogging Macomber and that he finally is forced to acknowledge.

In corroboration of Harris's view, Horst Breuer, in "Hemingway's 'Francis Macomber' in Pirandellian and Freudian Perspectives," argues that Margot, despite her culturally assigned role, is a controlling mother figure who wants Francis to be compliant and achieving, and that she punishes and humiliates him when he fails to meet her expectations (216). Baker ("Two African Stories" 119), Philip Young (42), Anne Greco (277), and Michelle Scalise Sugiyama (15), among others, all believe that sexual conflict is central to the story. Nadine Gordimer sums it up by saying that Francis and Margot live in "marital hell" (94).[3]

Nonetheless, change is possible. Susan M. Catalano believes that Macomber regains his manhood despite Margot's spousal tyranny. How this is possible is the subject of this chapter. Indeed, Margot is too beautiful to divorce, and he is too rich to leave (111–17). Furthermore, as a controlling mother figure, Margot punishes Francis by sleeping with the safari guide, Robert Wilson. The accelerating events give Macomber a profound psychological shock. He has publicly demonstrated that he is a coward, and being cuckolded is a private humiliation. Despite these blows to his self-esteem, or perhaps because of them, Macomber's subsequent actions demonstrate that he is capable of a dramatic about-face. How is this possible?

He changes because, despite his earlier fear of the lion, Macomber chooses to hunt buffalo, another dangerous animal. In choosing to face this challenge, he asserts a new identity and, in putting cowardice behind him, he defines an authentic self. He assumes his freedom. However, these new ontological states do not emerge spontaneously out of nothing. Or do they? Nothingness, contrary to what we may think, may indeed be the ontological state that rearranges everything. The lion symbolizes death, and facing it head on is enough to make any man or woman bolt. It's the suddenness of the confrontation that is so unnerving, and people like Macomber, with no prior experience hunting dangerous animals or intimate knowledge of mortality, are bound to be disoriented.

Macomber has led the conventional and protected life that money can buy. We must surmise, until the lion's charge, that he is not preoccupied with life and death as metaphysical entities. However, after his public display of cowardice, something changes dramatically as Macomber is forced to look into the abyss of nada, the being and nothingness that are the leitmotif of Sartre's oeuvre and Hemingway's. It is the nada of "A Clean, Well-Lighted Place" (1933), where Hemingway's excoriating travesty of the Lord's Prayer foregrounds suicide, old age, and death (383). In this story, light and cleanliness act as bulwarks against loneliness and the dissolution of being, because, in the course of the tale, a stoic old waiter, a brash young waiter, and a wealthy suicidal old man confront nothingness—the death that lurks in shadow, darkness, and the night. Baker says that the word "nothing" (or "nada") may be nothing for the young waiter but is something immense, terrible, and overbearing for the old waiter and, I would add, for the old man as well ("Two African Stories" 124). Steven K. Hoffman notes that the nada of "A Clean, Well-Lighted Place" echoes the nada of Hemingway's major short stories that precede it and adumbrates the nada of "The Short Happy Life of Francis Macomber" and "The Snows of Kilimanjaro." The story, says Hoffman, is a microcosm of the universe as defined by existentialist philosophers such as Sartre (173).

During the lion's charge, Macomber's fear of death and nothingness shows itself as panic. The fact that he bolted at the lion's charge is viewed by all as shameful, and he experiences humiliation and dejection. Indeed, the repercussions from his act of cowardice are immediate. Margot and Wilson, the white hunter, judge him harshly, and that night, she cuckolds her husband. Whatever Macomber's public image may have been, his fear reshapes it. His essence, his ontological self, is defined by the people around him. One act has altered it profoundly. Macomber knows it and so does everybody else. He wanted to save his life but he has lost face instead, and his flight, in Sartrian terms, is an example of bad faith.[4]

Bad faith is a state of being that men and women experience when they have chosen badly. It is the secular version of sin and is accompanied by varying degrees of suffering. Many Sartrian characters suffer the torments of bad faith because, for Sartre, to be judged by others is a living hell. Indeed, there is nothing worse. "Hell is other people" ("L'enfer, c'est les Autres"), says a character in his play *Huis clos* (167; *No Exit*). The room in which three people torment each other for previous acts of bad faith is their dead end, the hell in which they now find themselves. Garcin, Estelle, and Inez, the three characters in *Huis clos*, all suffer from inauthenticity and they strive in vain to alter their public personae. The irony of the play is that they will never succeed because they are dead (physically and psychologically), and yet they pursue each other relentlessly, striving to alter acts that have already defined them, inexorably: infanticide, desertion, suicide. This is also Margot and Francis's symbolic hell, and both, in the course of their marriage, have been acting in bad faith.

Macomber, the coward, may be suffering the torments of hell but, unlike the three characters in *Huis clos*, he is alive, and change is possible; indeed, everything is possible. What does this mean? It means that men and women are free to invent their lives and free to create their identities or essences. Men and women are free to choose and they are also responsible for their choices. In time, the choices they make define them as human beings, and this is what Sartre means when he says that "existence precedes essence" ("l'existence précède l'essence," *L'existentialisme* 17); that is, a person's biological presence precedes who he or she will become.

Nothing is determined except race, class, gender, nationality, and historical contingency. Except for race, all these categories can be changed, and even race is suspect. Thus, Macomber, a wealthy, white, married American male, is fit, handsome, and "good at court games" and has "a number of big-game fishing records" (4). This is his essence before he goes to Africa, and we might say that he has everything, except that Hemingway has cast him in the role of the bad boy who has failed to meet expectations and is being chastised by his mother-wife.

Although Macomber has lost everything—honor and love—everything, that is, that counts, except his money, he is given a reprieve, regains his manhood, and dies happy, fully integrated into himself. In a flip scenario, I can imagine the lion killing Macomber, and Sartre adding him to the characters in his play, where Macomber, like the others, will protest his guilt and strive vainly to redefine his essence. He is lucky that Wilson shoots the lion and that he, Macomber, by his subsequent actions, is able to persuade Wilson, his wife, and the natives that he is no longer a coward. Standing his ground before the buffalo redefines his essence. This is a radical turnaround and it occurs, in part, because he has looked into the abyss of nada and discovered that he has nothing more to lose. He has lost his previous essence, which was not much to begin with—certainly not by Sartrian standards—and he is now essentially a nobody.[5]

Orestes, in Sartre's play *Les mouches* (1943; *The Flies*), began as a no-body and, by committing himself to Argos, assumes the humanity of an entire city. He takes on the guilt of all the residents, who did nothing to oppose the assassination of their king, Agamemnon, and he does so by killing his mother and his stepfather. For Orestes, and perhaps also for Macomber, "human life begins on the far side of despair" ("la vie humaine commence de l'autre côté du désespoir," 102), but with one big difference. Orestes redeems the bad faith of the city in which he was born, whereas Macomber, by not running away a second time, redeems only himself. It is, nonetheless, a major redemption. Here, quite appropriately, and to good effect, Hemingway has Wilson quote Shakespeare: "By my troth, I care not; a man can die but once; we owe God a death and let it go which way it will he that dies this year is quit for the next" (32).

Sartre views death—his own, as well as God's—as the essential clue to facing life and living it authentically. It is this one "capital" possibility, always in view from the outset, from which all other possibilities derive their status of radical contingency. What dread or despair or alienation reveals to every man is that he is cast into the world in order to die there. To live with death as the supreme and normative possibility of existence is not to reject the world or to refuse participation in daily events. On the contrary, it is a refusal to be deceived. To accept death is to heighten the capacity for living, and that in turn leads to a heightened sense of authentic personal existence. Macomber, during his short and happy life, learns this lesson. He confronts nothingness.

"Nada" connotes the absence of transcendent authority and the absence of a priori values. It emphasizes meaninglessness, the contingency of life, and the impossibility of deliverance from any of these ontological states. This is, in essence, the nada of Sartre's "nausea," which reminds us that "we are born without reason, lead desultory lives and die by accident" ("tout existant naît sans raison, se prolonge par faiblesse et meurt par rencontre," *La nausée* 189).[6] This is the nada of the human condition, according to Sartre, and this condition, this nothing that is something, is, by definition, absurd (*La nausée* 182). John Killinger believes that Hemingway's nada is basically "the strange, unknowable, impending threat of nihilation, the *Nichts* of Heidegger, the *néant* of Sartre, and the *nada* of Unamuno" (21). Nonetheless, absurdity can give meaning to life because, if God is dead (Sartre and Nietzsche believe that He is), man and woman need no outside validation for their acts (Sartre, *L'existentialisme* 36). Because finitude represents the end of the self and of consciousness, every man and woman is cast in the world and there, in the absence of a priori morality, defines his or her essence.

Macomber ran from the charging lion because he was afraid of death, but he stands his ground while facing the charging buffalo. He was full of dread while hunting the lion, but while chasing the buffalo, he "felt a wild unreasonable happiness that he had never felt before" (32). Macomber's initial despondency is a form of death in life, and his bad faith and public censure are indeed painful. In any case, we may surmise that after his brush with death he discovers the meaning of life. The title of Hemingway's story implies as much, and the few remaining hours of Macomber's life are truly filled with happiness.

What is the source of a happiness that Macomber snatches so resolutely from the jaws of defeat or the horns of his dilemma? What happens to him between sunset and sunrise to have effected so profound a change in his weltanchauung? Fear and dread have given way to bravery, self-assurance, and keen anticipation. Hemingway does not probe the depths of Macomber's psyche, nor does he describe the seven-eighths of the iceberg below the surface of his mental processes. That is the reader's role and, in the context of existential anguish and lived experience, we can do it for him. This is an example of Hemingway's refusal to use "psychological analysis" or inner monologue—a refusal that Sartre admires.

Between the lion and the buffalo, Macomber's affective state can be viewed as a tabula rasa. Although his newly dramatized cowardice is no more than an extension of his marital cowardice and bad faith, his new essence does give him options: to live in shame, with all its consequences for his relationship with his wife and their friends, or to grab the buffalo by the horns and prove to everybody, himself included, that he does have cojones. What does he have to lose—his penis? Margot has already found another one and is likely to find others. Suddenly, Macomber is free, free to change, and he is responsible only to himself because, as Sartre says, he is his freedom. Such knowledge is liberating and Macomber exults in it. As he sets out on the buffalo hunt, his joy is boundless and he now has purpose and determination. His shame has pushed him up against the wall of no return (*Le mur* [*The Wall*]—also translated into English as *Intimacy*—is the title of the collection of Sartre's short stories), hence the desire to reinvent himself. He has cast off his fear and is free to act. Susan M. Catalano believes that Macomber has transcended his emasculating fear (115) and Joseph DeFalco asserts that Macomber "has severed the maternal-wife bond and achieved freedom from domination" (206). In both instances, because Macomber has rejected bad faith as an option, his courage represents a transition from an inauthentic self to an authentic one.

How is this possible? A brief look at Sartre's analysis of selfhood will explain the transition and Macomber's euphoria in transcending his past—both the bad faith of his marriage and the inauthenticity of his cowardice. Sartre equates authenticity with moral responsibility and the unwavering recognition that we are all free. The authentic person assumes full responsibility for past actions. Indeed, past choices define his or her essence. We must, however, also assume full responsibility for future choices. In this case, Macomber chooses to reject a previous cowardly essence in favor of a future self that is capable of standing its ground in the face of danger, be it physical or moral. Macomber transcends his past and makes himself anew because the future is now his and he recognizes its limitless possibilities. Sartre also believes that consciousness of death affirms our awareness of life and enhances it. The courageous person will therefore embrace this consciousness, not out of a sense of morbid anticipation, but because it is liberating. It enables men and women to discover their freedom and to invent their lives. As Macomber begins the hunt, we can empathize with his newly found happiness, which is a total anticipation of the future—the hunt, to be sure, but also his future life, with all its prospects for a new beginning. Macomber will not flee from the charging buffalo or from the anguish that accompanies the possibility of death.

It is this consciousness of his death and the authenticity that this consciousness confers that heighten our individuality and his. Macomber's exhilaration derives from his individuality and the knowledge that Margot can no longer influence his choices. He has passed through the valley of the shadow of death and come out on the other side, transformed.

The lion symbolizes death, and facing death reduces Macomber's life to its simplest terms: to run or not to run, to be or not to be a coward. Macomber's panic is instant and his flight spontaneous, and he is not, at the time, conscious of choice, although in hindsight he realizes, as with any binary contrast, that he might have gone left or right, forward or backward, or stood his ground. In hindsight he discovers his freedom in what Killinger calls "that ill-defined twilight between life and imminent death" (18). Only in retrospect does Macomber come to terms with his radical freedom, and his consciousness during the wild elation of the buffalo hunt shifts from dejection to happiness. The buffalo hunt occurs in a charged atmosphere of exuberance and sexual innuendo. Hemingway describes Macomber's change as a "wild unreasonable happiness" that feels "like a dam bursting inside himself" (32). Indeed, the orgasmic connotations of the dam bursting link virility to the authenticity of his newly found courage. And, adhering to the slippage between hunting and sex, Wilson calls Macomber's reaction "more of a change than any loss of virginity" (33). In this context, both Catalano (114) and Jeffrey Meyers (273) emphasize the connection between shooting and sex.

During the car chase, Macomber's entire being shifts into high gear and he now consciously chooses courage over cowardice. In *L'être et le néant* Sartre speaks to the crisis of every moment when he says that "man . . . is wholly and forever free or he is not free at all" (*Being and Nothingness* 441; "l'homme . . . est tout entier et toujours libre ou il n'est pas," *L'être et le néant* 511). His play *Morts sans sépulture* dramatizes the philosophical point: Resistance prisoners are being tortured so that they will reveal the identity of their leader. Their choice is clear: to reveal or not to reveal. "It's not fair," says Sorbier, "that a single minute should ruin a whole life" ("C'est injuste qu'une minute suffise à pourrir toute une vie," 194). It may not be fair, but every act occurs in the present and every choice defines our essence. Can the Resistance fighters face torture courageously? That is the question. Macomber makes his choice when he stands, facing the buffalo, "shooting a touch high each time and hitting the heavy horns, splintering and chipping them like hitting a slate roof" (36). At this moment of high drama, Margot, who has been sitting in the car, picks up the 6.5 Mannlicher and, although ostensibly shooting at the charging buffalo, kills her husband. In "Actually, I Felt Sorry for the Lion," Nina Baym says that "no careful and unprejudiced reader should doubt that she did so accidentally," because had she wanted her husband dead, the buffalo would have done it for her (114–15). Contrary to Baym's view, Theodore L. Gaillard Jr. asserts that "Macomber's death was anything but accidental" (70). She shoots at the buffalo "as it seemed about to gore Macomber and had hit her husband about two inches up and a little to one side of the base of the skull" ("Short Happy Life" 36). Gaillard argues that this is Margot's point of view as she aims at the back of Macomber's head, sighting through the rifle scope's crosshair. In her hands the rifle has become a "man licker" and her intentions are clear (Gaillard 71). She shoots to preserve her assets because, if he lives, he will leave her.

This debate is an old one, and it refuses to go away. Despite vigorous assertions both pro and con, the most plausible explanation is that the ending is undecidable, and it contains scenarios that accommodate both interpretations. Undecidability is a postmodern concept because, even as we argue for murder and place the accidental shooting theory under "erasure," its trace refuses to go away. Erasure does not eliminate the contradiction; it only blurs and defers it. This paradox is the product of a mating of opposites, whose fusion is unsettling because meaning is ambiguous. For Jacques Derrida, *la différance* is part of the undecidability of all meaning that is endlessly deferred and, therefore, never fixed (*Of Grammatology* 62). There is no doubt that Margot shot her husband. The question is, did she aim at him deliberately, or are the precise details of the bullet's penetration typical of Hemingway's accuracy in describing phenomenological events? The text provides sufficient information for us to argue both sides of the controversy.

Hemingway has compressed years of his own experience into Macomber's short life: his own brush with death on the Italian front in World War I, his reflections on killing bulls in *Death in the Afternoon,* and his ideas on killing animals in *Green Hills of Africa.* Macomber's euphoria may well be embedded in Hemingway's belief that killing animals gives the hunter feelings of transcendence that verge on immortality. This explains Hemingway's enthusiasm for the corrida, not as a cruel spectacle of bloodlust, but as idealized drama. William B. Dillingham says that Hemingway understood the ritual value of the bullfight, the purpose of which was to dramatize "the dignity of man facing death" (98). Macomber's euphoria is also enhanced by a heightened sense of being.

In *Green Hills of Africa* Hemingway takes pleasure in shooting animals because killing usurps one of God's prerogatives: the killer experiences a sense of exaltation. Shooting birds and hyenas also becomes a game laced with black humor. If Hemingway killed, the joke was on the birds, and M'Cola, his gun bearer, would shake his head and laugh. If Hemingway missed, he was the clown and M'Cola would look at him and shake with laughter. Whenever Hemingway missed, the joke was on him because he had claimed a power that he was unable to deliver. Usurping God's prerogative has reversed itself and the joke is now on the would-be killer. He has tried to play God but his incompetence has transformed him into a clown (*Green Hills* 36–37). None of this appears directly in "The Short Happy Life of Francis Macomber," but it is implied, and it helps to explain the joy Macomber feels as he sets out on the buffalo hunt, despite the danger and the threat of death.

Many commentators have noted that death is central to Hemingway's writing. Indeed, each character's identity is defined by how he or she faces it. In addition to facing death, Hemingway and Macomber also demonstrate that hunting and morality can be linked. In *Green Hills of Africa* Hemingway talks about writing against a background of hunting, and this equation links him with Sartre, who says that the common ground in art and morality is creation and invention (*L'existentialisme* 77). Life has no a priori meaning, says Sartre, and because this is so, it is incumbent on men and women to give it meaning. Humans create values and their choices determine meaning (*L'existentialisme* 89). Macomber chooses courage, and the joy he feels frees him from the constraints of his despondency. On the artistic level, Hemingway embeds this choice in the weave of his writing by dramatizing Macomber's dilemma.

In "Two African Stories" Baker says that the buffalo charge moves the story into a reversed moral situation. The lion's charge alerts the reader to the courage needed to face a wounded animal and it highlights Macomber's cowardice, whereas "the oncoming horns of the buffalo are the pronged forceps for Macomber's moral rebirth" (120). Thus, writing and morality are part of the existential fabric. You can choose anything as long as you choose freely, says Sartre (*L'existentialisme* 89). Not to choose is also a form of choice, as Macomber's involuntary panic demonstrates. Nonetheless, when choosing, every man or woman chooses not only for himself or herself but for all men and women, because choice implies responsibility and an acceptance of the consequences of that choice.

"The Short Happy Life of Francis Macomber" reveals the morality of Macomber's choices and their consequences. After his act of courage, Wilson revises his opinion of him and Margot now fears his newly found freedom. Macomber's bad faith has been erased as Hemingway fore-grounds the courage of his convictions, his own in writing the story and Macomber's while hunting. The morality of both is evident and it defines the authenticity (originality) of both men, the real one and the fictional one. Hemingway was justifiably proud of this story because it melds art and morality, creation and invention.[7] It is also a quintessential example of Sartre's philosophy in action. It is perhaps safe to assume that happiness is a byproduct of authentic behavior and that Macomber's euphoria is its manifestation.

Hemingway demonstrates conclusively that Macomber's courage is good for his self-esteem. He is choosing primarily for himself, but in choosing bravery, he sets up a paradigm that is good for all men and women. True, the balance of power has shifted and it is Margot who is now afraid—afraid that her husband may leave her, afraid of her own inauthentic behavior—but her response is also a consequence of bad faith.[8] Sartre believes that, although everything is allowed and all choices are possible, men and women must act not only for themselves but for all humans. Hemingway's story shows that cowardice has negative effects, whereas courage has positive ones. This sounds simplistic, but simple virtues are hard to ignore. Indeed, Sartre's and Hemingway's built-in self-correcting value systems postulate that in choosing for ourselves, we choose for others and that to eschew this process has consequences that we might prefer to reflect on and avoid.

"THE SNOWS OF KILIMANJARO"

"The Short Happy Life of Francis Macomber" is about one man's recovery from cowardice—the temporary death of his soul—whereas "The Snows of Kilimanjaro" is about death itself, with no recovery. "Snows" describes Harry's decline as a writer, his slide into failure and bad faith, and his death on the African plain. These two stories complement each other. One is all action while the other is contemplation, and both foreground death—Hemingway's favorite topic—death of the soul and death of the body.[9]

Harry has been "obsessed" with death for years (54), and now, as he lies dying in the shadow of Kilimanjaro, he acknowledges his many acts of omission: marrying for money, squandering his talent by not using it, and lying to himself and to others (60). He is, so to speak, on his last leg because one is gangrenous. He failed to put iodine on a scratch, the truck has broken down, and he is waiting to be rescued. Harry has chosen his fate, and he knows it. He is angry, he quarrels with his wife, he hallucinates, and he dies. But before he dies he remembers past events, and Hemingway writes many extraordinary passages for him—passages Harry wanted to write but can now only think about. "The Snows of Kilimanjaro" is about failure, bad faith, and Hemingway's recuperation of failure. Harry's creator understands the flaws in both of their lives, but unlike Harry, Hemingway triumphs by transforming failure into success.

Whatever Hemingway's personal deficiencies may have been, and there were many (bad temper, insecurity, drinking, paranoia), the one constant in his life was fidelity to writing and the subordination of almost everything else to it. When it comes to art, he is an authentic and original genius, and we admire the discipline that enabled him to create his masterpieces. This fidelity to an inner vision, the passage from the in-itself, the *en-soi,* to the for-itself, the *pour-soi,* as Sartre calls it, also defines him as an artist. That is Hemingway's essence: a Nobel laureate who altered the direction of twentieth-century writing. In "Vivienne de Watteville, Hemingway's Companion on Kilimanjaro," Robert W. Lewis notes that Hemingway's career was under the control of a discipline that almost never lapsed (108).

Meanwhile, Harry lies dying, surrounded by symbols of death: the buzzards and the hyena. Both are carrion eaters and Harry is almost already carrion. It is only a matter of time before the poison from the leg spreads throughout his body. The animals sense it and so does he. A rotting soul in a rotting body. It hasn't always been that way. In fact, the trip to Africa was designed to work the fat off his soul so that he could return to a career of writing—a neglected career—undermined by money, women, and drink. In this connection, Oliver Evans lists Hemingway's many works that stress the therapeutic value of immersion in nature (156–57). Prize fighters frequently train in the mountains to work the fat off their bodies, and Harry has gone to Africa on safari to train for another round of writing. But he is still on the slippery slope, the hell reserved for writers who fail to live up to their own expectations. Lewis believes that despite Harry's desire to recover his fitness as a writer, "it is too late. He will never redeem himself and his art" ("Vivienne de Watteville" 106).

Responsibility to the self as a writer is one of Sartre's tenets of good faith. Whereas Macomber, having recovered his honor, dies happy, Harry, like the characters in *Huis clos,* dies before his time and is unable to redeem his authentic self. He will go to hell, where he joins Inez, Estelle, and Garcin in their futile round-robin that would persuade the others of their good intentions. An authentic person is someone who lives in harmony with his or her choices, whereas Harry lies to himself and to his wife. He wanted to be a writer but he has sold his soul for lucre. An ironic clue to his damnation comes when Helen says, "Why do you have to turn into a devil now?" (58).

A number of commentators believe that Harry, in his delirium, dies happy. He dreams that he is being rescued and that the airplane takes him to the top of Kilimanjaro, the House of God. Harry is entitled to his dream, but it does not negate the fact that his life with Helen has been a sham and that he despised it:

> He had destroyed his talent by not using it, by betrayals of himself and what he believed in, by drinking so much that he blunted the edge of his perceptions, by laziness, by sloth, and by snobbery. . . . Instead of using [his talent], he had traded on it. It was never what he had done, but always what he could do. And he had chosen to make his living with something else instead of a pen or a pencil. (60)

That "something else" is his penis, and he should know, since "love is a dunghill . . . and I'm the cock that gets on it to crow" (57). Harry's safari was to have been the beginning of a new life, one that would reverse the slide and jump-start his deficient career. Kilimanjaro is there, in the distance, to remind him and us of the task ahead, of the arduous climb, and of the rigors facing him if he is to reach the pinnacle of success where the snow gleams in the sunshine. Kilimanjaro, in the story's epigraph, is called the House of God by the Masai, the "Ngàje Ngài," and immortality as a writer, for Hemingway, is to have gotten there, whereas Harry gets there only in his delirium. This is the ironic and contrasting ending that gives Hemingway the immortality he deserves and Harry the oblivion he has chosen. It is difficult to agree with Gloria R. Dussinger and others who say that Harry's "second chance" ends in victory (161). The "sensory impressions" of his journey toward the summit, like his earlier reminiscences, were written by Hemingway. They are admittedly Harry's point of view, examples of what he might have written had he been a better caretaker of his talent, but from a Sartrian point of view (Sartre says that you are what you do, not what you want to be), Harry is a failure. He has betrayed his authentic self. Even his best intentions or our goodwill cannot transform deficiencies, omissions, and decay into victory.

In addition to Hemingway's realism and crafted detail, which propel the story, Harry's flashbacks are carefully executed memories of the events and experiences that might have made him a great writer. They recapitulate significant events in Hemingway's life, thereby highlighting the differences between the two men. Hemingway nurtured his talent, whereas Harry squandered it. In Hemingway's brilliant narrative flashbacks, snow connotes both happiness and death: snow on the mountains in Bulgaria and Austria, where the soldiers died and where Harry skied with skill and precision; indeed, death at high altitudes replicates the death of the leopard near the summit of Kilimanjaro and Harry's death when the airplane of his dream flies toward the unbelievably white top of the mountain. But the white summit also connotes the joy of success and Hemingway's sense of triumph in achievement (see Gordon and Tate 421).[10] The flashbacks weave love, money, whoring, gambling, fighting, war, and pain into a nostalgia for Paris, Istanbul, the Black Forest, Michigan, and the West, a nostalgia for the places themselves and for all the stories Harry meant to write but never did. "He knew at least twenty . . . from out there and he had never written one. Why?" (72).

Why indeed. Harry lies to his wife about his love for her. He deceives her, he is conscious of his deception, and sometimes he pretends that he loves her because it gives him access to her money. He wanted to be a writer and, "at first, he never wanted to hurt any one and then it seemed as though there was enough to write without it" (66). Ultimately, he fails to engage in the ongoing process of putting words to paper and "now he never would" (66). Hemingway often reflected on the writer's need to survive. The death of a writer before his or her work is done, is, therefore, an apt topic. Baker notes that Hemingway's watchword, as well as the rule by which he lived, was "il faut (d'abord) durer" (*Life Story* 714).

Harry's wife, Helen, "this rich bitch, this kindly caretaker and destroyer of his talent" (60), is also a fine, marvelous woman (64). Her attributes belong to the generic leisure class that owns houses on Long Island and in Old Westbury, Saratoga, and Palm Beach. Her money is Harry's Swift and Armour. She has the good looks and "well-loved face from *Spur* and *Town and Country*" (67), and whenever Harry thinks about her, he thinks of death. She may be a fine woman, but "it occurred to him that he was going to die" (64), "and as he looked and saw her well known pleasant smile, he felt death come again" (67). Harry may lie to his wife, but he has no illusions about his imminent death. He faces it candidly and his big regret is the stories he has never written. But he still blames Helen and he equates her with death and his inability to write: "each day of not writing, of comfort, of being that which he despised, dulled his ability and softened his will to work so that, finally, he did no work at all" (59). Sartre says that when we hide the truth from ourselves we act in bad faith (*Being and Nothingness* 49), because "the goal of bad faith is to put oneself out of reach; it is an escape" (*Being and Nothingness* 65; "la mauvaise foi . . . a pour but de se mettre hors d'atteinte, c'est une fuite," *L'être et le néant* 106).

Harry says that he wants to be a writer but he does not write. Although he understands why he doesn't and he blames Helen, he pretends that he is a writer. Thus, blame and pretense are the parallel slopes of his bad faith. They have led to his demise as an artist and as a man because he did not assume responsibility for his choices or the consequences of his actions. But change is almost always possible, and Harry's desire to alter his condition prompts his safari to Africa—the first step toward recovery and authenticity. However, his negligence—not treating the scratch on his leg or attending to the mechanical details of the truck—is symptomatic of a certain indifference, perhaps even an unconscious death wish. We begin to question the veracity of Harry's intentions.

And so Harry escapes from himself as a writer either because he doubts his talent or because he lacks discipline. There is also that dark something, the nada that haunts him and that causes him to dwell obsessively on death. In any case, he trades what's left of his old life for security (62). He lies to himself by pretending it is his wife's fault and, all the more so, because he does not love her. So, finally, the immediate culprit is money, and if money has greased the slippery slopes, then it's no surprise that Harry can only reach the elusive summit of desire in the few delirious moments before death. He has been dead already for a long time and his rotting flesh is the analogue for his rotten soul. The excuses Harry gives for his inability to write are clear examples of bad faith, and his lying is a classic example of the escape that constitutes inauthentic behavior. Beatriz Penas Ibañez phrases it aptly when she says that Harry is a self-destructive writer who feeds on his own rotten and invented lies ("Ethics of Writing").[11]

To escape from oneself is a form of flight. In Macomber's case, Hemingway dramatizes his panic as a flight from death—his refusal to face his own mortality. "But," says Sartre, "the first act of bad faith is to flee what it can not flee, to flee what it is" (*Being and Nothingness* 70; "Mais l'acte premier de mauvaise foi est pour fuir ce qu'on ne peut pas fuir, pour fuir ce qu'on est," *L'être et le néant* 111). In Harry's case he is fleeing from himself as a writer and he masks this flight with money, booze, and women. However, says Sartre, such escape is a form of inner disintegration because good faith, or authenticity, moves away from this disintegration of being "in the direction of the in-itself which it should be and is not" (*Being and Nothingness* 70; "vers l'en-soi qu'elle devrait être et n'est point," *L'être et le néant* 111).

Self-transcendence—or, in Harry's case, putting words to paper—is the most important feature of Sartre's human reality. Robert G. Olson maintains that "Sartre is more concerned about the problem of moral responsibility than about the problem of death," and the individual, for Sartre, is someone "who has the courage to make authentic decisions" (211). Harry has not had the courage to make authentic decisions and he is therefore, by Sartre's standards, not an individual. Worse than that, he is dying.

We must presume that the leopard in the story's epigraph, when it froze, was after prey near the summit of the mountain. For an artist, writing is like hunting because you don't always know what kind of prey you will get. Thus, Harry, like the leopard, is an unsuccessful hunter. He also dies, whereas Hemingway, the eventual Nobel laureate, uses failure and transforms it into success. Hemingway's life reveals periods of bad faith, but his essence as a writer, that is, his sense of himself as a champion who could go any number of rounds in the ring with Tolstoy, Turgenev, Maupassant, or Stendhal and win, reveals purpose and discipline[12]—the constant self-recovery that Sartre names authenticity (*Being and Nothingness* 70).

Like Mallarmé agonizing over the creative process because the conception and execution of a poem can never match the purity of the vision or of the white page, Hemingway transforms Harry's death on the "unbelievably white . . . top of Kilimanjaro" into literary life. Moreover, the irony of Hemingway's ending reminds us of the irony in Flaubert's story

"Un cœur simple ("A Simple Heart"), in which Félicité adores her parrot, Loulou. When the bird dies, she stuffs it, mounts it, and makes a shrine for it, and eventually, in her delirium, just before she dies, enveloped in the blue, mystic vapors of incense and the last rites, Félicité "believed she saw a gigantic parrot circling in the opening skies above her head" ("crut voir, dans les cieux entr'ouverts, un perroquet gigantesque, planant au-dessus de sa tête," 73).

Félicité knows she is going to heaven and Harry "knew that [the House of God] was where he was going" ("Snows" 76). However, both stories sub-vert the realism of the descriptions. The protagonists may die happy but the reader does not share the illusion. For Félicité, the parrot is the Holy Ghost, and Harry goes to heaven in an airplane.

Sartre titled his biography of Flaubert *L'idiot de la famille* (*The Family Idiot*) and he was no fan of the author of *Madame Bovary* because Flaubert did not engage himself, that is, actively participate in the historical events of 1848 that caused such upheaval and turmoil in France. It is indeed ironic that Sartre should write a three-volume treatise on a man who, contrary to Sartre, showed no interest in sociopolitical commitment. Flaubert was committed only to his writing and, in large measure, so was Hemingway, and it was Flaubert's art that influenced the American writer.[13]

The mountain, for Flaubert, was a symbol of challenge and achieve-ment, and many of Hemingway's statements about prose and poetry sound as though they were written by the French master. It is perhaps no accident that the snows of Kilimanjaro and the mountains of Austria and Italy should loom over the Hemingway landscape.[14] In one of his letters to Louise Colet, Flaubert compares the completion of a work of art to the ascent of a tall mountain—a task that requires a dogged will and total discipline. "Never mind! May we die in the snow, may we perish in the white pain of our desire." ("N'importe! Mourons dans la neige, périssons dans la blanche douleur de notre désir," *Correspondance* 432.)[15]

In light of Flaubert's statement, Hemingway's epigraph takes on new meaning because both Flaubert and Hemingway compare prose to po-etry, and, as such, Hemingway's leopard becomes a metaphor for desire. Harry and the leopard die, but Hemingway and Flaubert, when they succeed, that is, when they reach the summit, "look down on mankind from twenty-thousand feet" ("à vingt mille pieds sous soi on aperçoit les hommes," *Correspondance* 432)—Kilimanjaro is 19,710 feet high—fill their giant lungs with the Olympian breeze, and feel like colossi because they have the world for a pedestal. Harry dies in the plain, but from the airplane he sees the square top of Kilimanjaro "as wide as all the world" ("Snows" 76).[16] Are these similarities coincidental? In *A Farewell to Arms* Catherine dies while it is raining in the Swiss Alps, and in "Snows," as Harry is dying and the airplane begins to climb, the skies "darkened and they were in a storm, the rain so thick it seemed like flying through a waterfall" (76). Bad weather, an example of T. S. Eliot's objective correlative (124), is a convention that frequently accompanies the misfortunes of fictional characters.

Earlier, as death moves closer, Harry tells his wife that he has been writing (74), when in fact he has only been thinking of the stories he wanted to write. This is the beginning of the end, the final moments of delirium and delusion that make it possible for him to think that he is being rescued, that the stories have been written, and that he is on his way to the summit, where he and God will be one. The leopard near the summit is one of the objects in the chain of animal events, death, and sensory impressions that contributes to what Eliot calls the *particular* emotion of the story. The epigraph states that no one has explained the presence of the leopard at that altitude, but Hemingway's story is the answer to the riddle and it explains the cat's presence.[17]

Leopards must kill to eat and writers must write if they are to be writers. Harry and the animal die, but they die for different reasons. Leopards hunt and they do what leopards do, whereas Harry, the would-be writer, does everything except write. In the end, Compton, the rescue pilot, sums up Harry's essence when he says: "What's the matter, old cock?" (75). Everything is the matter and his death is the final gasp in a long chain of events—money, booze, women, and bad faith—that has destroyed him. Harry's essence, in Sartrian terms, is the accumulation of bad choices, and his failure is the combined effect of his actions, all of which—except his decision to go to Africa, and even that is tainted with irresponsibility—paint the picture of an inauthentic being whose bad faith is as high as Kilimanjaro and as wide as all the world.

In conclusion, Macomber recovers his courage and his honor, erases his bad faith, and dies happy, whereas Harry dies unable to redeem himself as a writer and thus never escapes the lies and the personal dishonor of his bad faith. The African stories embody the "objective style" and the lived experience that Sartre admired and that he believed would express the new sensibilities of men and women in the twentieth century. Although Hemingway was not a politically engaged writer,[18] his preoccupation with death and the consequences of inauthentic behavior adumbrate many of Sartre's preoccupations as well as the philosophy of being that he was to write about in such detail and with such passion. These transatlantic affinities are genuine and deeply felt and Sartre was right to salute the influence of the American author. By the same token, Sartre's philosophical explorations go a long way toward illuminating the work of Ernest Hemingway.

Sartre wanted to be and was, in fact, a committed writer, that is, someone who was engaged in the sociopolitical struggle to transform the world. Sartre wanted to change history, and writing, for him, was an instrument in the class struggle. For Hemingway, writing was everything; that is, he was committed to the aesthetics of his art. Although Hemingway spoke out against Fascism during the Spanish civil war in 1937, his goal, unlike Sartre's, was not to change history. Nonetheless, he was keenly aware of injustice and his sympathies were not with the Right. In *To Have and Have Not* he criticizes the rich, and in *The Fifth Column* he dramatizes the conflict in Spain between the warring factions. We look next at how Hemingway's two attempts to engage himself socially and politically mesh with the ideas of engagement that both Sartre and Camus were advocating.

Six

Camus and Sartre

Rebellion, Commitment, and History in

To Have and Have Not *and* The Fifth Column

How can one make himself a man in, by, and for history?
—Jean-Paul Sartre, *Qu'est-ce que la littérature?*

I rebel, therefore we are.
—Albert Camus, *L'homme révolté*

*S*artre went through two distinct literary periods. The first, the aesthetic period of *La nausée* (1938; *Nausea*) and the short stories, focused
on the ontology of self, whereas the second period, primarily one of theatrical production, distanced him from the psychology of being in order
to focus on the possibilities of commitment in the political arena. Sartre
wanted to change history.

Unlike Sartre, Hemingway was not interested in changing history, and
his stab at sociopolitical commitment in *To Have and Have Not* resulted
in a flawed novel. Hemingway was above all an artist, whereas Sartre,
although also a good novelist, was primarily a philosopher who wanted
to change the world.

Camus was both an artist and a philosopher and, with *L'étranger* (1942;
The Stranger), he wrote a novel that was every bit as good as *The Sun Also*

Rises. As for *L'homme révolté* (1951; *The Rebel*)—his book on political history and philosophy—his analyses have proved more enduring than those of Sartre.

In his 1946 essay in the *Atlantic,* Sartre said that *L'étranger* would not be what it is if Camus had not read *The Sun Also Rises* ("American Novelists" 114). However, although there is rebellion of sorts in both works, neither novel displays much human solidarity. *The Sun Also Rises* narrates the erratic behavior of "the lost generation," and Meursault's passive aggression in *L'étranger* is his attempt to cope with alienation and the absurd.

The absurd describes the state of mind of individuals who are conscious of a discrepancy between desire and reality: the desire for freedom, happiness, and immortality, and the knowledge that life imposes limits on desire even as death anticipates finitude. In fact, death in an absurd world is one of the themes that Camus and Hemingway develop in their fiction and in their essays.

In *L'homme révolté,* Camus' longest and perhaps most important book, he moves beyond solipsism, suicide, and death—the major themes of *Le mythe de Sisyphe*—to address the issues of social oppression, tyranny, and state-sponsored murder. He believes that people who rebel against these dehumanizing forces assert a value that transcends them as individuals. His group *cogito,* "I rebel, therefore we are" ("Je me révolte, donc nous sommes," 432), posits a collective ontology based on the fact that rebellion defines and conditions human solidarity. Camus says that in order to exist, men and women must rebel, and he postulates the need for metaphysical as well as sociopolitical revolt. However, in defending freedom, the rebel strives not to violate the freedom of others. There is, in fact, an enormous distance between the rebel and the revolutionary. The rebel respects life, including the enemy's, whereas the revolutionary believes that the means, no matter how bloody, justify the ends. The rebel, because he or she empathizes with the victim(s), stops short of terror and murder, whereas the revolutionary believes that if the world is to be transformed, the death of opponents is both just and inevitable. But, says Camus, the world is sundered whenever rebellion turns violent (685).

Revolutions are therefore doomed to fail. Indeed, all modern revolutions, says Camus, have reinforced state control and, from human and historical vantage points, they have been disasters. The French Revolution of 1789 gave birth to Napoleon, and 1848 to Napoleon III; the Russian revolution of 1917 produced Stalin; in Italy, the difficult years of the 1920s spawned Mussolini; and the Weimar Republic gave us Hitler. The ensuing state terror, murder, and suppression of human rights, although perhaps not inevitable, were at least predictable (*L'homme révolté* 583).

Both Hemingway (1954) and Camus (1957) won the Nobel Prize for literature, a fact that attests to a high degree of artistic integrity, and both men had a social conscience. At one time or another they were both journalists, Camus as editor of *Combat* during World War II, and Hemingway as a reporter for the Toronto *Star* after World War I. Camus was in the Resistance in the early 1940s and Hemingway was wounded on the Italian front during World War I.

Despite similarities between Hemingway's and Camus' lives and works, it is not my purpose to show influence. I am interested in the points of join of their oeuvres that reflect social conscience, because *L'homme révolté* develops the parameters and the logic of a collective *cogito* that Hemingway's characters in *For Whom the Bell Tolls, To Have and Have Not,* and *The Fifth Column,* all from the 1930s, and even Hemingway himself, put into practice years before 1951, the year *L'homme révolté* was published, albeit with important differences. Furthermore, despite the exhortations of this important work, most of Camus' books, while striving toward the kingdom of collective emancipation, deal with exile, solitude, and the absurd.

In *La peste* (1947; *The Plague*) rebellion is metaphysical and social. All of Dr. Rieux's efforts and those of the sanitary squadrons are directed against the ravages of a disease that kills children and adults before their time. The novel's evil, however, is not social injustice, except perhaps allegorically, but death—the tyranny of mortality. Death's random selection, similar in many ways to Caligula's whimsical executions, is an arbitrary oppressor and Rieux does all he can to diminish its force.

Although death is also present in *Les justes* (*The Just Assassins*) and *L'état de siège* (*State of Siege*), produced in 1949 and 1948, respectively, Camus' two plays explore political oppression and the social commitment of people who oppose the dehumanizing effects of totalitarian regimes. Only in *Les justes* and *L'état de siège* does oppression elicit collective revolt against tyranny and social injustice. *L'état de siège,* a "spectacle" based on the myth of the plague (not to be confused with the novel), is set in Cadiz, Spain, where the entire population rebels against a bureaucratic dictatorship. *Les justes,* an historical play set in Moscow in 1905, dramatizes the assassination of Grand Duke Sergei Alexandrovitch by a terrorist group in order to establish justice and advance the cause of the revolution.

There is rebellion in the play *Caligula,* but the tyrant's assassination has few positive connotations, and Scipio and Cherea do not share the resolve of the conspirators. In "Réflexions sur la guillotine" Camus argues against the death penalty, and his reasons for rejecting it echo his passionate indictment of collective murder—the twentieth-century scourge that he chronicles in *L'homme révolté.* Indeed, few of his fictional and theatrical works develop the theme of rebellion as a group endeavor. As Germaine Brée points out in her book *Camus,* his essential dramatic theme is "the fall incurred by individuals and societies who . . . lose touch with the mystery of man's concrete presence and incarnation in the flesh" (160).

In two of Hemingway's works, *For Whom the Bell Tolls* and *The Fifth Column,* the protagonists, Robert Jordan and Philip Rawlings, rebel against political oppression, and their commitment to the Republican cause during the Spanish civil war is tangible. Likewise, the Cuban rebels of the 1930s, in the novel *To Have and Have Not,* rebel against the tyranny of the dictator Fulgencio Batista.

Robert Jordan is an American scholar who has taught Spanish at the University of Montana. He goes to Spain in order to defend Spanish Republicanism against the Fascists. As E. San Juan Jr. points out, Spain, in the 1930s, was a "Third World competitive market of alienated labor" where the opposing forces were "overdetermined by the global conflict between fascist Germany and Italy, on the one hand, and the anti-fascist camp of the Soviet Union and the International volunteers, on the other" (121). Hemingway's Jordan is fighting with the popular forces of peasants, workers, and elements of the petty bourgeoisie, and the novel was written in order to elucidate, defend, and justify that particular political position.

Although Jordan, like Hemingway, was not a member of the party, the Communists were the most disciplined group on the Republican side, and the Soviets, who were organizing the International Brigades and forwarding arms and ammunition to the Madrid government, were seen as best able to mold the various Loyalist groups into a unified force that could achieve victory. Despite this alliance, Hemingway chips away at the idea of the Communist Party as an organized effort to promote solidarity among the masses, and he rejects Communism as a philosophy. Although Jordan respects the party, works under its orders, and admires

some of its leaders, he portrays the majority of them as "maniacs, pho-
nies, fakes, murderers, and propaganda-make-ups" (*Bell* 73). Hemingway is also highly critical of Franco and Fascism, as attested by his 1937
speech to the American Writers Congress, in which he excoriates the
movement as one condemned to literary sterility ("Fascism").

Camus' criticism of Fascism and Communism is equally harsh. Fascism, he says, never wanted to free all of mankind. Its goal was to liberate
a few while subjugating the rest. As for Communism, its purpose was to
free all men by provisionally enslaving them all (*L'homme révolté* 648). In
denouncing revolutionary causes, he says that every revolutionary ends
up as an oppressor (651). It's clear now that Hemingway felt the need to
oppose the greater of two evils, whereas Camus denounced both.

Both Camus and Hemingway quote Dolores Ibárruri, the Spanish Communist deputy during the civil war, better known as La Pasionaria, who
said that "it's better to die on your feet than live on your knees" (*L'homme
révolté* 425; *Across the River* 40). These words stress the value of rebellion
and the dignity of the individual, because those who are willing to die for
the general good affirm a value that transcends them as individuals. However, in "La pensée de midi," Camus draws the line between self-sacrifice
and the arrogance of power, which, in killing, denies the freedom of others
and nullifies the logic of rebellion (*L'homme révolté* 687–89). Murder destroys the collective *cogito* and the bond of solidarity that validates history
and life: "when rebellion foments destruction, it is illogical. As long as it
stresses the unity of the human condition, it is a force for life, not death"
(688). The logic of rebellion, says Camus, is the logic of creation, not destruction.

In *The Fifth Column*, Rawlings, an American, and Max, a German, are
both revolutionaries fighting on the side of the Republicans. They want
to change the world so that men and women can live in a classless society
and the poor will not go hungry; nor will they fear the indignities of ill
health and old age. Their beliefs echo Karl Marx's egalitarian doctrine,
and Hemingway's rebels, like Camus', are born and emerge out of the
spectacle of human folly (*L'homme révolté* 419). Hemingway's revolutionaries want to change history, but change requires action and action
means killing. They are committed to obey their Communist leaders,
who believe that killing is legitimate, and it is this false legitimacy that
Camus argues against in *L'homme révolté*. For him, Hitler's concentra-

tion camps and Stalin's gulags represent a fatal chapter in what he calls "Europe's pride" (420).

In 1938, Hemingway wrote an article for *Pravda,* the organ of Soviet propaganda and Moscow's most prominent newspaper. It was entitled "Humanity Will Not Forgive This," and it appeared on page 4 of the August issue, along with articles by Mikhail Koltsov, the former *Pravda* correspondent in Spain; Upton Sinclair; Zhou Enlai; and Mao Zedong. The *Pravda* article read very much like Hemingway's war stories and his NANA dispatches, all of which equated Fascism with the killing of civilians and children, and he opposed it mainly on humanitarian grounds.

In *To Have and Have Not,* Hemingway blames corporate America for the economic repression in Cuba as well as Harry Morgan's demise. During the Depression years, some of the have-nots have turned to crime in order to survive, while the "haves" cruise in luxury, oblivious to the needs of the working poor. When Harry Morgan says that "a man alone ain't got . . . no bloody fucking chance" (225), he is desperately seeking a communal solution to deprivation, and his words echo Camus' collective *cogito.*

The Cubans in Florida have turned to crime, and one gang robs a bank in Key West in order to help finance the revolution. One of the rebels says: "We want to do away with all the old politicians, with all the American imperialism that strangles us, with the tyranny of the army. . . . We want to end the slavery of the *guajiros,* you know, the peasants, and divide the big sugar estates among the people that work them" (*To Have* 166).

Despite Hemingway's professed disinterest in politics, he had studied how revolutions work for over fifteen years (Reynolds, *The 1930s* 261). In *To Have and Have Not* there is an allusion to Spartacus, who was the leader of the Gladiatorial War against Rome from 73 to 71 B.C.E., and thus indirectly to his army of 90,000 Roman slaves. Allusively, the reader is asked to compare the Roman slaves, who could rebel, with the plight of the displaced vets in their holding camps, who could not because they have been brutalized by neglect. The vets can't organize because they are rummies, because their solace is in booze and in the pleasure of "taking it" (206).

However, as Camus points out, despite Spartacus's discipline, the revolt failed because instead of attacking Rome immediately, he retreated to Sicily, where he was eventually defeated by Crassus. Because Spartacus crucified one Roman citizen, Crassus crucified thousands of defeated slaves. Camus' point is that Spartacus's revolt contributed nothing new to Roman society and that retribution and bloodshed, the hallmark of all revolutions, did not advance the cause of human solidarity. Spartacus was killed by mercenary slaves, who, in killing him, were also killing their own freedom. Camus concludes that Spartacus's revolt failed because the rebels were repeating the mistakes of all previous servile revolts in which the slaves were freed and their masters enslaved (*L'homme révolté* 518–20).

Why rebel, asks Camus, if there is nothing permanent to preserve (*L'homme révolté* 425)? Spartacus's rebellion confirms the slave's need and desire for dignity. In saying no to slavery, he says yes to freedom, and he thereby asserts the solidarity of humans, who affirm these inalienable rights. Spartacus fails to fulfill the premise of the collective *cogito* because he failed to grasp the metaphysical implications of "La pensée de midi." This is also the flaw of Hemingway's rebels, who fight and shed blood for good causes but do not articulate the essence that binds them together. One man's tribulation is everybody's plague, says Camus (432), and when we deny the rights of others, particularly the right to life, we do not eradicate the plague—we perpetuate it.

In conclusion, the affinity between Hemingway and Camus is both artistic and moral. The main difference is that in writing about rebels and revolutionaries, Hemingway dramatizes the praxis of social engagement and revolutionary endeavor, whereas Camus, in *L'homme révolté*, transcends the expediency of the present in order to focus on the metaphysical dilemma that confronts all individuals, who, of necessity, must solve the exigencies of living and dying in a totalitarian age.

Sartre also addresses the exigencies of living and dying in a totalitarian age but, unlike Camus, he discusses them primarily in a political and historical context.[1] In *Qu'est-ce que la littérature?* (*What Is Literature?*) he says that the world and the people who inhabit it are known by their acts. All human endeavor can be reduced to one single enterprise: to make *history*. Our praxis, he says, is to act within history and on history in order to bring about a classless society. Sartre goes on to say that literature must contribute to this praxis and that the writer will be remembered for his commitment (265).

Although Sartre was a sociopolitically committed writer, Hemingway was not, except perhaps during the 1930s, when he was being criticized for his lack of involvement in such matters. It is not without misgivings that I link Hemingway and Sartre, knowing that in 1970 Sartre was arrested by the French police in Paris for distributing Maoist tracts, whereas in fleeing from the notoriety of his Nobel Prize in literature, Hemingway tried to insulate himself from the public.[2]

Nonetheless, works such as *The Fifth Column, To Have and Have Not, For Whom the Bell Tolls,* and Hemingway's NANA dispatches during the Spanish civil war display a high degree of social consciousness, and they can be compared with Sartre's oeuvre. In *For Whom the Bell Tolls,* Robert Jordan, an American, is fighting against Franco's forces. In *To Have and Have Not,* the have-nots—American workers, displaced vets, and the Cuban people—although not at war, are the victims of the Depression era on one hand and savage capitalism on the other. Finally, Hemingway's presence in Spain, during which time he sent war dispatches to the North American Newspaper Alliance (NANA), and his collaboration with Joris Ivens on the film documentary *The Spanish Earth* attest to his deep commitment to the Republican cause.

Although Hemingway empathized with the suffering of the Spanish people, as his NANA dispatches clearly indicate, his own views, unlike Sartre's, were neither Marxist nor revolutionary.[3] Nonetheless, as Michael Reynolds points out, after years of insisting upon his political disinterest, Hemingway "was now publicly committed to antifascism, if not to communism itself" (*The 1930s* 271). In his 1937 speech for the American Writers Congress in Carnegie Hall, entitled "Fascism Is a Lie," and published that same year in the *New Masses,* Hemingway said that "fascism . . . will have no history except the bloody history of murder."

In his 1938 article for *Pravda*—*pravda* in Russian means "truth"— Hemingway excoriates the indiscriminate shelling of civilians, the "murdered" children, the dead women "looking like bloodied bundles of rags," and a hungry dog "rushing up the street with a four-foot piece of intestine trailing from his jaws" ("Humanity").[4] The *Pravda* article was not unlike many of his NANA dispatches—dispatches that read like war stories, not Marxist propaganda.

More to the point, as William Braasch Watson points out, is the fact that Hemingway was incensed at the United States government and the Western Powers for their refusal to aid the Spanish Republicans (he had been active for over a year in fund-raising, speech making, and letter writing), and the *Pravda* invitation gave him the opportunity to vent his anger openly at Fascist atrocities and Western indifference ("War Dispatches" 115). Neither Sartre nor Hemingway was ever a member of the Communist Party but, unlike Sartre, who frequently proselytized the Marxist cause in his writings and public appearances, Hemingway was a reluctant activist. However, the Spanish civil war, its civilian casualties, and Fascist atrocities aroused his animosity against Fascism.

Both Hemingway and Sartre opposed Fascism in Spain and its dictatorial consequences: the authority of the church in collusion with industry and big landholders, and the ongoing repression of the workers, who wanted to improve their standard of living. But Hemingway seems to equate Fascism primarily with the killing of civilians and innocent children and he opposed it on humanitarian grounds, whereas Sartre, as a philosopher, always defended the praxis of Marxism-Leninism despite its abuses and misuses by Stalin. Ultimately, as the French historian Raymond Aaron points out, in *L'opium des intellectuels,* the human toll was enormous, whether Hitler's or Stalin's, and a Communist dictatorship was no better than a Fascist one (26). But in 1937, in Spain, the lines between the good guys and the bad guys were so clearly drawn that Hemingway was in fact defending the Communists. Although he admired them for their discipline when fighting the Fascists, "there's only one thing about duty," says Philip Rawlings in *The Fifth Column.* "You have to do it. And there's only one thing about orders. THEY ARE TO BE OBEYED" (18). Nonetheless, Hemingway had little of Sartre's zeal for defending left-wing causes.

In *The Fifth Column* civilian casualties are high, in keeping with the war casualties that Hemingway was reporting in his dispatches to NANA. But the casualties in *To Have and Have Not* are also high, although not for the same reasons. If the Depression years took their toll on ordinary people and the displaced vets, Hemingway allusively attributes the blame to the excesses of capitalism, and it is these excesses that, according to Sartre, were also responsible for the wretched state of the people in Cuba—conditions that eventually led to Fidel Castro's revolution in 1956 and its triumph in 1959.

Not only did Sartre defend Castro's revolution against Fulgencio Batista, but he also attacked American economic practices. The United States, said Sartre in his book *Ouragan sur le* sucre (*On Cuba*) freed the country from Spain only to impose a string of dictators who decreed that sugarcane and nothing else would be grown on the island. The United States bought the

Cuban sugar and, in return, supplied Cuba with all its necessities. Cuba was thus dependent exclusively on the United States for its manufactured goods. In addition, absentee plantation owners lived in Europe while the Cuban people slaved in abject poverty. The role of the Cuban army was to enforce these practices and protect the status quo. For Sartre, Cuba was an example of Marxist theory at work, a classic case of exploitation, not only of Cuba itself but of the proletariat (*On Cuba* 155–59).

In *To Have and Have Not*, Hemingway's assessment of the Cuban situation is not that different from Sartre's. If corporate America is directly responsible for economic repression in Cuba, it is also indirectly responsible for Harry Morgan's demise. These are the Depression years, and some of the have-nots have turned to crime in order to survive. The "haves" cruise in luxury, oblivious to the needs of the working poor, and their slogan is "You win; somebody's got to lose, and only suckers worry" (238). A sixty-year-old grain broker yachtsman thinks "in shares, in bales, in thousands of bushels, in options, holding companies, trusts, and subsidiary corporations" (235). The wealthy seem to live in another country and they have insulated themselves from the vicissitudes of want because their money comes "from selling something everybody uses by the millions" (240). By contrast and in order to survive and fund the revolution in Cuba, the Cubans have turned to crime, and they rob a bank in Key West. One of the rebels says: "You do not know how bad things are" (167). He is not a Communist but he uses the language of the Left, the same language that Sartre uses when defending Castro, when denouncing American imperialism and the excesses of the Cuban army.

As for *The Fifth Column*, it is worth noting that it is more overtly Marxist than *To Have and Have Not*, and it may have influenced Sartre's screenplay entitled *Les jeux sont faits* (*The Chips Are Down*), which was published in 1946, the same year the translation of Hemingway's play hit the Paris bookstores and newsstands. The love stories in the two works resemble each other, the narrative styles are similar, and there is a curious parallelism of specific detail and events: the revolution, class differences, commitment to a cause, and fox furs. In the 1930s, fox furs were a symbol of upper-class affluence, and Dorothy Bridges in *The Fifth Column* and Eve Charlier in *Les jeux sont faits* both wear them, and they are criticized for their extravagance. Furthermore, when Dorothy and Philip are together in the hotel room in Madrid, they sometimes play a Chopin ballad on the Victrola. Philip lifts the needle off the disk and "the record goes round and round on the turntable" (*Fifth Column* 32). Similarly, when Pierre Dumaine, the leader of the insurrection, is shot while riding his bicycle and falls in the middle of the road, the front wheel continues to revolve (*Les jeux* 14). The revolving disk and bicycle wheel are arresting images, and both Hemingway and Sartre use them to good effect by emphasizing their silent revolutions. Revolution is, in fact, the subject matter of *The Fifth Column* and *Les jeux sont faits*.

Max's agenda in *The Fifth Column*, like Marx's and Sartre's, is to change the world. Max has become a Communist so no one will ever go hungry, so men and women will not fear ill health and old age, "so they can live and work in dignity and not as slaves" (68). And Philip, who agrees with him, has signed up for fifty years of undeclared wars (95) so that men, women, and children will not be the victims of Fascist atrocities. When the world has been changed, and men and women live in a classless society, no one will be exploited by rich capitalists. Max and Philip speak like confirmed Marxists because they are opposed to all dehumanizing regimes. Sartre also consistently framed his social concerns within a Marxist ideology and, from all appearances, so did Hemingway, although not frequently. Nor did Hemingway articulate his humanitarianism within a coherent philosophical system the way Sartre did, and that is no doubt one of the differences between the philosopher and the novelist. However, in the 1930s, Hemingway's social conscience, within his fiction and his activism on behalf of the Republican cause in Spain, echoes Marx's egalitarian doctrine, not to mention Sartre's.[5]

Sartre believed that revolutions were necessary in order to transform the world and bring about the classless society (see Brée, *Camus and Sartre* 7, 176).[6] When Philip Rawlings says that "we're in for fifty years of undeclared wars and I've signed up for the duration" (*Fifth Column* 80), both he and Max know that they derive their strength and unity from the proletariat in opposition to those classes that exploit the workers.

Specifically, Sartre believed that Castro and the Cuban revolution could redress injustice. In his play *Le diable et le bon Dieu* (*The Devil and the Good Lord*), Goetz, the main character, assumes his role as general of the peasant army in insurrection against the feudal lords. This play dramatizes the idea that the future belongs to the masses fighting to secure freedom from oppressors. Indirectly, it also foregrounded Sartre's decision to side with the Soviet Union in order to foment political revolution in France, because, by 1952, he had aligned himself politically with Moscow. Sartre was convinced that Marxism-Leninism combined theory and practice and that it was, as Brée says, in paraphrasing him, "the only rational guide to the future, and to responsible action" (*Camus and Sartre* 7). Sartre believed that men could direct the course of history and that such action could serve rational human purposes. In his plays, novels, articles, and essays he was demonstrating that men could influence events and that they should be held responsible not only for their actions but for history as well. Sartre believed that freedom was the inescapable human reality and it could only be achieved through revolution.

During the Spanish civil war, Sartre, like Hemingway, was anti-Fascist and against the Franco forces. But unlike Hemingway, he also, throughout the decades, took positions on the issues of the day. In post–World War II France, Sartre signed petitions, joined demonstrations, and supported victims of political injustice. All this took time and energy, and to each cause he brought the benefit of his name and notoriety. His writing, however, suffered, and a number of projects, such as the fourth volume of *Les chemins de la liberté* (*The Roads to Freedom*), were never completed. Although many of Hemingway's projects also remained unfinished, as the now frequent publication of his posthumous works attests, it was not because of his activism. The reasons are complex. Suffice it to say that he was a more private person than Sartre, that he lived primarily for his writing, that he did not work as actively as Sartre did to change the world, and that he eschewed the publicity of social causes. This is not to say that he did not cultivate a public persona, only that, except for in the case of the Spanish civil war, he did not actively espouse political causes. His literary output, unlike most of Sartre's, was apolitical.

Hemingway was a reluctant activist. The flaws in *To Have and Have Not* and *The Fifth Column* confirm the suspicion that a writer who uses his or her art in order to effect social change runs the risk of compromising the integrity of the art. Sartre's first novel, *La nausée,* and Camus' first novel, *L'étranger,* are their best fiction, perhaps because these novels are apolitical. A writer's primary duty should be to his or her art. This is not to say that an author should not be an activist. Indeed, it is desirable that he or she engage in social causes, but if this engagement spills over into the art, the art suffers. The unevenness of *To Have and Have Not* is no doubt a reflection of this dilemma. How do you engage in social causes artistically without affecting the art negatively?

Fortunately, *For Whom the Bell Tolls* transcends this difficulty. In the next chapter we shall see how Hemingway manages to do so while comparing his novel about the Spanish civil war with André Malraux's *L'espoir*. By 1937, both writers were not only seasoned travelers and admirers of T. E. Lawrence but also consummate novelists. Whereas Malraux went to Asia and the Middle East as an adventurer, Hemingway went to Africa as a big game hunter. Geography and history played their roles in both men's writings. Like Hemingway, Malraux gravitated to centers of war and conflict. He wrote about the Communist resistance in Asia and two novels, *Les conquérants* (1928; *The Conquerors*) as well as *La condition humaine* (1933; *Man's Fate*, which won the Prix Goncourt, France's most prestigious literary award), which are fictionalized versions of historical events. *La voie royale* (1930; *The Royal Way*) is also fiction and it corresponds to an earlier period when Malraux tried to smuggle Cambodian bas-reliefs from remote Buddhist temples out of the country. He was apprehended, imprisoned briefly, and released when it was discovered that the French government had no title to the statuary.

Hemingway's youthful adventures and dangers were less flamboyant and they were limited to distributing candy to the troops on the Italian front, where he was seriously wounded by the explosion of an Austrian shell, during World War I. He spent time convalescing in the Milan hospital, and *A Farewell to Arms*, perhaps his best novel, was the result of this encounter with the war and Italy.

In time, both men received the highest honors: Hemingway, the Nobel Prize, and Malraux, interment in the Panthéon, where France's greatest heroes are buried. Meanwhile, their posthumous rivalry lives on.

Seven

Malraux, Spain, *L'espoir,* and
For Whom The Bell Tolls

The artist's voice draws its force and is born from a solitude that invokes
the universe in order to impose its human accent on it; in the great arts
of the past we recognize the invincible inner voice of lost civilizations.
This surviving and not immortal voice lifts its sacred song over the endless orchestra of death.

—ANDRÉ MALRAUX, *Les voix du silence*

In the case of an execution by a firing squad, or a hanging . . . if these
very simple things were to be made permanent, as, say, Goya tried to
make them in *Los Desastros de la Guerra,* it could not be done with any
shutting of the eyes.

—ERNEST HEMINGWAY, *Death in the Afternoon*

*T*his chapter blends historical facts, political attitudes, biographical
events, and aesthetic preoccupations. It organizes and focuses information from a variety of sources into a narrative that highlights the rivalry
between Ernest Hemingway and André Malraux. It also analyzes the artistic differences that emerge from a comparison of *For Whom the Bell Tolls*
(1940) and *L'espoir* (1937), translated into English as *Man's Hope* (1938).

Hemingway's novel, with occasional metafictional digressions, is written in the classic realist tradition, and it describes one event, the blowing

up of a bridge in the Guadarrama mountains of central Spain, whereas Malraux's novel transcends conventional narrative form in order to communicate the simultaneity of the Spanish conflict on all military fronts. His novel is decentered in ways that anticipate postmodern attitudes, and this dispersal of narrative perspective contrasts markedly with Hemingway's unitary vision of an event that, for him, revolves around one main character, Robert Jordan, in contrast with some six or seven characters for Malraux, all of whom are more or less equal. Hemingway describes individuals in action, whereas Malraux's most memorable scenes involve groups, collective action, and fraternal endeavor. The Unanimism of *L'espoir* is not to be found in the isolated events and circumscribed interactions of the characters in *For Whom the Bell Tolls*.

The biographical information is not new, but my organization of it is, and it helps to explain the animus between the two writers. Although essays have been written comparing *For Whom the Bell Tolls* and *L'espoir*, none combines the historical, political, biographical, and aesthetic categories using individual and Unanimist molds or frames the differences in the context of classic realism and postmodernism.

When the Spanish civil war broke out in July 1936, André Malraux was purposefully engaged in Spain less than a week after the rebel uprising of July 17. He organized a foreign volunteer air force for the Loyalists, assumed its command in battle, collected French bombers for the España Squadron, and personally flew sixty-five missions. Jules Segnaire, who was with Malraux in the España Squadron, says: "I was with him over Teruel when we had flak all around us. Malraux risked his life as much as any of the comrades. But his role was obviously more important, first because he had to command the squadron, and secondly because he had to supply it. If there were planes, it was thanks to him" (qtd. by Lacouture 242–43). Meanwhile, Ernest Hemingway was writing *To Have and Have Not* and slugging it out with Wallace Stevens in Key West (Garrick 9). In November, when Malraux's squadron had been put out of action by Franco's superior air power, Malraux traveled to the United States to raise funds for the Republican cause (Wilkinson 6–7). In the course of his visit he met Hemingway and gave him a list of people to see in Spain (Madsen 195).

Hemingway arrived in March 1937, along with fellow journalist Martha Gellhorn and co-worker Joris Ivens, with whom he would collaborate on a fund-raising film for the Republic. Meanwhile, Malraux had returned to France in early 1937 and went back to Spain again in July. Hemingway, unlike Malraux, had missed the decisive first eight months of the war, on which Malraux's novel *L'espoir* is based. When Malraux returned to France for its publication in 1937, Hemingway, perhaps envious, accused him of pulling out of the war too soon, "of pussyfooting off to resume his career of opportunist, high-wire artist, and political charlatan . . . while the Spanish Republic bled to death from its wounds" (Garrick 9–10).[1]

Despite their emerging antipathy, Malraux and Hemingway were much alike. In their lives and works they projected a total artistic construct, what Bickford Sylvester calls "an orchestrated amalgamation of fictional texts and fictionalized authorial persona," and they manipulated the public into identifying their novels with their lives (19). They were also cat lovers, middle class, and short on formal education and had fathers who had committed suicide. They were both going through marital breakup in Spain and were starting over with new partners. They mistrusted intellectuals and they adored T. E. Lawrence, the quintessential man of action, who was also a writer (Garrick 14–15).

The protagonists of *L'espoir* and *For Whom the Bell Tolls,* like their authors, opposed Fascism in general while engaging in the specific struggle against Franco. Hemingway had once admired *La condition humaine* (1933; translated as *Man's Fate* in 1934), stating that it was the best book he had read in a decade, and Malraux had said that *A Farewell to Arms* (1929) was the best love novel to have been written since Stendhal. Malraux also admired Hemingway for being a warrior-writer, particularly the action passages in *For Whom the Bell Tolls,* where his descriptions and style were, according to Malraux, "the language of action" (qtd. by Lewis, "Hemingway, Malraux" 66). After the war in Spain, and by the end of World War II, the exploits of both writers loomed larger than life. Indeed, they were both credited with liberating Paris, however exaggerated that claim may have been. Baker notes that their rivalry surfaced again when they met at the Ritz and Malraux announced that he had commanded two thousand men compared with Hemingway's ten or twelve (*Life Story* 532).

Earlier, Hemingway had referred derogatorily to Malraux's novels as "masterpisses" even as Malraux criticized the love story in *For Whom the Bell Tolls* as "the intrusion of fiction on reality" (qtd. by Lewis, "Hemingway, Malraux" 67). After the war, both men went their separate ways,

Hemingway to Cuba and Ketchum, Idaho, where he died in 1961. Malraux remained in Paris, eventually to become Charles de Gaulle's minister of culture. He died in 1976. In November 1996, Malraux was reinterred in the Panthéon, on the Left Bank in Paris, where he now rests in the company of other great Frenchmen, such as Jean-Jacques Rousseau and Victor Hugo. This honor serves to reinforce the striking contrast between France and America and the way the two countries treat their artists. France respects its intellectuals, whereas America neglects them. In fact, artists in America tend not to be intellectuals. There is the mystique of the innocent creative genius. Hemingway, for one, shunned eggheads, preferring the friendship of soldiers, hunters, ranchers, matadors, and fishermen. Commenting on this phenomenon, Malraux stated that "to my mind, the essential characteristic of contemporary American writing is that it is the only literature whose creators are not intellectuals" (qtd. by Peyre 218). And he wondered how American literature could intellectualize itself without losing its direct approach. It was precisely this direct approach that French writers and critics such as Sartre ("American Novelists"), Camus, and Claude-Edmonde Magny (see introduction) had admired.

Although in his fiction, Malraux prefers men of action to intellectuals, he himself was an intimidating interlocutor. Stephen Spender, André Gide, A. J. Ayer, and François Mauriac, among others, attest to Malraux's brilliance and dynamism as a conversationalist (Garrick 12). That an intellectual's intellectual such as Gide could feel humbled by Malraux's verbal pyrotechnics suggests that Hemingway would also take offense. Personal idiosyncrasies aside, Hemingway should have approved of the tendency of Malraux's characters to devalue the intellect. Moreno, in *L'espoir*, has learned that neither thoughts nor deep truths exist when shells begin to fall. Unamuno, Spain's great philosopher, is criticized for thinking and not acting. One of the characters in *Les noyers de l'Altenburg* (1948) says that "intellectuals are like women. . . . Soldiers make them dream" (qtd. by Brombert, "Malraux" 65). Malraux even dismisses Sartre as a man who has never fought. In *L'espoir* Malraux has taken the scholar out of the study and given him an active role in the midst of war. The aviator Scali was a professor of art history in Italy and the author of the most important study on Piero della Francesca. Garcia, perhaps Spain's foremost ethnologist, heads the Loyalists' military intelligence. Lopez, the sculptor, and Shade, the journalist, discuss the values of contemporary art. Magnin, like Malraux, organized and leads one of the air squadrons. The way he takes off his glasses betrays the gesture of the intellectual (Brombert, "Malraux" 68). And Guernico, the leader of Madrid's ambulance corps, is one of Spain's well-known Catholic writers. There is a great concentration of intellectuals in action.

In *For Whom the Bell Tolls* Hemingway has also cast Robert Jordan as an intellectual and a man of action. Erik Nakjavani points out that Jordan is an academic, a scholar, and a courageous militant. He has taught Spanish at the University of Montana in Missoula and he has written a book on Spain. He "carries his considerable knowledge to Spain in order to defend that country and the political ideal which it embodies in the form of Spanish Republicanism" (Nakjavani, "Knowledge as Power" 135–36). Both Hemingway's and Malraux's characters are in Spain fighting against the regressive forces of the Church and the feudal landlord class as represented by the "nationalist" military machine.

Hemingway's Jordan and Malraux's many characters were all fighting with the popular forces of peasants, workers, and elements of the petty bourgeoisie. And both novels were written in order to elucidate, defend, and justify that particular political position. Although neither Hemingway nor Malraux was a member of the party, the Communists were the most disciplined group on the Republican side, and the Soviets, who were organizing the International Brigades and forwarding arms and ammunition to the Madrid government, were seen as best able to mold the various Loyalist groups into a unified force that could achieve victory (Thornberry 226). Also, intellectuals of the 1920s and 1930s were attracted to Communism because they saw it as a vast destructive operation, a political adjunct to the literary movements of Dada and surrealism. It was a time of political violence and defeat: the defeat of the Comintern in China, of the Loyalists in Spain, and of France as a nation in 1940 (Brée and Guiton 181–82).

However, Malraux's anti-Fascist commitment, as expressed in *L'espoir,* is neither Stalinist nor counterrevolutionary. His defense of democratic values is accompanied by an ongoing critique of Communism and Stalinist ideology (Thornberry 229). Gaëtan Picon (91) and Armand Hoog ("Malraux" 89) concur, stating that the Malraux of the 1930s was not a Marxist any more than the Malraux of 1948 was a Fascist.[2] In *For Whom the Bell Tolls,* Hemingway chips away at the idea of the Communist Party as an organized effort to promote solidarity among the masses and he rejects Communism as a philosophy (Fleming 146). Both novels critique Communism while admiring the heroism of the men who fought under the party's leaders. *L'espoir* culminates in the battle of Guadalajara (March 1937), the most important victory won by the Republican forces during the war, whereas *For Whom the Bell Tolls* describes an operation of support in a localized abortive offensive. The courage, heroism, and sacrifice of the protagonists of *L'espoir* are meaningful because they adumbrate the final triumph over Fascism, whereas Jordan's failed effort, from beginning to end, is a struggle against overwhelming odds. In both novels, history is the stage on which the heroes are defined, and the civil war is the backdrop against which they test themselves. But the novels are very different in sweep and in structure.

L'espoir is a fictionalized chronicle of the first months of the war. There are many characters, and the events are described alternately in Barcelona, Madrid, Toledo, and Guadalajara. Malraux is telling the story of the men who fought the war, but he is also describing the events as they occurred. He uses changing perspectives from one city to another, highlighting the points of view of the ground forces, the aviators, and the main characters in order to provide different and, at times, simultaneous perspectives from which the events are narrated. There is a triple movement to the action of the novel: first, the initial euphoria of the "lyric illusion"; second, the leaders striving to harness the energy in order to give the disorganized factions greater power and cohesion; and third, the Loyalists succumbing to the superior military power of Franco's forces. Malraux alternates scenes of war with philosophical and political conversations. Altogether, there are fifteen major dialogues, each one separated from the other by scenes of action. Each conversation shuffles the participants in order to focus on a different topic. Magnin is the commander of the International Air Force. Garcia is an ethnologist turned intelligence chief. Hernandez is an idealistic captain at the siege of the Alcazar and the fall of Toledo. Scali is an Italian art historian who becomes a bombardier. Ximénès is a devout Spanish Catholic Loyalist, and Manuel is perhaps the closest thing to a central character. As a result, the reader views events "through one great, multifaceted compound eye that absorbs all possible angles of vision" (Wilkinson 80).

In contrast to the panoramic landscapes of *L'espoir,* with its descriptions of crowds, fraternal virility, and group solidarity, *For Whom the*

Bell Tolls is a fictional account of one episode describing the Spanish Republican guerrilla warfare in May 1937, in the Sierra de Guadarrama in Spain, in the province of Segovia. Jordan is sent on a secret mission behind enemy lines, where he preaches Communist ideology to Pablo's band. He persuades them to help him blow up a bridge over a mountain gorge, where he will die defending the Republican cause.

Despite this fundamental difference in narrative approach, the lines between tyranny and change are clearly drawn. Both authors describe the people's challenge to the state and the Church as well as the bone-breaking poverty that serving the wealthy landowners has reduced them to living in. In *L'espoir,* Ximénès believes the Church has forced the Spanish people into a sort of mindless childhood. The peasants accuse the Church of supporting the nobility and repressing the masses, and of preaching the virtues of poverty and submission while supporting the Fascists, who are killing them (130–31). And Jordan, who is on the side of the people, believes that he is fighting "for all the poor in the world, against all tyranny" (*Bell* 236). There is also the protagonists' sense of commitment to something that transcends them—freedom, justice, dignity, an idealized Spain—ideals that regulate their actions in life and define their essences in death. Nonetheless, these two novels are very different in tone and concept—differences that, to some degree, also explain the antagonisms of the two authors.

Malraux spurns conventional narrative techniques that emphasize plot, linear chronology, and character development in favor of a different aesthetic. Although he believes that the novelist should create a coherent world, he does not believe in creating characters (Picon 38).[3] "Great artists are not transcribers of the scheme of things, they are its rivals" (qtd. by Hartman 128).[4] Malraux devalues the French tradition of psychological analysis that runs from *La princesse de Clèves* to *A la recherche du temps perdu* and, in doing so, he also moves beyond Hemingway's "objective style," the directness that the French admired so much. Hemingway's influence on world writing has been remarkable: short sentences, dialogue, the iceberg technique, and the fourth and fifth dimensions that connote so much more than meets the eye or ear. Except for works such as *Green Hills of Africa, A Moveable Feast,* and *Under Kilimanjaro,* in which life and art overlap, he believes in the illusion of fiction, although *Death in the Afternoon,* which is ostensibly about bullfighting, is also very much about writing and how writing apprehends the world while encompassing the artist, the observer, and language. Such writing is transgressive because it is more than fiction. In many ways it is postmodern, and it is here that Hemingway and Malraux resemble each other the most. Fiction, autobiography, and art criticism are all cast in the same mold. "When I try to express what the Spanish Revolution revealed to me, I write L'espoir; when I try to express what art and its current metamorphosis have revealed to me, I write Les voix du silence" (qtd. by Picon 15). These events and insights belong to the same domain. As Picon points out, there is a symbiotic relationship between the images of art and the images of life (15). In his writing, Malraux has suppressed the trappings of the conventional novel and replaced them with shifting images that radically alter the artistic process. Instead of a love story between Jordan and Maria, or the psychological conflict between Jordan and Pablo, or the suspense between success and failure in blowing up the bridge, Malraux, as R. M. Albérès puts it, registers "lightning flashes of awareness and anguish" (53).

Rodolphe Lacasse notes that Hemingway's characters, although they know they are going to die, are forever trying to figure out how to live in this world. In contrast, Malraux's characters are more interested in transforming experience into consciousness in order to give meaning to the human condition (213). Malraux is less interested in telling a story than in presenting moments of crisis when men become aware of destiny, when they become aware of their human condition as tragedy.[5] This insight into "man's fate" is what Malraux calls consciousness. In one of the many dialogues that punctuate L'espoir, Scali asks Garcia what the best thing is in life that a person can do. Garcia's answer is "To transform into consciousness as vast an experience as possible" (282), and the novel ends with the statement that "an anemic Spain was at last becoming conscious of herself" (360). The struggle of the Loyalists will not have been in vain and in due course the defeat of Fascism will have vindicated their effort and their belief that the enemy of man should not be other men but whatever diminishes him or them. This conclusion reminds us of John Donne's epigraph to For Whom the Bell Tolls, except that Hemingway's novel is so different from Malraux's. It expresses similar values and pursues similar goals, but on a fictional plane that bears little resemblance to the Frenchman's work.

For Whom the Bell Tolls is for the most part a classic realist text; that is, it follows the conventions of realism in which plot, characters, and place govern the writing and the reader's involvement. All the characters, even the secondary ones, are fully developed through dialogue, description, flashback, and inner monologue. Jordan, the main character, is a flesh-and-blood entity, someone readers can relate to, whose hand they could shake if necessary, and whom they would wish luck when he goes to blow up the bridge. This is the function of realism in writing. We see it at work not only in Jordan but also in the other characters as Hemingway portrays the identities of Pilar, Pablo, Maria, and Anselmo—the family of guerrilla fighters whom circumstance and necessity have brought together. Hemingway's characters, his descriptions of places and events, and his use of plot to move the action toward climax clearly serve a dual function. The individuals come alive but they also embody essential characteristics of the Spanish people.

Pilar, though not a virgin anymore, is named after the Virgin of Pilar. In many evocative passages she describes the mob execution of the Fascists in Pablo's village and her life with Finito, the bullfighter, before she meets Pablo. She provides essential background information about life in Spain. Her narratives help to situate specific events and the Spanish value system.

Pablo, like Pilar, is a Gypsy, and he is the fading leader of a guerrilla band that operates in the mountains. In Pablo, Hemingway gives us a complex and nuanced character weakened by age, events, and wine, a foil for Pilar's strength and pride. His deviousness is as defined as Anselmo's loyalty and Maria's love. Each character embodies one trait or more of a collective psyche. Although each one is portrayed as an individual, together, they form a collective portrait.

Maria, shaved and raped by the Falangists, is the symbol of a country that is being raped by Franco. By falling in love with her, Jordan loves the beauty, honesty, and devotion of the land for which he gives his life. We understand why he is willing to die for Spain and why, at the end, after blowing up the bridge, despite the pain of his broken leg and the threat of torture by his captors, he does not commit suicide (thereby highlighting the cowardice of his father's suicide) but engages the enemy in a rearguard action that will ensure the safe passage of Maria and his adoptive family.

Jordan is an American who understands the idiosyncrasies of the Spanish people and who, therefore, because he also speaks the language, can become a member of Pilar's family. He is also a part of Iberia and he has heard the tolling of the peninsular bells. However, despite the symbolism of John Donne's epigraph and the symbolism of character (Maria is also the name of the Virgin Mother, and Jordan is the name of a river in the Holy Land, where T. E. Lawrence blew up trains) and place, *For Whom the Bell Tolls* is a work that is personal, intense, and highly focused. The tragic love story between Robert and Maria—two people ground up in the machinery of the civil war—involves the reader in a profound way. Although Hemingway gives us a lot of information about other places and events, the action centers on the remote mountain canyon, the cave, the road, and the bridge. This is where things happen.

Blowing up the bridge severs the link between the left and right banks of the river, both physically and politically. It is a symbolic act that exposes the chasm between the opposing sides. It is the visual dramatization of events that have been moving inexorably toward the novel's climax. The river that flows beneath the broken and twisted supports and girders represents also both space-time and cosmic indifference to the tragic circumstances that have been staged on both sides of the divide.

Hemingway's characters all fit into a narrative aesthetic that is primarily referential. However, I do not mean to imply that, for all its realism, *For Whom the Bell Tolls* is devoid of self-reflexive elements, the three most memorable ones being Pilar's account of the killing of the Fascists, the flashback to the corrida, and her description of life with the matador Finito. These accounts are narratives within the main narrative and they have their specular value; that is, they complicate any simplistic view of the novel as pure classic realism. In a self-conscious nod to his writerly genius, Hemingway/Jordan says that Pilar is a better storyteller than Quevedo, even as Jordan wishes he could write well enough to tell the story of the killing of the Fascists, if only he could get it down the way she told it. But since Jordan has not written it, and Pilar can't, and we know that Hemingway has, it is Hemingway himself who is telling the reader, in an oblique way, that he is better than Quevedo (134).

Furthermore, I don't believe that Hemingway wants to undermine the realism of the novel. He may want the reader to acknowledge his superior writing abilities, but these are highlighted not to devalue the larger narrative but to enhance it. Jordan's determination to blow up the bridge is never in doubt, and Hemingway, unlike postmodern writers, particularly the metafictionists, does not cast doubt on the veracity of events. If he fabulates, it is not to call attention to language, the way Robert Coover does in *Spanking the Maid* (1982) or as Raymond Federman does in *Double or Nothing* (1971), but to contribute to the suspense of the story. Nor does Malraux foreground language per se. The differences between him and Hemingway reside primarily in the way they describe collective action.

In *For Whom the Bell Tolls* Pilar's description of the drunken mob that is killing the Fascists is a negative portrayal of group behavior, and it is very different from Malraux's positive descriptions of groups. Hemingway's portrayal of the peasants is not Malraux's idealized portrait of them in *L'espoir,* as, for instance, when after the airplane crash, the rescue party brings the dead aviators down the mountain. The fraternal voices of the Spanish peasants meld with the rhythms of death and renewal on the mountain in order to oppose the dehumanizing and destructive forces of the war. For Malraux, a person's commitment to the cause is as imperious as the rocks and as ephemeral as the decaying apples around the trunk of the tree. Decay may symbolize death, but the tree symbolizes life. There is a fraternal consciousness that raises its collective voice above the forces that debase man (*L'espoir* 341–42). By "man," Malraux means all men and women who work toward a common goal, hence his animation of crowds, streets, barracks, and churches. Only the concerted endeavor of all human beings can counteract the absurd, alienation, and aloneness.

The closest Hemingway comes to Malraux's vision of solidarity in action is when he compares the discipline of resistance in the Sierras to taking part in a crusade, when the participants fight with a true sense of comradeship. Hemingway compares the combatants' feelings to religious faith and the beatitudes of artistic experience (*Bell* 235). Typical, perhaps, and in sharp contrast, is his portrayal of Gordo's solitary stand on the hill, an isolation that contrasts with Malraux's description of people, places, and equipment, all of which are group oriented. By comparison, Malraux's characters are flattened out, as in modern painting, where depth and perspective are abolished. According to R. M. Albérès, "Malraux has suppressed the immobile setting favored in the traditional art of story and novel, replacing it by confused, vibrant, shifting images" (48).[6]

In contrast to *For Whom the Bell Tolls, L'espoir* evolves over a period of months, not days; it is not set in one place, except perhaps for Spain in general; and it has no love story to sustain it. It does not fit the mold of classic realism. Malraux is less interested in the subtleties of human interaction, the way Hemingway is, than by the chance to use fiction as a means of exploring and highlighting ideas. His purpose in writing the book was to help the reader empathize with the Republican cause, in short, to give as broad an experience as possible by describing the multi-faceted nature of the war that was being fought simultaneously on many fronts. Malraux's most lyrical passages center not on one man or one unit but on descriptions of fighting that are panoramic and that involve crowd action: street encounters, tank battles, airplane sorties. It's not the psychology of the individual that interests Malraux, but the ideology of the group. The novel dramatizes fraternal endeavor and collective movement in line with Unanimist premises that were laid down by Jules Romains, a twentieth-century predecessor who wrote a twenty-seven-volume novel entitled *Les hommes de bonne volonté*.

According to Romains, a Unanimist writer can tap into the psychology of the crowd in a street, a square, or a theater and, in doing so, write the poetics of the group. It was Romains and Georges Chennevière who, from 1903 on, particularly throughout the fauve and cubist periods of French art, strove to imbue their writing with the consciousness of group behavior. According to them, a crowd had a life and dynamic rhythm of its own. These two writers emphasized the positive force elicited by collective beings and they strove to direct this energy through their essays, poetry, fiction, and mass gatherings, such as Chennevière's Fêtes du Peuple (see Stoltzfus, "Georges Chennevière"). Romains' *Vie unanime, Knock,* and *Puissances de Paris* evoke the consciousness of groups, and he poeticizes the agglomerations and noises of people, streets, cities, trains, ports, barracks, stores, and churches.

André Cuisenier (*Jules Romains et l'unanimisme* and *L'art de Jules Romains*) and others have described the theory of Unanimism in great detail (see also Stoltzfus, *Georges Chennevière*), and this literary movement has clearly left its imprint on Malraux. In *L'espoir,* its influence is discernible in his descriptions of street scenes, ground and air battles, and the vocabulary of hope within the fraternal endeavor of the combatants. Instead of individuals, he depicts a crowd thrashing about with an exhausted and dejected sense of rage (194). In his description of the insurrectionists' attack on the Fascist barracks, he animates a battering ram, which then functions as a synecdoche of crowd action. The battering ram *does not see* the flag of surrender and, in *its zeal,* breaks down the door that the Fascists have just opened (36). In like manner, Malraux animates the barracks, which are *vibrating with cries,* explosions, and smoke, like a sonorous convent (35). In yet another Unanimist image he compares the city to a living body that is being drained of its lifeblood by the people leaving it (176). Madrid, illuminated and disguised by the props and costumes of the revolution, is described as one immense nocturnal studio (38). Elsewhere, lights give the bombing of a city a muted existence, but when the lights are extinguished, the life of the city is even more intense (159). In another bombing scene Malraux compares the city to a blind man *crying out* in self-defense (198). Castille *sleeps* with one eye open (211), and Madrid, not the individuals in it, is invested with enormous powers to resist the enemy (224). Moreover, the hope that gives the novel its resonance stems from the discipline and fraternity of men engaged in a common cause (197). This awareness of themselves in groups and in cities, as Malraux portrays it, evolves slowly into the optimism with which the novel ends. If, at last, Spain is becoming conscious of itself, it is because the efforts of each enclave coalesce into resisting Franco's machine, the war that is tearing the country apart.

All these descriptions belong to the panoramic simultaneity that makes *L'espoir* so different from *For Whom the Bell Tolls.* Whereas Hemingway strives to give each one of his characters specific and different personality traits, Malraux is working toward a definition of history, political action, and group behavior. Although, as we have seen, Malraux develops many characters, none is as clearly delineated and memorable as Hemingway's. Indeed, the most memorable characters in *L'espoir* are not individuals, but the people, the refugees, the combatants, the airplane crews, the bombed cities, and ultimately Spain itself. Unanimists believe that a nation, like any entity, can become a "god." For that reason, there is hope for a divided country whenever it becomes conscious of itself and its collective purpose. In 1937, Spain was shattered, and Franco eventually won the civil war, and it is ironic that during this same period Hitler was able to give Germany a Nazi identity—one that would set the stage for World War II—a calamity adumbrated by the war in Spain.

Picon phrases it aptly when he states that the story of Malraux is in essence the encounter between Malraux and history. Indeed, Malraux's fictions, like *A Farewell to Arms* and *For Whom the Bell Tolls,* emerge from the bloody and tumultuous history of the twentieth century, which Friedrich

Nietzsche prophetically defined as "the classical era of war" (qtd. by Ginsberg 47). Malraux, who liked to quote Napoleon's dictum that "tragedy is
now Politics," drew on the defining myth of the twentieth century in order to
write *La condition humaine* and *L'espoir,* in a context of tragedy (Picon 19).

According to Germaine Brée, history is the stage on which Malraux's
heroes are defined. The author's purpose is to create a myth of redemption
more eloquent than the silence of the cosmos (Brée, *Twentieth-Century*
256). Malrucian heroes then define themselves through fraternal action in
combat by opposing dictators such as Franco or through an art that exalts
the human in opposition to cosmic indifference. Malraux's perception that
life is both tragic and absurd leads him toward political commitment on
one hand and, on the other, to the conclusion that only art can survive
death. Not only do the masterpieces of the past—Malraux calls them "the
voices of silence"—speak of human greatness, but they also manifest the
continuity of conscious engagement.

Malraux's art foregrounds humanity's inherent greatness as it strives
to unveil its sense of destiny. In this connection the artist is greater than
the revolutionary because he or she is not bound by the straitjacket of
expediency. While the artist, like the revolutionary, is mortal, the artist's
work transcends finitude. Art may not be eternal, but it is the supreme
expression of a culture that, "ever since man has confronted the Cosmos
alone, aspires to inherit the nobility of the world" (Picon 103). Although
in *L'espoir* Manuel implies that fraternal revolutionary action is as strong
as art (360), and Moreno says that when the bombs begin to fall and
people die, the masterpieces of the world seem inconsequential, revolutions are, nonetheless, by their very nature ephemeral and also deadly,
whereas not only does art endow mankind with the mantle of true nobility, but it also defies the vicissitudes of time.

Hemingway, like Malraux, writes of the Republicans' sense of brotherhood under fire and of their dedication and, like Malraux, he juxtaposes political commitment and art. For Jordan, the feeling of fraternal
endeavor is as authentic as listening to Bach or standing in the cathedral
of Chartres or looking at Mantegna, El Greco, or Brueghel (*Bell* 235).
Despite their differences, both Hemingway and Malraux strove to transform lived experience into an art that would be truer than life and whose
reality would rival everyday existence.

In opposition to Fascism's destructive image of humanity—one that
privileges certain men and women at the expense of minorities and the

oppressed—both Hemingway and Malraux committed themselves early on to oppose totalitarianism.[7] It is ironic that these two great writers who were engaged in the struggle against Fascism preferred to duke it out rather than acknowledge their similarities. Jordan, Magnin, Scali, Hernandez, Garcia, Jimenez, and Manuel, like their progenitors, are of the same cloth. Because Hemingway's lone hero resembles Malraux's many warriors, it's time, once again, to sound the bell: "No man is an *Iland*. . . . Every man is a piece of the *Continent*."[8]

In conclusion, despite Hemingway's and Malraux's commitment to the Republican cause, their novels are very different in form and style. Whereas Hemingway strives to give each one of his characters a specific personality, Malraux is working toward a definition of history and political action. Although Jordan succeeds in blowing up the bridge over the gorge, the ending of Hemingway's novel is tragic because Jordan and Maria are separated and we know that he will die while guarding the retreat of his Gypsy friends. Malraux's ending is hopeful because Spain, despite the agony of the war, is developing a consciousness of itself. This consciousness belongs to Malraux's generic optimism and faith in the efficacy of group endeavor and fraternal action, and it contrasts with the overriding pessimism of Hemingway's novels, in which winners are always losers. Hemingway's heroes and heroines may save their dignity, but they either die, lose the person they love, or end up impotent. Their tragedies, although they function as a metaphor for the human condition, are solitary endings, like Jordan's rearguard action, whereas Malraux's tragedies are potential victories because they are fueled by a collective spirit that transcends the individual.

I suspect Hemingway and Malraux understood their differences. Their artistic temperaments, in addition to their professional rivalry, probably tainted a relationship that could have been more harmonious. In any case, Hemingway always eventually distanced himself, even from friends such as F. Scott Fitzgerald and John Dos Passos. Not only was Hemingway more aggressive than Malraux in vilifying his rivals; he also structured his fiction and his characters in ways that reflect a fundamental sense of alienation. In contrast, Malraux's initial sense of alienation in novels such as *La voie royale* (1930; *The Royal Way*) altered radically in order to impose the stamp of man on nature, as in *La condition humaine* and *L'espoir*.

Despite Camus' preference for *L'espoir* over *For Whom the Bell Tolls*, the latter is far superior to *To Have and Have Not*, the work in which

Hemingway failed to master his material. In defending the cause of the displaced veterans and in comparing the plight of the down-and-out to the luxurious living of the rich, Hemingway fails to bring the different components of the novel together in a way that addresses the exigencies of art and politics. Not so with *For Whom the Bell Tolls,* where all the characters and all the elements of the story coalesce in order to highlight the action in a country under siege.

Ten years after the publication of *For Whom the Bell Tolls,* Hemingway published *Across the River and into the Trees* (1950), an ambitious novel that was panned by the critics, but one that deserves better than it got. In the next chapter I compare Hemingway's calculus of time, place, and memory with Proust's similar accomplishments in *A la recherche du temps perdu.*

Again, the centrality of Malraux and Hemingway in literary space is worth emphasizing because their achievements, whatever their differences may be, highlight the competition for excellence and, ultimately, the definition of literature itself.

Eight

The Stones of Venice, Time, and Remembrance

Calculus and Proust in Across the River and into the Trees

For the writer, an impression is what experimentation is for the scientist.
—MARCEL PROUST, *A la recherche du temps perdu*

In writing I have moved through arithmetic, through plane geometry
and algebra, and now I am in calculus.
—ERNEST HEMINGWAY

When *Across the River and into the Trees* was published in 1950, criticism was almost unanimously negative. Some 150 newspaper and magazine critics reviewed the book and most of them panned it. The novel was characterized as disappointing, trivial, garrulous, and tired. In an interview in the *New York Times Book Review* Hemingway defended himself by saying that the critics were confused by the novel's experimental complexity (Breit 14). "In writing I have moved through arithmetic, through plane geometry and algebra, and now I am in calculus" (qtd. by Bruccoli 62). More than fifty years after Hemingway's statement, readers familiar with metafiction and the *nouveau roman* have little difficulty with *Across the River*'s circular structure, time shifts, and inner resonance, and the complexity of the novel is no longer daunting or, worse, dismissible. At the time, Hemingway's frustration at not being understood stemmed from the fact that in his final years, his subjects of war, love, and remembrance were "all explorations into death's fusion with a creative consciousness" (Listoe 94).

Although *Across the River and into the Trees* is a flawed novel, Hemingway, according to Reynolds, believed it was the best book he had ever written (*The Final Years* 212). The best it is not, but its experimental complexity has elicited a number of revaluations that may indeed reveal a calculus of writing.[1] In this connection, Venice, stones, time, and remembrance are the elements of a narrative convergence between Hemingway and Proust that deserves analysis. Marcel, the intermittent narrator of Proust's novel, and Richard Cantwell, the implied narrator of Hemingway's novel—a novel narrated from a third-person limited point of view—remember the past as though it were the present and they compress time by reliving events that dramatize love and death. This is not to say that *Across the River and into the Trees* and *A la recherche du temps perdu* (*In Search of Lost Time*) are stylistically and structurally identical. They are not, and the differences are striking. *Across the River and into the Trees* is 308 pages long, whereas the three volumes of Proust's novel are 3,134 pages. Proust's long sentences, inner monologue, and psychological analyses of events, time, and remembrance contrast with Hemingway's short sentences and absence of narrative commentary. Proust explores connections and draws conclusions, whereas Hemingway describes events, places, and people, using an allusive vocabulary that does not theorize. His narrative forces the reader to connect the parts by analyzing the poetic resonance of the floating signifiers. Indeed, Hemingway's iceberg technique of writing is at odds with Proust's long passages, in which he explicitly analyzes the meaning of hidden relationships. For Proust, more is more, whereas for Hemingway less is more, and he asks the reader to solve the relationships between the parts and the whole. Proust crosses the bridges for the reader, whereas, in Venice, along the canals, Hemingway walks the reader to the bridges that he or she must cross alone without the narrator's help. Hemingway does not theorize, and his refusal may explain, in part, the incomprehension that greeted *Across the River* when it was first published.

Venice is the city that Colonel Cantwell has fought for in two world wars. He loves the city and he feels that it is his. Renata, whom he also loves, is his eighteen-year-old "Venus rising from the sea." He was approximately her age during World War I when he defended Venice against the

Austrians and now, at fifty, during World War II, he has helped liberate the city from the Fascists. He is outspoken, gruff, an art connoisseur, and a gastronome.

Throughout his narration, Cantwell describes military blunders and the stupidity of superiors who were responsible for the death of many soldiers. Cantwell is an experienced strategist who loves history, literature, and art. His references to Dante, Shakespeare, Villon, Blake, Byron, Browning, Rimbaud, Verlaine, and d'Annunzio complement his allusions to artists and the history of Venice, and they serve in part to define the rich heritage of the city.

Unlike Cantwell, Proust's Marcel is a social-climbing aesthete. Nonetheless, these two characters, like Proust and Hemingway, share a predilection for complex narrative patterns in which memory and space-time coalesce. Both of them experience a geometry of space and a psychology of time. Entropy erodes events and it diminishes people, but memory preserves them, and it is their so-called resurrection that highlights the present-tense immediacy of both novels.

In *Le temps retrouvé* (*Time Regained*) Venice figures prominently in Marcel's narrative equation—an equation that conflates the past and the present into a timelessness that defies death. His remembrance of the uneven paving stones of St. Mark's is one of a series of privileged moments that provide access to the meaning and structure of the novel. Other privileged moments are the episode of the madeleine, Vinteuil's sonata, the sound of a spoon tinkling against a plate, and the feel of a starched napkin against his lips at the Guermantes' château.

All these sensory contacts—taste, sound, touch, and feel—are mnemonic catalysts that revive the past with great intensity and affective joy, and none is attributable to voluntary memory. On the contrary, the key to the happiness Marcel feels is that these memories are involuntary. They occur spontaneously and are the result of chance encounter. Marcel relives these past events as though they were in the present, and because he has the illusion of escaping from time, he no longer "feels mediocre, contingent, or mortal" (*A la recherche* 1:45). In fact, he feels immortal and, in due course, he imbues the art that organizes and captures these privileged moments with the immortality that will survive death. Indeed, for Proust, art in the broadest sense is the only immortality that men and women can hope for. In a secular world nothing lasts forever, but great artists live posthumous lives that mere mortals never will. The renown of Proust and Hemingway guarantees their survival, at least for awhile, and it is interesting that both men, despite their profound stylistic differences and lifestyles, incorporated a consciousness of survival into their writing.

For Cantwell, the stones of St. Mark's and the emeralds Renata gives him also connote continuity. Proust, however, unlike Hemingway, who devotes little space in *Across the River and into the Trees* to analysis or inner monologue, dissects memory in order to draw conclusions about the psychology of time, namely, that the body is a reservoir of forgotten events, which, like Celtic souls held captive in a tree, a plant, an animal, or a stone, can, at the propitious moment, respond and emerge.

The taste of the madeleine, the sound of Vinteuil's sonata on the violin in the salon of the Princess Mathilde, and the feel of uneven paving stones in the Guermantes' courtyard are bridges to the past, and as Marcel relives an afternoon as a boy with his aunt, the room, the street, and the town appear miraculously from the cup of tea, like a miniature Japanese landscape that was nothing more than a paper pellet that, immersed in water, unfolds to become the houses and trees of a wonderful landscape. Also, the little phrase of Vinteuil's sonata that was the "national anthem" of Swann and Odette's love, one that he considered long forgotten, resurrects his feelings for her with all the sweetness and pain of their former relationship when he hears it again (*A la recherche* 1:345). Thus, also, in the Guermantes' courtyard, the feel of the uneven paving stones connects Marcel, across space and time, with the stones of St. Mark's baptistery. The tinkle of the spoon and plate elicits the metallic sound of a trainman's hammer against a wheel, and the feel of the starched napkin conjures a moment in the past when Marcel stood in front of a window in Balbec, admiring the landscape. The happiness Marcel feels in seeing the trees and the spires of Martinville and the euphoria elicited by images of Combray or the paving stones of Venice make death seem distant and illusory (*A la recherche* 3:866–73). Proust concludes that time is elastic: the love we feel sometimes expands it, the passions we inspire in others shrink it, and habit fills the rest. As though to confirm these conclusions, Cantwell's love for Renata occupies 214 pages of the 308-page novel, and his love for Venice fills the entire novel.

Cantwell's memories, as bridges to the past, are not involuntary, as Marcel's are, because Cantwell's remembrances can be verbal, even actual. For example, his pejorative use of the word "boy," in referring to himself in the duck blind at the end of chapter 1, introduces the first sentence of chapter 2, "But he was not a boy," and the flashback to the physical examination of the day before in Trieste, when he had taken enough mannitol hexanitrate to pass the physical that would give him a three-day pass to Venice. Chapter 2 goes back in time one day, but the dialogues of all the chapters in the novel, including the first two, are in the present. Despite the time shifts of a third-person narrator sliding into a first-person narrator, the reader has the illusion that everything is occurring in the present, even though Cantwell's time with Renata exists only in his memory. Hemingway's frequent use of the word "now" reinforces the illusion.

Although sight, in Proust's novel, does not activate involuntary memory, sight in *Across the River* plays an important role in recapturing the past. While Jackson, the chauffeur, is driving the big Buick toward Venice, Cantwell remembers and describes the bridge, the Piave, the river banks, and the *ossario* by Nervesa, where he fought in the Italian army during World War I. The simultaneity of the past and the present is tangible, but Proust's sense of euphoria is absent, and it would be difficult to construe Cantwell's memories of World War I as involuntary. Nonetheless, this country means very much to him and he remembers his "loss of immortality . . . that is quite a lot to lose" (33). However, the closer he gets to Venice, the younger he feels and he remembers immortal writers such as Lord Byron, Browning, and d'Annunzio. And as Cantwell describes a speech by d'Annunzio during World War I, when he and his platoon had stopped to listen, Hemingway's prose moves the past into the present and conflates it with the "small villa on the left" that belonged to the great writer (51).

Throughout *Across the River and into the Trees* the battles of World War I and World War II are described in vivid detail and in ways that dovetail, and Cantwell becomes the center of an overlapping simultaneity. Time seems to stop as his consciousness oscillates between events that are separated by thirty years. In the duck blind, time does in fact stop as Cantwell telescopes two days into hours, as the fifty-year-old man remembers and experiences love and life with a fresh and renewed intensity. In Proust's novel, while recalling his love for Odette, Swann comments on love's rejuvenating effects and the feelings it generates. The outlines of things become sharper; the air is crisper; and, for Cantwell, the houses are "as clear and sharp as on a winter day" (48). However, for Hemingway, unlike Proust, sight does trigger involuntary memories. When Cantwell contemplates the play of light from the canal on the ceiling, "he was completely desperate at the remembrance of his loss of his battalions, and of individual people" (242). Earlier, his descriptions of the Piave, the Rapido, Fossalta, and the Hürtgen Forest were quite objective and certainly not desperate. In *Across the River and into the Trees,* touch, feel, and sound, as in Proust's novel, also generate happy images of remembrance, and Venice is their touchstone.

For Cantwell, Venice is the most important link with the past, and the city, like the emeralds in his pocket, is also a jewel, with its Grand Canal, gondolas, houses, churches (Santa Maria del Giglio and St. Mark's), frescoes, and squares, and the Gritti Palace Hotel, Harry's Bar, and the marketplace with produce on display as vivid as still lifes, food, drink, and love. All this and Giotto, Piero della Francesca, Mantegna, Michelangelo, Titian, Tintoretto, Botticelli, and, by extension, other European painters such as Bosch, Velázquez, Goya, Degas, and Cézanne. In addition to Proust and the elements of time, death, and remembrance, and in order to fully grasp the complexity of *Across the River* and Venice within the context of Hemingway's calculus, we need to incorporate analyses of the historical, literary, and artistic references as they resonate throughout the novel like the bells from the church towers.

Venice exists in time. Indeed, Cantwell imbues the city with layers of history, from the Visigoths and the Lombards to the time a boy from Torcello located the body of St. Mark in Alexandria and smuggled it into Venice under a load of fresh pork. It is perhaps symbolic that Venice was built from the stones of an abandoned Torcello, and Hemingway's use of the word "stones" for emeralds is not without premeditation. Emeralds, stones, houses, squares, and churches all resonate with the connotations of time, duration, and place. They are all jewels. Like Combray, the village that emerges from the taste of the madeleine, Venice emerges from the stones in Cantwell's pocket. The architecture of the city and the architecture of the novel resemble each other, which is not surprising because both Proust and Hemingway wanted their work to have symmetry. "Prose is architecture, not interior decoration," says Hemingway in *Death in the Afternoon* (191), and, in a letter to Jean de Gaigneron, Proust says that he constructed his book as if it were a cathedral, in which the solidity of the smallest part was an essential piece of the whole (Maurois 175). For example, as a boy at his uncle's house, Marcel sees a woman in a rose dress who, in due course, becomes Miss Sacripant, then Odette de Crécy, Madame Swann, and Madame de Forcheville. At the Verdurins' salon there is a painter named "Biche" who, in time, will become the great and talented Elstir. In a house of ill repute the narrator meets a girl of easy virtue who will become Rachel, then Saint-Loup's wife, and, eventually, one of the greatest actresses of her time, La Berma. André Maurois says that the Gothic arches of Proust's first volume rise above the whole and descend gracefully into the final volume (176). In *Le temps retrouvé,* the title of the last volume, the theme of the madeleine echoes throughout thousands of pages as it resonates with the uneven paving stones of Venice.

In addition to paving stones, Cantwell's Venice has love, friends, gastronomy, art, and architecture, all the movable pleasures that contribute to the feast of Cantwell's "one and only life" (*Across the River* 94). He and Renata are determined to have fun, and because he does not believe in hell (250), there can be no impediment to the satisfactions they pursue. The only hell the colonel has known is war and with it the stupidity of military hierarchies. Venice offers a reprieve and he is determined, at fifty, to recapture all the youth and happiness he can. "No one," he says to himself, "is ever old in Venice" (93). Being souped up on nitroglycerin gives him the heart of an eighteen-year-old, the same age as Renata. Besides, in Venice, as in heaven, everybody stays young, even the eighty-year-old Contessa Dandolo, who is as vivacious as a girl and has no fear of dying (47). Neither does the colonel. As in Proust's *Le temps retrouvé,* Venice defies death and so do its residents.

Hemingway was wise to resist Charles Scribner's request that he introduce Renata into the novel before page 80 (Reynolds, *The Final Years* 212), because it would have altered the symmetry of the book. Venice (and its environs) is the main character, and Cantwell loves the city and duck shooting perhaps even more than he loves Renata. Otherwise, why would he not spend his three-day pass exclusively with her? We know and he knows that he is dying. All the symptoms and symbols are there: symptoms such as his failing heart, the doctor's admonitions, Cantwell's temper and physical exertions that are bad for his heart, his age, his ten concussions, and his overdose of mannitol hexanitrate, and symbols such as the canals and bridges of Venice; the channels of the marshes, which, like Dante's circles of hell, are closing in with Charon, the ill-tempered boatman, ferrying the souls of the dead across the river Styx to Hades; the ice on the marsh; the cold wind blowing from the north and "somewhere else" (52); the snow on the mountains; and Cantwell's driver, Jackson, who, like Stonewall Jackson, is the source of the novel's title.

Furthermore, Cantwell's heart sounds like "a marine conversion of a tiny Fiat engine" that has "served its allotted time" (43). Its every move "is a triumph of the gallantry of the aging machine" (52). At the Gritti Palace the elevator halts "with slight hydraulic inaccuracy at the top floor" because "the current is not stable" (66). Later, when the tide is in, Cantwell, Renata, and the gondolier clear the space under the bridges with barely enough room to spare. Baker believes that the failing engine, the unstable current, and the rising tide are all tropes for Cantwell's failing heart (*Writer as Artist* 280–82).

As Cantwell enters Venice along the canal leading into the Rio Nuovo, he feels rejuvenated, and the engine of the boat, like his heart, "commenced its metallic agony that produced a slight increase in speed" (46). He knows the houses, the palaces, and their occupants, and the city moves him again "as it had when he . . . had seen it first, understanding nothing of it and only knowing that it was beautiful" (31). Venice is "my town," says the colonel (20), and Renata is his girl. He loves everything about them. Renata's "dark hair [is] of an alive texture" and hangs "down over her shoulders," and her body, her olive-colored skin, and her profile break his heart (80). In the portrait, Renata's hair is twice as long as it has ever been and there she looks like Botticelli's *Venus Rising from the Sea* (97). But Venice also rises from the sea (45) and because Cantwell loves both Venice and Renata, they have an overlapping and simultaneous beauty. The hair of Botticelli's *Venus* hangs down to her knees. Never mind that she is a honey blonde and Renata is a brunette. Venus is the metaphorical pearl on the half shell and she dates from 1480, but Renata's emeralds are also old and they once belonged to her great-great-grandmother. When the colonel says that he loves her "on these water-worn, cold and old stones" of the wind-swept square (161), we hear stones, jewels, and emeralds resonating like the bells from the campaniles of St. Mark's, Murano, and Burano, and the squared tower of the church at Torcello. "You're a Torcello Boy," says Renata to Cantwell (161), and he has the stones to prove it, and when he sleeps he keeps them in the pocket close to his heart, where Renata's beauty reverberates. Her presence is mesmerizing, and when he looks at her his heart turns over inside him (83). His joy in love is comparable to Marcel's joy when he tastes the madeleine, which also has the shape of the scallop shell in Botticelli's painting, and the taste reverberates along the ridges and grooves to recapture the precious moment that abolishes time. Venus, Venice, and Renata rising from the sea on a scallop shell are arresting images, and their visual impact on Cantwell is comparable to the madeleine's gustatory effect on Marcel. This is perhaps the calculus of writing that Hemingway refers to when he says that he has gone beyond arithmetic, algebra, and plane geometry.

For Marcel, the scallop shell of the madeleine is the joyful source of remembrance. For Cantwell, the scallop shell that is Venice rising is the joy of his love for the city and Renata and their dual beauty. Here, the similarities between Proust and Hemingway are striking. The taste of the madeleine, like falling in love, has made life's brevity illusory and its disasters inoffensive (*A la recherche* 1:45), and that is precisely Cantwell's reaction. In Renata's embrace, he is supremely happy and he repeatedly takes tablets of mannitol hexanitrate to keep him going, even though he knows that the overdose will kill him. The movable feast that is Venice overrides every mundane concern. Indeed, he would rather "live one day as a lion than a hundred years as a sheep" (*Across the River* 40). Cantwell's passion reminds us of the writer Bergotte, in Proust's *La prisonnière* (1923; *The Prisoner*), who gets so excited by a review he reads in the newspaper of Vermeer's *View of Delft* that, despite his bad heart, he goes to the exhibition that has been lent by the Hague Museum in order to contemplate a yellow section of the painting whose beauty is so totally self-contained that it resembles a precious Chinese work of art. "This is how I should have written," says Bergotte to himself. "My last books are much too dry and they needed several layers of color to render the phrasing as precious as this small section of yellow wall." And while looking at the yellow surface of Vermeer's painting, Bergotte keels over dead, stricken by a heart attack (*A la recherche* 3:187).

Cantwell does not die while looking at the play of light on the ceiling of his hotel room but, as an art connoisseur, he could have. Instead, Hemingway completes the circle of time remembered in the duck blind, a circle as perfect as any Giotto might have drawn, as Cantwell succumbs and dies in the backseat of the Buick.

If Proust's novel depends in part on involuntary memory for its architectural design, for Hemingway, the building blocks of *Across the River* are shaped by a consciousness based on the play of writing and its dramatic effects. "If you loved the city of Venice," says Cantwell on his way to the marketplace, *solitaire ambulante* is an excellent game "and what you win is the happiness of your eye and heart" (185). Later, he asks Renata if she would like to play historical personages and she says, "Let us play that you are you and I am me," and the colonel says, "Let's play" (261), a game he has been playing all along because he is enamored with Venice, the city's history, and her gustatory delights. "Produce a few smells or something from your off-stage kitchen," says Cantwell to the man he calls *gran maestro* (273).

Finally, shortly before he dies, in keeping with writing as drama and the theatricality of language, Cantwell refers to the "noise heard off stage in [his] heart" (294). When it stops, everything stops, and the machinery of the novel grinds to a halt. The heart is a chambered muscle and when Richard "the lion-hearted" dies, time stops, and with it, all the memories and all the happiness. A stone will mark his grave and it will be as lifeless as the emeralds and Renata's portrait. Only the beating heart remembers. The dead are like the reflected shadows of light on the ceiling of the hotel room where Cantwell and Renata once loved each other.

Hemingway's novel is constructed stone by stone and the different pieces of its structure, like Venice or St. Mark's, articulate his writing and its calculus. Each theme fits into the other as the different building blocks dovetail into the architectural whole. The soul of Venice, like the Celtic souls to which Proust refers, is in its stones, buildings, artists, and people. To possess Venice, as Cantwell does, is to become a part of the city; to be reenergized, even if only for three days; and, like Marcel and the madeleine, to have the feeling of never growing old. The immortality that Marcel discovers when his involuntary memory manifests its magic is experienced by Cantwell as he remembers Venice. Venice and Renata are the love and beauty that give meaning to his life. In their presence he no longer feels mediocre, contingent, or mortal. They are his happiness. Time and youth have been regained.

The calculus of writing that structures *Across the River and into the Trees* echoes the proleptic images in *A Farewell to Arms;* the ironic repetitions in *The Sun Also Rises;* and the melding of art, writing, and the corrida in

Death in the Afternoon. In *Across the River and into the Trees* Hemingway has crafted an ambitious novel that almost lives up to our expectations. Indeed, the space-time comparison with Proust gives it a heretofore unexplored dimension that should redeem it even in the eyes of the most jaundiced critics.

We look next at *The Old Man and the Sea* (1952), the novella in which Hemingway's prose poetry colors Santiago's pride with Christological images and pagan allusions. Like Oedipus in Gide's play *Oedipe* (1930), Santiago, the fisherman, imposes a human stamp on endeavor in order to affirm the strength and dignity of man.

$\mathcal{N}ine$

Pride

André Gide's Oedipe *and* The Old Man and the Sea

Pride . . . is a Christian sin and a pagan virtue.
—ERNEST HEMINGWAY, *Death in the Afternoon*

I am glad above all that I owe nothing to anyone but myself.
Happiness was not given to me: I conquered it.
—ANDRÉ GIDE, *Oedipe*

$\mathcal{I}$n 1951, the year of André Gide's death, Sartre wrote that "all of French thought in these past thirty years, willing or not, whatever its coordinates may have been elsewhere—Marx, Hegel, Kierkegaard—must also be defined in relation to Gide" ("The Living Gide" 50).[1] As for Hemingway, prose fiction will no doubt forever bear the imprint of his style, which draws attention not only to itself but also to the experience behind it. Both men received national and international recognition and were formally honored with the Nobel Prize, Gide in 1947 and Hemingway in 1954. Both men are at the center of literary space, and this convergence enriches their works by amplifying the themes and the craft of each artist. They also draw on the centrality of Sophocles' *Oedipus Rex,* perhaps the greatest classic of world literature.

Despite common ground, their differences were pronounced. Gide typifies the French intellectual, whereas Hemingway typifies the American anti-intellectual. For all of Hemingway's virile posturing, he felt obliged, from time to time, to question the virility of alleged or suspected homosexuals.[2] Gide, himself an avowed homosexual, felt no shame or guilt about his gay persuasion. Indeed, what he admired most about contemporary American literature was its "direct contact with life" (*Journal* 225).[3] Hemingway, the soldier, bullring aficionado, African hunter, and man of action, wrote novels and short stories about death, violence, and safari travels and became a myth in his own lifetime, whereas Gide, although of robust health, eschewed action per se in favor of the more abstract battles of religion and the intellect. Gide joined the Communist Party, traveled to the USSR, and upon his return repudiated the party, engaging in open polemic with Communist ideology. Although Hemingway was never a member of the party, during the Spanish civil war he was a war correspondent and a sympathetic reporter of the Republican cause and its allied Communist ideology.

Considering their differences, notoriety and fame are not sufficient reasons for comparing the two writers. In addition to their celebrity, they are both also innovative, rebellious, and original. It is each writer's idiosyncratic revolt that is interesting, stemming as it does from their intimate knowledge of the Bible and the Western cultural tradition. But even here there are differences. Hemingway was converted to Catholicism and, at least outwardly, observed many of the conventions of religion, whereas Gide's so-called dialogue with his Catholic opponents (Paul Claudel, Jacques Rivière, Henri Massis, and others) reveals a profound distrust of all forms of institutionalized belief and practice.[4] Underlying their differences, however, are several common sources of inspiration. Both writers exhibit a faith in men and women and what they can accomplish: joy in being alive and a desire to fulfill a specifically human potential. These attitudes, directly and indirectly, lead both writers to challenge convention, social values, and ready-made ideas. The invisible thread that connects Gide and Hemingway is their need to assert a human stamp against the forces of destiny—death itself—and, in doing so, to assert pride in achievement—the essence that each one has created for himself.

This pride in human achievement is evident in their work, most specifically in Hemingway's novella, *The Old Man and the Sea* (1952), and in Gide's play *Oedipe* (1930).[5] In these works, the two protagonists, Santiago and Oedipus, have created an essence they are loath to relinquish. They each have an identity of which they are proud—an identity they have worked hard to define—and which is being challenged by bad luck for Santiago and by the gods for Oedipus. Santiago, the old Cuban fisherman, has not caught a fish in eighty-four days and he is *"salao,* which is the worst form of unlucky" (*Old Man* 9), and Oedipus, the king of Thebes, has to cope with an outbreak of the plague. In order to safeguard an essence that is now under threat, Santiago outfits his skiff, goes far out into the Gulf Stream, and catches the largest marlin in the sea. And Oedipus, in order to faithfully exercise his regal duties, launches an investigation into the causes of the gods' displeasure. Pride motivates both men and each will perform heroic deeds in order to retain his identity. Also, they are both overreachers, and the tragedy of their actions stems from the fact that in pursuing their goals, they destroy the prize. If the old adage that pride goes before a fall is true, then, once again, by their extreme endeavors, they prove it correct. Santiago lands a fish he cannot bring back intact, and Oedipus concludes a successful criminal investigation that destroys his happiness. He wants to know who killed Laius, the king; the sharks eat Santiago's marlin; and Jocasta, Oedipus's wife and mother, hangs herself. Santiago suffers a heart attack while fighting the sharks and Oedipus blinds himself out of guilt, rage, and pride. Santiago needs to prove that he is still the champion and Oedipus needs to prove that Man is still the answer to the Sphinx's riddle.

In "The Mask of Humble Perfection" Jackson J. Benson says that "a threat to selfhood is the threat, involving the ultimate horror that the irrational forces of the world can accomplish" (*The Writer's Art* 130). Men who feel this threat, and the ultimate threat is death, carry the painful responsibility of constantly proving themselves. Santiago's code requires that he catch fish. Francis Macomber, during his short and happy life, must prove that he is not a coward; Harry, of Kilimanjaro fame, wants, perhaps belatedly, to prove that he is still a writer; and Oedipus needs to prove that men and women, rather than the gods, can determine their own fate. Because the gods have humiliated him, Oedipus wants to convince Tiresias, the high priest, that man, not God, can, despite adversity, solve life's recurring problems. Each time is a new time, regardless of age, and men such as Santiago and Oedipus act in ways that will reassert their essence. Oedipus blinds himself in order to reaffirm it, and Santiago, who fishes for three days straight in order to remain *el campeón,* has a heart attack.

Santiago believes that he was "born to be a fisherman" (*Old Man* 50). His entire being is bound up in his occupational identity. Other men, less proud, might accept the decline that comes with old age—might even assent to the natural and inevitable rhythm of life and death—but Santiago does not. Although attuned to nature, he is in rebellion against creation. He says he must kill the marlin (75) and he is thankful that he does not also have to kill the stars or the moon or the sun (75). These strange thoughts imply that if the stars were as accessible as fish, he would want to kill them too. Whatever for?

Man takes pleasure in giving death, says Hemingway, because in this way he can usurp one of the godlike attributes (*Death* 233). Hemingway enjoyed killing animals, birds, and fish, and his fictional characters share his predilection. To usurp one of God's attributes in order to heighten the feeling of being alive suggests that life is perhaps too boring or empty without the power of life and death over animals and things. The desire to assert such strength and dominion, although perhaps heroic, is surely also a manifestation of pride. Santiago wants to prove that he is still the best fisherman around and that he can kill marlin in order to prove it. In short, he kills to maintain his essence and his pride.

Although Oedipus kills his father, Laius, because he, the king of Thebes, was blocking the road on which Oedipus was traveling, this act was not motivated by pride. It was the result of anger and, in due course, a courageous Oedipus answers the Sphinx's riddle and unwittingly marries his mother. Despite being abandoned at birth by his parents, he fulfills the oracle's prophesy. Unlike Santiago, for Oedipus his pride and essence derive not from killing, but from his accomplishments, his satisfaction in having bested the Sphinx; married the queen; and, in turn, become king of Thebes: "I am Oedipus. Forty years old and for twenty years a king. By sheer strength I have reached the summit of happiness. A waif and a foundling, without citizenship or papers, I am glad above all that I owe nothing to anyone but myself. Happiness was not given to me: I conquered it" (*Oedipe* 253). Oedipus believes that he has forged his own destiny. The answer to the Sphinx's riddle was Man, and Oedipus feels justifiably proud to be that person, a child raised by Polybus, the king of Corinth, a man without baggage, someone who is now the most important person in Thebes. He says he is happy that his origin is unknown because as long as he thought he was Polybus's son, he listened to him and mimed his virtues. After Oedipus realizes that he has no known past and no legitimate family role model to guide him, he concludes that he is free to create and invent everything: even himself, a country, and ancestors. "Not to know one's parents is a call to glory" (272).

In many ways Oedipus's language adumbrates Sartre's. He begins with existence, nothing more, and by virtue of his strength and intelligence creates a formidable essence: king, husband, father, and opponent of Tiresias—the gods' high priest. Whereas Tiresias believes in God's word, Oedipus believes only in himself. Indeed, the play's central theme is the opposition between man-made values and a so-called higher authority that transcends the human. Oedipus thus embodies Sartre's ideas about an existence that precedes essence and the dizzying consequences engendered by the freedom to choose. We can readily understand why he, Sartre, would say that French thought between 1920 and 1950 must be defined in relation to Gide.

The conflict between God and man, between independence and submission, freedom and guilt, is the subject of Oedipus and Tiresias's encounters. "All science that begins with man and not with God is worthless," says Tiresias. All you can teach your sons is pride (284). Which is true. Oedipus believes that God is superfluous and that he has all the answers. And why wouldn't he? He has bested the Sphinx and he is now the king. Why shouldn't he trust his own superior powers? Besides, he believes in happiness, whereas Tiresias believes in salvation.

Although Gide's play is ostensibly set in ancient Greece, the characters' dialogues echo twentieth-century values. Oedipus is cast as an existential hero who predates existentialism, and Tiresias is cast as a Catholic priest who embodies the values of the church. Whereas Oedipus stresses freedom, independence, self-creation, and self-reliance, Tiresias's vocabulary reflects the faith of a Catholic moralist: God, guilt, original sin, and submission to authority.

Oedipus, the king, and Santiago, the fisherman, both believe that they are free to act in their own best interests, but Oedipus cannot elude the oracle's prophesy—the fatal flaw that destroys his happiness—nor can Santiago elude the sharks that track the blood scent of the marlin and destroy the fish. Both men are buffeted by forces beyond their control. Although they fail, their honor remains intact. Santiago loses the marlin but he proves that he can catch him, and Oedipus loses his wife-mother and his sight, but in blinding himself he atones for not seeing what was staring him in the face: that he was the one who had offended the gods and that everything had already been foretold.

By refusing to submit to the faith of Tiresias—a Tiresias who claimed that his blindness enabled him to hear the voice of God—Oedipus asserts his independence from both, because now, also blind, he can remain faithful to his own inner vision. "Like you [Tiresias] I now contemplate the divine obscurity" (*Oedipe* 301). This is a typical Gidean irony and oxymoron that echoes one of his *Journal* entries: "Faith moves mountains; yes: mountains of absurdities" (1285). Tiresias responds by saying, once again, that pride made Oedipus blind himself (301). In short, Gide's play has a dual conclusion: first, that happiness cannot be built on blind premises, that is, on ignorance of the past, and second, that the gods are to blame for stacking the deck against him. Clearly, Oedipus and Santiago are proud men. But pride, as Hemingway himself has stated, "is a Christian sin and a pagan virtue" (*Death* 233), and both protagonists behave more like pagan heroes than Christian devotees.

Santiago's *pundonor* (a Spanish word meaning honor, probity, courage, self-respect, and pride) makes him go out too far, question the notion of sin, fight "evil" sharks, and return half dead yet somehow triumphant. Santiago is not just fishing for food. The Christ motif and symbolism are too pronounced, in fact so pronounced that commentators have alluded to the Eucharist, the Crucifixion, and in some cases a fish-Christ identity. However, the Christ motif embedded in Santiago's pagan quest asserts strength and pride, not submission and humility, and we, as readers, must necessarily question Hemingway's motive, whether conscious or unconscious, in structuring such clear-cut dichotomies.[6]

The Christ motif in *The Old Man and the Sea* is Hemingway's. Santiago is unaware of the metaphors or the iceberg theory of writing, where connotation overrides denotation. Santiago is proud to be a fisherman. From his boyhood days he has always been self-reliant. He knows the ocean, he knows the weather, and he fishes with precision. The laws and moral code that he observes, except for the perfunctory and ritual use of prayer, are his own and those of the sea. The marlin will teach him dignity and nobility, but the law of the sea is survival, and Santiago adheres to that code. Moreover, Hemingway's precise, naturalistic descriptions of life on the Gulf Stream give us more than local color. Man-o'-war birds and dolphins eat the flying fish, turtles eat the man-o'-war birds, and dolphins eat the flying fish; turtles eat the Portuguese man-of-wars, and sharks eat the flippers of the sleeping turtles. Sea hawks eat the little birds, and so on. Santiago, at the top of the food chain, catches and destroys a 1,600-pound marlin.

Santiago, like the marlin that swims in the Gulf Stream for three days, can, as long as he is alive, resist death and affirm his dignity by "swimming against the current." There is symbolic value for Hemingway and Gide in endurance because adversity allows them to define themselves. Santiago, like Sisyphus rolling his rock up the mountain, affirms his identity as a fisherman by repeatedly proving it. "Ten thousand times that he had proved it meant nothing. Now he was proving it again. Each time was a new time" (*Old Man* 66), and each occurrence takes place in the here and now. Indeed, Hemingway seems to have been acutely aware of the present, and the present has an elasticity that affects duration. Carlos Baker says that the phrase "our one and only life" runs through Hemingway's correspondence with Charles T. Lanham like a theme song (Dillingham 101). E. M. Halliday says that Hemingway's suspicion of ultimate doom increased his "passionate fondness for being alive" (53). For Macomber and Oedipus, to reflect on the meaning of being alive has ontological consequences. They would rather face death or disfigurement than live without honor.

Both men have an acute sense of being cast adrift in a contingent universe, a condition that Sartre names forlornness. Whatever sense of despair we may feel at being abandoned by God, it transforms itself eventually into an awareness of our dreadful freedom, one that is full of opportunity and promise. Oedipus looks forward to the challenge of creating an identity from scratch, and he succeeds, whereas Santiago, who believes he was born to be a fisherman, is happiest when he fishes and triumphs over nature. Besides, who could be more alone or forlorn than Santiago on the Gulf Stream with only his courage, his determination, his skill, and his knowledge to guide him? Santiago, the tenacious, precise, intelligent fisherman, shows that man can endure extraordinary privation and suffering in order to prove that he, of all the beasts, even the lions and the marlin, has the greatest pride and dignity. Baker states that Hemingway considered *The Dignity of Man* as the working title for the novella (*Critiques* 196).

Santiago kills fish because he is a fisherman and also because killing affirms his superiority. This is metaphysical revolt, not Christian humility, because it questions the ultimate ends of creation and protests conditions of mortality imposed on man. The rebel challenges the power that forces him to acknowledge his human condition. Accordingly, Santiago defies creation by wanting to kill the stars and he challenges heaven in order to experience the feeling of dominion that comes with killing. There is tragedy in such desperate intensity: "Christ, I did not know he was so big. I'll kill him though . . . in all his greatness and his glory" (*Old Man* 66).

"Christ," "greatness," and "glory" connote "the Kingdom and the power, and the glory" of the Lord's Prayer. Here and elsewhere the Christian and pagan themes of the novella overlap. "Christ" is Santiago's exclamation, but Hemingway is equating the fish with the Deity. The word "Christ" is an interjection and also a word of identification. Meaning exists simultaneously on two levels, but such ambiguity is not the result of carelessness. It is intentional and, according to William Empson, the result of the richness of poetic speech and verbal nuance. In the proper context it elicits alternative reactions to the same piece of language. Therefore, in the context of ambiguity and the poetic dimension of prose, we need to pursue the Christian and pagan dichotomies.

In primitive and mediaeval Christian art, the fish was a symbol of Christ. The origin is to be found in the initial letters of the names and titles of Jesus in Greek: Jesus Christ, Son of God, and Savior, which spell the Greek word for "fish": ΙΧΘΥΣ. The Christ motif permeates the novella. Santiago carries the fish in his right hand. The traitorous left hand is like a claw. Two robbers were crucified with Christ, a traitorous one on the left, and a faithful one on the right. Santiago, like Christ, settles against the wood and takes "his suffering as it came" (*Old Man* 64). When the fish is killed, it hangs momentarily motionless in the air, a harpoon in its side. A Roman soldier pierced Christ's side as He too hung motionless on the cross.[7] There is a startling contrast, however, between the Christ motif and the act of killing, because if killing fish and animals is to usurp one of God's prerogatives, then, says Camus in *L'homme révolté* (*The Rebel*), such an uprising is "organized into an over-zealous expedition against heaven with the intent of bringing back a prisoner-king whose fall will be proclaimed first, and his death sentence next" (41). Toward the end of his struggle with the fish, Santiago sees the marlin "come out of the water and hang motionless in the sky before he fell" (*Old Man* 98).

Proud men such as Hemingway and Santiago feel the need to heighten their sense of manhood by confronting forces that challenge them. If you are proud of your selfhood and nature conspires to do you in, then it is important that you defend yourself and the concept of man. Too proud to be the laughingstock of the village, Santiago will challenge nature and die if necessary. Such actions explain why he was not tempted to let go of the line that held the marlin, not even for one moment. He, like Macomber, who stands his ground while shooting the buffalo, risks death rather than live without honor. Better to die than live with the indifferent, mocking, or pitying glances of the villagers. Sartre's play *Huis clos* (*No Exit*) posits that our identity is mirrored in the eyes of others, and old age failure is not something he is ready to accept.

Finally, on the question of pride, everyone, perhaps especially Hemingway, knows that a family of lions is called a pride. For Santiago, the lions are "the main thing that is left" (*Old Man* 66), and in the last sentence of the novella he is again dreaming of lions. Clearly, the word "lions" denotes animals but connotes Santiago's *pundonor*. If we extend the Christ motif to include the lions, we are reminded that Christ is "the great, mighty, and invincible lion of the tribe of Judah" (Rev. 5:5) and that the line of Boaz, Jesse, and David that produced Jesus is of "that tribe" (Luke 3:30). The name Santiago is also of that tribe, since Santiago is the Spanish for Saint James. We remember that one of the Jameses referred to in the Bible is Christ's brother and that throughout the narrative Santiago keeps calling the fish his brother. The word "brother" works on the naturalistic level as well as on the symbolic level.

Despite the biblical connotations of words and metaphors, we are left with the overriding impression that honor, pride, and even anger regulate Santiago's actions. Yes, anger, based on his desire to kill the stars and the marlin, not to mention the sharks. His anger derives from frustration: eighty-four fishless days, an essence under threat, and the unsettling pity he sees in the gaze of the other fishermen. His anger is understandable and Santiago is not yet ready to give up. But there is more. There is also the anger that lurks in the unconscious, the metaphysical anger directed at creation for having made us mortal. This is the anger that cries out in protest against death, against conditions that Camus names the absurd— the disproportionate gap between man's longing for immortality and the nada of his human condition. Finally, there is the repressed anger of the Oedipus complex that coils in the unconscious and that reveals itself occasionally in puns and in slips of the tongue or of the trigger finger of

Macomber's wife when she shoots her husband. This is also the sudden anger of Oedipus, who kills his father, Laius. For Hemingway, the biological trap—mortality—also generates anger, and the pleasure he derives from killing animals is a manifestation of repressed anger. God or nature has created us mortal and Santiago (a veiled Hemingway) acts out his displeasure by killing fish far out on the Gulf Stream.

And so Santiago kills in order to reassert strength in his own eyes as well as dominance in the eyes of the community. He may be a fisherman, not a king, but, like Oedipus, he perseveres against all odds and succeeds in preserving his essence. Like Oedipus, his rebellion encompasses the Oedipus myth, but with a difference. Oedipus kills Laius, his father, whereas Santiago kills the marlin. Oedipus loves his mother, Jocasta, whereas the mother Santiago loves is the sea, *la mar,* which is what fishermen call her when they love her (*Old Man* 29).

Santiago was born to be a fisherman (*Old Man* 40), as Oedipus was born to be a king. Santiago, the old man, is abandoned by his fellow fishermen, as Oedipus, the infant, was abandoned by his parents. Santiago, a man of inordinate pride, leaves the security of the coastal waters because he must restore his honor. Oedipus leaves the home of his foster parents in search of his identity, but his name, meaning "swollen foot," is symptomatic of his swollen ego, his pride, which results in patricide and incest—his downfall.

Despite multiple ordeals and overwhelming odds, Oedipus battles against his destiny, and Santiago strives to defeat nature and the marlin. In the end, both men are destroyed but not defeated. Hemingway also was destroyed, although not defeated, because his work survives as a lasting literary achievement, and it is this survival that the conclusion to this book addresses.

Conclusion

Suicide, Sisyphus, and the Leopard

No one has explained what the leopard was seeking at that altitude.
—ERNEST HEMINGWAY, "The Snows of Kilimanjaro"

We must imagine Sisyphus happy.
—ALBERT CAMUS, *Le mythe de Sisyphe*

*S*hould a person commit suicide or not? To die or not to die—that is the question Camus asks in *Le mythe de Sisyphe* (1942; *The Myth of Sisyphus*). Not only does his essay relate to Hemingway's life, but it also generates answers that even the leopard of Kilimanjaro might understand.

To begin with, Camus believes that the world is absurd, that we are born by chance, live by encounter, and die by accident. Although we crave happiness on earth and immortality after death, the disproportion between desire and fulfillment defines the parameters of the absurd. An absurd world is a world without necessity, without purpose, and without essence. Whatever meaning it has, we ourselves must provide it. Existentialists believe that, because there is no a priori morality, men's choices and actions fill the void that was left by the disappearance of God. However, says Camus, man's forlornness should not be construed as a source of despair. On the contrary, God's death should be viewed not as tragedy but as a liberation, and it is this newly found freedom that gives men and women the strength to invent themselves. In an absurd world all choices are possible, even suicide.[1]

In Dostoevsky's novel *The Possessed,* Kirilov is obsessed with the idea of freedom and, in due course, he kills himself in order to prove that God does not exist. By philosophizing his suicide, he believes he is liberating himself from the chains of God's commandments. He dies in order to prove his freedom, and Camus views Kirilov's reasoning as an important prelude to the type of reasoning that defines the absurd. Henceforth, says Camus, no one need duplicate Kirilov's suicide.

It is ironic, therefore, that Hemingway, after leading a full life of writing, travel, and adventure should have taken his own life, a gesture that some critics construe as weakness, cowardice, and a mortal sin. The flip side is that killing a person, oneself included, is a choice that requires the strength and courage that only a seasoned professional can muster. Hemingway was a consummate hunter and he liked to kill.[2] That, and his experience as a young man on the Italian front during World War I, had brought him face to face with death. He knew what death was; he had written extensively about it in *Death in the Afternoon*—an extended meditation on death as a ritual performance that is both mythic and artistic. The bullfighter, says Hemingway, is an artist, and his performance is to be admired for its elegance, courage, and precision.[3] It is not a bloodletting, as so many uninformed spectators allege, but a dramatic confrontation of life and death, a reenactment of the most elemental aspect of the human condition, namely, that death regulates life. The corrida, says Hemingway, has a message for all men: fear can be overcome, cowardice is odious, craft is everything, and, when allied with courage, the performance can ennoble life (*Death* 213). Hemingway's suicide, like Montherlant's suicide, has to be viewed in this context.

However, Camus says that it matters little whether we die at twenty or at fifty or, for that matter, at sixty. Why not commit suicide right away and be done with it? And yet, although suicide is theoretically possible because in the context of the absurd there are no sanctions to proscribe it, Camus rejects it. And he does so because the idea of the absurd leads him to postulate three premises: freedom, passion, and rebellion (*Le mythe* 145). In the final analysis suicide is redundant because it destroys all future choices, it negates the individual's emerging passion for life, and it contradicts a person's nascent rebellion. Camus wants to exercise a person's freedom, he realizes that he loves the world passionately, he feels free to create himself, and he is in revolt against all forces that debase human beings. Death in its various disguises dehumanizes, and suicide represents an alliance with the absurd that he is now rebelling against. Instead of concluding that the absurd leads to nihilism, Camus believes that it is an invitation to live. Freedom and passion color life with meaning, hope reappears on the horizon, and purpose is a mountain that invites ascent.

Sisyphus has become Camus' metaphor for twentieth-century man—for all those who persevere despite the knowledge that everybody is mortal. Sisyphus rolls his rock upward knowing that purpose, dignity, and happiness are the rewards of endeavor. He has chosen his cause (the rock) and he is committed to it. Despite all difficulties, he pushes upward toward the summit, aware that when he reaches the top, the rock will roll down into the valley and he will have to begin the ascent all over again (*Le mythe* 193–98). Such is the inevitable labor of human beings and of their successive generations. Some individuals, however, reach higher peaks than others, and the Nobel Prize was Camus' reward for his efforts, as it was Hemingway's. Not all men are equally endowed, although many are also insufficiently rewarded. Still, it is the effort that counts and it is the struggle toward the heights that gives meaning to life in a world without purpose. The absurd is not an obstacle; it is a catalyst. We live in a world in which death is the arbiter of life: we create meaning, we invent ourselves, and we act out the dramas of our existence. For writers, the theater of language, be it comedy or tragedy, determines success or failure.

Although Hemingway does not develop his thinking as systematically as Camus does, his life and career illustrate many of the ideas that Camus explores in *The Myth of Sisyphus*. The leopard epigraph for "The Snows of Kilimanjaro" is Hemingway's metaphor for the writer committed to his craft. Although the epigraph states that no one knows what the leopard was seeking at that altitude, Hemingway's writings suggest that he knows exactly what the metaphoric presence of the leopard signifies. Indeed, there is a connection in Hemingway's mind between hunting and writing. In *Green Hills of Africa* there is a clear link between hunting big game and literary success. The fourth and fifth dimensions to which he alludes represent the summit of writerly achievement because he is as hungry for artistic perfection as the leopard is for prey.[4] It is only the symbolic altitude of Kilimanjaro or its sudden blizzards that can interfere with the sought-after prize. The skill it takes to shoot a kudu or, as in *The Old Man and the Sea*, land the biggest marlin is not unlike the craft of fiction: the bigger the prize, the better you appear to be, and your self-esteem goes up accordingly. In Hemingway's mind the analogy between hunting and writing is evident, and it is not by chance, in *Green Hills of Africa,* that he juxtaposes hunting and achieving a fourth and fifth dimension, a form of writing that is "much more difficult than poetry" (27).

Ultimately, the leopard's death and Hemingway's death are reminiscent of the effort that Sisyphus puts into rolling his rock toward the summit. In order to survive, the writer must write, and the leopard must catch its prey. We know the high premium that Hemingway placed on achievement. His personal and public dignity depended on recognition and success. Like Flaubert, he believes that producing a work of *Art* is like climbing a high mountain. The artist ascends, persevering, even if it means dying in the snow, near the summit, "in the white pain of desire" (Flaubert, *Correspondance* 431–32).[5] Flaubert also compares his writing style, prose particularly, to Sisyphus rolling his stone (447). The irony in "The Snows of Kilimanjaro" is that Harry has gone to pot as a writer. He is nowhere near the summit and he dies on the plain because he did not take the necessary field precautions that would enable him to survive. As Harry lies dying, reminiscing about the highlights of his past, Hemingway transforms Harry's failure into his own success. Harry, like the leopard, may ascend to the House of God in death, but Hemingway gets there in life, and it is this real and, at the same time, metaphorical achievement that allows Hemingway, the knowledgeable African hunter, to triumph as a writer. He knows what he is seeking at the higher elevations and how to get the prize.

Indeed, Hemingway's life and work are a testimonial to his ability, endurance, and tenacity. Jake Barnes perseveres despite his impotence. Frederic Henry survives despite the war. Francis Macomber regains his courage. Robert Jordan remains committed to Maria and the cause for which he is fighting. The old man of the sea demonstrates that, despite his age and bad luck, he is still *el campeón.* We could argue that Hemingway's female protagonists are less fortunate than their male counterparts, but the fact remains that selected personae embody praiseworthy characteristics: courage, nobility, skill, endurance, fidelity, and faith—traits that are manifest against all odds, even when you end up with nothing. In his life and in his work Hemingway had explored and come to terms with the three premises of the absurd (freedom, passion, and rebellion), he had endured as long as he could, and he was "'fraid a nothing" (qtd. by Baker, *Life Story* 12), not even death. Like many of his characters, Hemingway knew what death was and, like them, he had done his share of killing. The old man of the sea's determination to kill the marlin despite "his power and his beauty" (*Old Man* 94) echoes the tone in *Green Hills of Africa,* where Hemingway derives great satisfaction from the shooting of animals. Hemingway's entire oeuvre is an ongoing dialogue with death, and he and his killers usurp the role of God (or nature) because, whenever they kill, they assert the power of man.

This Nietzschean striving for the Übermensch, when coupled with the idea that "man is a rope . . . stretched across an abyss" (Nietzsche 7), manifests a human will that opposes the existential void. Life may be nada, but the will to confront the nothings that dehumanize it is an important trait of Hemingway's protagonists. Hemingway is fascinated by death and his work is one continuous dramatization of it. The corrida in *The Sun Also Rises* and in *Death in the Afternoon* stages death as spectacle, life as tragedy, and the matador—man the artist—as the mediator between the two. Courage, skill, and endurance are the attributes of the bullfighter as well as the artist, and the writer capable of bringing his life's work to term manifests all three. Art, says André Malraux, is a revolt against fate, because after the writer's death, only the voices of art survive—"the voices of silence" that speak through the work (*Les voix* 628).

Although death is an important leitmotif in *Green Hills of Africa,* the landscape is also significant. Hemingway loved Africa and he felt at home there, "and where a man feels at home, outside of where he's born, is where he's meant to go" (284). There was game and plenty of birds, and he liked the natives. "That, and writing, and reading, and seeing pictures was all I cared about doing. . . . That and ski-ing" (285). The fact that Hemingway's heightened sense of well-being depends in part on killing animals underscores the Nietzschean motif of the superman. But killing aside, Hemingway's primal contact with nature is an essential part of the "moveable feast" that regulates his pleasures. The natural world is an important trope for Hemingway and Camus, and both authors use nature as an objective correlative: their landscapes situate characters not only in space but also in time, where beliefs, attitudes, and values are defined.

Fishing, hunting, skiing, and boating occupy Hemingway and his protagonists in significant ways. To participate in these activities is to eschew the city, society, and the mundane in order to engage in pleasures that can only be fulfilled when one is in touch with mountains, hills, valleys, plains, rivers, and seas. Although he was not as consummate a sportsman as Hemingway (Camus was a star soccer player), Camus' work is nonetheless marked by lyrical passages in which the sea, the sun, and the earth can rejuvenate a person because they engender meaningful contact not only with nature but also with the inner self.

Although the environment is an elemental force in the works of both writers, its corollary is death. Hemingway and Camus use the landscape and death contrapuntally in order to emphasize first one and then the other. Their themes oscillate between the pleasure principle and reality. However, the pleasures of nature and the specter of death are often conjoined, and this melding enriches their symbolic language with layers of ambivalence.

There is arguably less ambivalence in Camus' writing than in Hemingway's. Indeed, Camus' categorical rejection of suicide is theoretically at odds with Hemingway's death by suicide. Nonetheless, despite this fundamental difference, certain themes in their oeuvres are so similar as to belie the opposition. The "moveable feast" syndrome, using death as its backdrop, is an element they both share.

Like Hemingway, Camus' Caligula, in the play *Caligula* (1958), blends nature and death into a plot designed to teach all of Rome that life is absurd and that he, Caligula, with his deadly imperial freedom, has usurped the power of the gods. I am not implying that Hemingway wanted to teach the animals or his readers lessons in the absurd. I am saying that during a certain period in his life he took pleasure in killing and that killing enhanced his sense of worth and well-being because he too was usurping the power of God (*Death* 233). The killing of animals in the bullring or in the wild appealed to Hemingway in ways that he sometimes trivializes, for example, as in the joke of killing birds and hyenas (*Green Hills* 36–37), or that, at other times, he prefers not to verbalize: "Killing is not a feeling that you share" (*Green Hills* 120). Nonetheless, both Hemingway and Camus believe that an awareness of death heightens their feeling for life.

Near the end of *Caligula*, the Roman emperor and his patricians play a game of "exquisite corpse." It is a group poem whose theme, assigned by Caligula, is death. A number of inept lines are interrupted by Caligula's insults until it is Scipio's turn to recite his lines: "A quest for happiness that purifies, / A sky where the sun is streaming, / Unusual and savage celebrations, my delirium / devoid of hope!" (100). Caligula's response is that Scipio is too young to understand the true lessons of death. But what are these true lessons if not the passion for life that flows from the absurd? Once we accept the inevitability of death and understand that we are free to invent ourselves, we are also authorized to partake of life's pleasures. Once these lessons have been internalized, we can experience pleasure whenever and wherever we are in touch with simple, physical, and elemental realities. The narrator of Camus' essay "Noces" (1950; "Nuptials") derives as much joy from swimming in the sea as Hemingway's narrators do from fishing and skiing (55–60). Mara, one of the characters in Camus' play *Le malentendu* (1947; *The Misunderstanding*), will rob and kill in order to buy happiness on the sunlit shores of the Mediterranean, where she imagines it can be found. Death's urgent lesson for Camus is that as long as man is alive he should enjoy his honeymoon on earth. Although *La peste* (1947; *The Plague*) demonstrates that there are other demands on man's allegiance, such as commitment to a cause and to others, the text also makes clear that the idea of commitment loses its purpose unless there is something worth fighting for. At the height of the plague, Dr. Rieux goes for a swim in the Mediterranean and it is this contact with the sea that revives him and makes it possible for him to continue the struggle against the disease (1427). The plague is a detour, sometimes a permanent one, in man's quest for happiness, but men who are committed must persevere and endure in this never-ending confrontation.

Hemingway's commitment to his writing was total, but his involvement in sociopolitical causes, compared to Camus', was minor.[6] Indeed, Hemingway's service on the Italian front during World War I seems to have contributed to a certain distancing. Hemingway survived his wounds on the Italian front, but instead of nudging him toward social commitment, the way Camus' early brush with tuberculosis had, Hemingway's experience with death reinforced his commitment to himself and to writing (*Green Hills* 148). Whereas, in my judgment, Hemingway is the better fiction writer, Camus is a much more interesting thinker. The point in all this is that the confrontation with death leads Hemingway to commit himself to writing, and for Camus, to commit himself to writing and to the sociopolitical arena.

Camus' death (in an automobile accident) is as absurd as Hemingway's; that is, both events underscore the absence of providential purpose, at least one we can discern. Camus, the nonbeliever, died at the height of his creative powers, whereas Hemingway, a professed Catholic, died in a state of so-called mortal sin. How are we to resolve his alleged Catholicism and suicide as a deliberate choice that contravenes the teachings of the church? Sartre maintains that choices define a person's essence. If Hemingway's suicide represents a deliberate choice, then that act contradicts earlier professions of faith. It is the final chapter and there is no turning back. In Sartre's play *Huis Clos* (*No Exit*), Garcin "suffers" because desertion, his final act before he dies, marks him as a coward. Estelle also suffers because she cannot undo her infanticide, and this act defines her essence as a murderess. This hell on earth, this death in life, is the punishment for their bad faith (111–68).

Hemingway's suicide is an indelible act, and in retrospect it defines his entire life. His death is not an aberration, nor is it an act of bad faith. On the contrary, it is consistent with a lifestyle that he chose to exercise up to the very end. Successive choices create an essence, and this essence, when lived authentically, is sufficient for any man. Hemingway chose to become a writer, he exercised his craft with consummate skill, he lived his life passionately, and when his body and mind could no longer live up to his expectations, he pulled the trigger. To commit suicide is to take matters of life and death into your own hands. If physical and intellectual debility destroy everything that makes life worth living, who is to say that the fateful shot early Sunday morning, July 2, 1961, was not an assertion of courage, mastery, and control? Surely Hemingway preferred death to the indignities and infirmities of old age, and it is this shot that still resonates with M'Cola's laugh—M'Cola, the gun bearer in *Green Hills of Africa*—whenever Hemingway killed birds and hyenas. Whenever he killed, the joke was on the animal; whenever he missed, the joke was on Hemingway (36–37). But the tragedy of Hemingway's death, whichever way we look at it (he is now the animal, and he does not miss), is that the joke, ultimately, is on him because M'Cola's laughter invites speculations about Hemingway's ego, selfishness, callousness, and insensitivity. However, I leave this reverse scenario for others to explore. More interesting, I think, is the drama of life and death that Hemingway pursued against a backdrop of natural settings, a drama that allowed him to explore the full range of his physical prowess and writerly genius.

Before he died, Hemingway, like Montherlant, was neither physically nor intellectually capable of doing what he had always done so well. Old age and his various accidents had caught up with him. His passion for life, his freedom to choose, and his revolt against death, attributes that had shaped his life and his work as long as his energies were intact, all were weighing him down. At the end, life had stopped being "a moveable feast." Metaphorically speaking, a new ascent toward another summit was beyond him. Writing well, shooting big game, and killing large fish were no longer possible. This is perhaps a form of pride, but Hemingway had always been proud of his achievements. However, as with the leopard of Kilimanjaro, prey was now beyond his grasp. Baker phrases it aptly when he says that for years Hemingway's maxim had been: "'il faut (d'abord) durer.' Now it had been succeeded by another: 'il faut (après tout) mourir'" (*Life Story* 714).[7]

If death is the sovereign remedy for the misfortunes of life and you are obsessed, as Hemingway was, with pride, honor, and dignity and, on top of that, if you are an artist who, like the bullfighter, can no longer perform, then killing, even if it is the self, must have singular appeal. To lose your memory, one of the most important elements in writing, would be unbearable. It is not difficult to imagine Hemingway the artist administering death in the arena of life, in order to dramatize his life and death. Using the corrida as metaphor, it is possible to envisage Hemingway playing the dual role of matador and bull simultaneously, a consummate artist and sacrificial animal. Celestino's death in the afternoon, in Montherlant's novel *Le chaos et la nuit* (*Chaos and Night*), echoes the title of the Spanish translation, *La muerte en la tarde*.

In his art, Hemingway achieved the fourth and fifth dimensions to which he aspired. However, the debility of old age and his inability to continue writing (he had undergone shock treatments at the Mayo Clinic) had curtailed his freedom and virtually eliminated his passion. All he had left was rebellion, the third element in Camus' triad. Hemingway had constructed his life vigorously, but at the end, his body and his mind were spent. No further achievement seemed possible and there were no summits on the horizon, except perhaps the House of God, toward which, like the dying protagonist in "The Snows of Kilimanjaro," he could aspire. This melding of art and life, of triumph and defeat, of a winner at the end of the line, is the sublime, although tragic, image of Hemingway in his final hour.

His famous Gulf Stream passage in *Green Hills of Africa,* whatever else it is, can be read as a paradigm of the absurd and of Sisyphus's eternal and renewable defeat: "and the palm fronds of our victories, the worn light bulbs of our discoveries and the empty condoms of our great loves float with no significance against one single, lasting thing—the stream" (150). Despite the absurd, Hemingway's achievement—the craft of his writing—proves that there is a difference between dying at the age of twenty and dying at the age of sixty-one. Both his life and Camus' life demonstrate that Sisyphus's endeavors can fill the void with meaning and purpose.

In conclusion, Hemingway, like Flaubert, uses proleptic images, repetition, and the ongoing present (Flaubert used the ongoing past). As in Proust's writing, memory compresses time, both accelerating events and slowing them down. This elasticity expands and contracts the ontology of narration and the experience of reading. The immediacy and beguiling simplicity of Gide's style has its counterpart in Hemingway's. It communicates deep pride in man and what man can accomplish. Hemingway's iceberg theory of writing, with its massive, unstated, and invisible narrative component, melds with Lacan's theories, in which the unconscious is structured like a language. Deliberate stylistic repetitions echo unconscious metaphorical discoveries. Hemingway's enthusiasm for Spain and the corrida is matched only by Montherlant's, and both men wrote vivid accounts of tauromachia. Malraux's ability to be present at and write about war, conflict, and insurrection parallels Hemingway's knack for inserting himself into and being part of important historical events. Hemingway's existential obsession with death imbues his fiction with the ontology that Sartre's writings transform into epistemology. Death is the warp against which Malraux, Sartre, Camus, and Hemingway weave the woof of life. Camus wrote about suicide, and Hemingway, like Montherlant, shot himself, yet all these men, from Flaubert on, like Sisyphus, led reasonably happy lives reaching for the summit. Each one of these authors is a wordsmith of extraordinary vitality, and their craft and writings have enriched literature in immeasurable ways.

Flaubert, Proust, Gide, Lacan, Montherlant, Malraux, Sartre, Camus, and Hemingway have all made original contributions to the republic of letters. Their importance is measured by publications, translations, and the critical attention their work generates not only in relation to themselves, but in relation to the work of other writers. That is why comparisons are useful. They highlight differences and similarities, and our understanding of each author is enhanced when we pass him or her through the prism of comparative scrutiny. The colors and nuances of each are highlighted as they shift, blend, and refract according to the angle of vision and the quality of light brought to bear on the subject.

In this context, the historical and geographical records are important; that is, who came first and from where, and in what language(s) did he or she write? The historical primacy accorded French and English is an advantage for those already writing in these languages, although the impact of writers such as Mario Vargas Llosa and Gabriel García Márquez from Latin America and Carlos Fuentes and Octávio Paz from Mexico, among many others, all of them writing in Spanish, is changing the literary landscape. The Russian writers of the nineteenth century—Tolstoy, Dostoevsky, and Chekhov, among others—left their mark, as did German, Czech, and Austrian writers of the nineteenth and twentieth centuries: Goethe, Kafka, and Thomas Bernhard, again, among many others. In Asia, India has its laureates, but Japan is a relative newcomer to the republic of letters, China is trying to break in, and South Korea's recent putsch to take control of the ICLA (International Comparative Literature Association) is indicative that centrality in literary space and access to it are critical factors for nations striving to achieve literary recognition.

The number of Nobel laureates from each nation is part of that recognition. Although the Nobel Prize Committee has striven for diversity by recognizing writers from the periphery, such as Iceland's Halldor K. Laxness (1955) and Egypt's Naguib Mahfouz (1988), the concentration of awards given to authors writing in English, French, Spanish, and German is striking.

Clearly Hemingway belongs to an elite group of artists. But before gaining access to the center, he, too, came from the periphery and he underwent the necessary apprenticeship, both physically and mentally. Paris is where he discovered the classics, Paris is where he learned how to write, and Paris is the city that made him famous. Without Paris and the French, Hemingway would not be the renowned writer that he is today.

Finally, France's discovery of Hemingway in the 1930s was the result of his discovery of France in the 1920s. Both discoveries would have a profound and lasting impact on the world republic of letters.

Notes

INTRODUCTION

1. Hily-Mane lists all the books published in France by and about Hemingway, including translations, articles, essays, and book reviews—an invaluable source of information; see also Roger Asselineau, "Hemingway's Reputation."

2. "American fiction," says Richard Lehan, "was new and different to the French. It was distinct from any narrative genre France had yet known" (37).

3. See Stein's epigraph to *The Sun Also Rises:* "You are all a lost generation."

4. "Meetings of first-rate minds are as rare as renderings by first-rate translators, and such shocks of recognition deserve to be studied for their own sake. The shift in atmospheric conditions, when moving between the hemispheres either way, produces a refraction which must be allowed for and reckoned with by comparative literature" (Levin 219).

5. Sainte-Beuve wanted to be a novelist but he discovered his superior talents as a literary critic while writing *Volupté,* an introspective account of his affair with Madame Victor Hugo. Sainte-Beuve also had an affair with Louise Colet, the poet, salon hostess, and Flaubert's estranged mistress and literary confidante. Sainte-Beuve was acquainted (through translations) with the works of Cooper, Longfellow, Bryant, Harriet Beecher Stowe, Melville, and Emerson. He had also read the literary essays of Washington Irving and Poe's stories in Baudelaire's translations and, in due course, became France's preeminent literary critic of the nineteenth century (M. Baym 131).

6. In 1918, Duhamel received the prestigious Prix Goncourt for *Civilization,* a book in which he describes the tragedy and human suffering he observed in hospitals during World War I.

7. In his finest novel, *Le chant du monde* (1934), Giono exalts men's and women's intuitive links with nature, cosmic forces, and cyclical patterns. He advocated a pastoral utopia while also condemning modern civilization, the machine age, and war.

8. See Dwight Eddins, "Of Rocks and Marlin." See also Robert O. Stephens, "Hemingway and Stendhal"; Carolina Donadio Lawson, "Hemingway, Stendhal, and War"; Paul W. Miller, "Hemingway vs. Stendhal"; Dana Dragunoiu, "Hemingway's Debt" 868–69; and Jack Jobst and W. J. Williamson, "Hemingway and Maupassant."

1. HEMINGWAY AND FRENCH LITERATURE

1. "Until I read the *Chartreuse de Parme* by Stendhal I had never read of war as it was except in Tolstoi, and the wonderful Waterloo account by Stendhal was an accidental piece in a book that had much dullness" (Hemingway, *A Moveable Feast* 132). See Robert O. Stephens as well as Paul W. Miller.

2. Stein says that she and Anderson formed Hemingway, even though Hemingway repudiated Anderson's influence and minimized hers. In a pejorative aside, Stein says that she and Anderson had a weakness for Hemingway because he was such a good pupil: "he takes training and anybody who takes training is a favorite pupil" (*Autobiography* 216).

3. From Pound, Hemingway borrowed his "maximal compression" of language, his imagery, and his rhythm, and from Stein, her requirement that language submit to a basic restructuring in its overlapping compounds and participles. Both mentors taught Hemingway, as Milton A. Cohen notes, how "to convey the freshness and intensity of physical experience within the tension and tautness of constructed form" (20–21). Hemingway says that Pound was the most generous writer he had ever known because he helped poets, painters, sculptors, and prose writers whom he believed in (*A Moveable Feast* 110). "Pound didn't so much champion his peers as take them by the scruff of the neck and shake them till they did their best" (James R2).

4. For Cézanne's influence on Hemingway, see Ron Berman. See also Theodore L. Gaillard Jr., "Hemingway's Debt"; Emily Stipes Watts, *Ernest Hemingway* 29–50; and Erik Nakjavani, "Aesthetics."

5. In 1924, Adrienne Monnier's new magazine, *Commerce,* published *Ulysses* in French translation, and Hemingway subscribed to his copy of the first issue (Reynolds, *The Paris Years* 232).

6. Bradbury calls it a temple of love, but the inscription over the portico on the four-columned Greek-style monument in the garden is dedicated to friendship—A L'AMITIÉ. See photo in Gajdusek 85.

7. In Romains, *Manuel* 53. Romains did not capitalize the word "god" because he uses it in a secular sense to refer to a group of people. For him the smallest unit would be a couple. Larger units could be a line of commuters waiting for the bus, the spectators in an auditorium before or during a performance, or the residents of a city. Either Monnier or the printer erred when inserting the capital letter G.

8. "Le cimetière marin" was first published in 1920 in *La Nouvelle Revue Française.* Jacques Rivière, a friend of Gide's, was the new editor.

9. Gide records the stages of Michel's recovery in his novel *L'immoraliste,* and Hemingway records the near-death experience of Frederic Henry and his recovery in *A Farewell to Arms.*

10. In 1922, Gide translated *The Marriage of Heaven and Hell* into French as *Le mariage du ciel et de l'enfer.*

11. See Emily Stipes Watts, who says "that Hemingway probably borrowed at least four methods from Cézanne for landscape descriptions: the use of a series of planes often cut across by a diagonal line, the careful delineation of even the most distant mountains and ridges, the emphasis upon volumes of space with the use of simple geometrical forms as the basis of definition, and the occasional use of color modulation" (40).

12. In *A Farewell to Arms,* Frederic Henry refers to Barbusse's *Le feu* (261), and this means that Hemingway had probably read the novel.

13. For a satisfying overview of Dada and surrealism in relation to Hemingway, see Watts 3–28.

14. See also Milton A. Cohen, who says that "the perspective of the chapters—pointillistic glimpses of four realms 'in our time': war, crime, politics, and the bullfight—sharply contrasts with the 'quiet,' close-up narratives of individuals in the stories" (x).

15. See H. R. Stoneback, who argues that Montherlant "may well be one of Hemingway's best-concealed and most important sources and influences" ("Hemingway and the Camargue" 189).

2. *MADAME BOVARY* AND POETRY

1. See Brombert (*The Novels* 80), who quotes from Valéry's essay on Flaubert, "La tentation de (saint) Flaubert": "Realism curiously led to giving the impression of the most contrived artifice" (*Variété* 5:614).

3. JACQUES LACAN READS *THE SUN ALSO RISES*

1. There are over three hundred essays, articles, and book chapters devoted to Hemingway's first novel, *The Sun Also Rises.* Two books, Frederic Joseph Svoboda's *Hemingway and* The Sun Also Rises: *The Crafting of a Style* (1983) and Michael S. Reynolds's The Sun Also Rises: *A Novel of the Twenties* (1988), chronicle the novel's genesis and historical context, respectively. H. R. Stoneback's *Reading Hemingway's* The Sun Also Rises: *Glossary and Commentary* (2007) provides a close reading of the novel and, most important, exposes the seven-eighths of the iceberg below the surface. Not surprisingly there is a lack of unanimity among commentators concerning the novel's central character or what that centrality means. Opinions on the central character range from Jake Barnes, the narrator; to Robert Cohn, the romantic anti-hero; to Pedro Romero, the code hero;

to Bill Gorton as code hero; to Brett Ashley as love goddess. There are essays on Count Mippipopolous, Mike Campbell, Wilson-Harris, money, values, manners, humor, France, Spain, bullfighting, irony and pity, tragedy, comedy, terror, art, travel, religion, the beginning, the ending, and Pamplona, to name the more frequent ones. Perhaps adumbrating this lack of unanimity, Hemingway himself viewed the earth as the novel's abiding hero.

2. In a letter dated December 9, 1951, Hemingway explained to a Rinehart editor that the genesis of *The Sun Also Rises* was a wound he had received that resulted in a subsequent infection due to pieces of wool cloth that had been driven into the scrotum. Hemingway wondered what life would be like if he had lost his penis but his testicles and spermatic cord remained intact, particularly if he were in love with a woman who was also in love with him. Hemingway insisted that his own wound healed rapidly and that he was not Jake Barnes (*Selected Letters* 745).

3. In *Metafiction: The Theory and Practice of Self-Conscious Fiction*, Patricia Waugh defines metafiction as "a term given to fictional writing which self-consciously and systematically draws attention to its status as an artefact in order to pose questions about the relationship between fiction and reality. In providing a critique of their own methods of construction, such writings not only examine the fundamental structures of narrative fiction, they also explore the possible fictionality of the world outside the literary fictional text" (2).

4. For many commentators Jake is an active hero, whereas for others he is a passive recorder of events, chronicling the decadent lives of "the lost generation" that contrast with Spanish *afición*. For some Jake is a trustworthy narrator, whereas for others he is untrustworthy. For some he is an existential hero, whereas for others he is a Catholic believer on a pilgrim's mission. For some the novel's conclusion is a dead end, whereas for others it is upbeat. For some Brett is a nymphomaniac, whereas for others she is merely promiscuous. For some she is spoiled and self-centered, whereas for others she is a caring, liberated woman. Some believe that Jake dominates Brett, whereas others see him as submissive to her whims. Some believe that the novel is circular and that Jake and Brett's relationship goes nowhere, whereas others argue that Jake changes after his disgrace in Pamplona and his "cleansing" experience in San Sebastian. Some argue that Jake's love for Brett is as romantic as Robert Cohn's, whereas others believe that Jake, the narrator of the novel, has the grace and control of Pedro Romero, the bullfighter. Some view Jake's infirmity in tragic terms; others stress the dialogues of "irony and pity" as manifestations of comedy. Some believe that Cohn deserves the ostracism he receives, whereas others see it as a reflection of anti-Semitism. Some view Hemingway's celebrated dialogues as an expression of artistic realism, others as the quintessence of stylistic compression and omission.

4. *DEATH IN THE AFTERNOON* AND *THE DANGEROUS SUMMER*

1. Pedro Romero is the fictional name of the real bullfighter Cayetano, and a faena is the work done by the matador with the muleta. The muleta is the heart-shaped scarlet cloth that is used to defend the man and tire the bull as the matador performs a series of passes.

2. *Toreo* means the art of fighting bulls, and the corrida almost always ends with the death of the animal and sometimes of the matador. The event is a quintessentially Spanish performance and Hemingway describes it as tragedy, and not sport (*Death* 16), because death unites man and bull "in the emotional, aesthetic and artistic climax of the fight" (*Death* 247). See Allen Josephs for an insightful account of the role and meaning of bullfighting in Spanish culture and in Hemingway's thinking and art. Josephs notes that *toreo* in Spain is frequently described "as the tragedy of the death of the bull" (229).

3. Mithras is a god mentioned in Sanskrit and old Persian documents. The cult of the bull was the foundation of Mithraism and that legacy has been passed down through the ages and transmuted into the tragedy and spectacle of bullfighting in Spain. Mithraism and Christianity developed simultaneously and they share common symbols: blood, wine, and the sun. In Catholicism, the eucharistic wine represents the blood of Christ. The host recalls the solar circle. In Spain, all three symbols converge around the bull, which bled, was sacrificed, and was worshiped as a god for millennia.

4. In 1959—the year of the "dangerous summer"—Hemingway followed the rivalry between two great matadors, Luis Miguel Dominguín and Antonio Ordóñez, from one corner of Spain to the other. What made the rivalry so personal was that Carmen, Antonio's wife, was also Luis Miguel's sister. Month after month, from May to September, Hemingway describes the competition between the two men and the eventual triumph, at least in Hemingway's mind, of Ordóñez. Their dueling is intense, and while it lasts, both matadors are gored several times.

5. For historical information and references on Mithraism I am indebted to Francesca Rochberg, professor of history at the University of California, Berkeley.

5. SARTRE, NADA, AND THE "AFRICAN STORIES"

1. In "The Prose of Life: Lived Experience in the Fiction of Hemingway, Sartre and Beauvoir," Erik Nakjavani reminds us that Sartre and Hemingway had met at the Ritz in 1944, and again at the Finca Vigía in 1949; that Hemingway had praised Sartre's collection of short stories, entitled *Le mur* (1939), as excellent and first rate; and that Hemingway would read any book Sartre sent him (142). Nakjavani maintains that the concept of lived experience fulfills the requirements of compression and omission in Hemingway's fiction as well as the requirements

of existentialism in Sartre's writing. Lived experience, according to Sartre, is "the idea of an ensemble, a whole, whose surface is completely conscious and the rest of which is opaque to this consciousness, and without belonging to the unconscious, is hidden from you" (qtd. by Nakjavani 155). "What Sartre and Beauvoir philosophically understood about lived experience had not only been perceived and practiced by Hemingway and bodied forth in his fiction, as it is now evident, it had been in reality formulated by him" (148).

2. In *Hemingway: The Writer as Artist,* Carlos Baker notes that "Macomber dies at the very moment he is commencing to live" (187).

3. Edmund Wilson praised "The Short Happy Life of Francis Macomber" as "a terrific fable of the impossible civilized woman who despises the civilized man for his failure in initiative and nerve and then jealously tries to break him down as soon as he begins to exhibit any" (qtd. by N. Baym 114). Seventeen years after the story was published, Hemingway, in a 1953 interview, stated that "Francis' wife hates him because he's a coward. . . . But when he gets his guts back, she fears him so much she has to kill him—shoots him in the head" (qtd. by N. Baym 114).

4. For Sartre, bad faith is a lie to oneself through which one seeks to escape the responsible freedom of being-for-itself, which is a desire for Being. Bad faith depends on a vacillation between transcendence (the process whereby the for-itself goes beyond the given in a further project of itself) and facticity (the for-itself's necessary connection with the in-itself) and the failure to recognize either one for what it really is. Being-in-itself is non-conscious Being (*Being and Nothingness* 628–29, 634).

5. Macomber has been a playboy and therefore, by Sartre's Marxist standards, a nobody, because he has done nothing to ameliorate the human condition. According to Sartre's hierarchy of values, men and women must work actively to abolish class differences; that is, they must commit themselves to the class struggle. See *Qu'est-ce que la littérature?* where Sartre says that "the historical situation drives us to join the proletariat in order to construct a classless society" (*What Is Literature?* 271; "la situation historique nous incite à nous joindre au prolétariat pour construire une société sans classes," *Qu'est-ce que* 298).

6. In *Being and Nothingness* Sartre speaks of the nothingness that lies coiled like a worm at the heart of all true existence (21).

7. "The Short Happy Life of Francis Macomber" was Hemingway's choice for *This Is My Best,* edited by Whit Burnett (letter from Hemingway to Burnett dated May 12, 1942).

8. For an intelligent and nuanced analysis of Margot Macomber, see Warren Beck.

9. Granville Hicks writes that "it would be difficult to find an author who has written of death as often and as consistently as has Hemingway. At one time or another he has described the death of ants, salamanders, grasshoppers and fish; how hyenas die, how to kill *kudu,* the proper way to execute horses, how bulls are slain, how soldiers die, death in Italy, in Cuba, in Africa and in Spain, death in childbirth and death by suicide, death alone and death in a group; selfish death, sacrificing death, and graceful death" (524). *La mort dans l'âme,* the title

of Sartre's third volume in the *Les Chemins de la liberté* series, is itself symptomatic of Sartre's own preoccupation with death, actual and symbolic.

10. It's difficult to agree with the authors who believe that Kilimanjaro is a symbol of death. See Marion Montgomery, who says that we are "not sufficiently prepared for the . . . sudden symbolic use of the mountain" (149). Clearly, the mountain signifies different things to different readers. I believe, in the context of the epigraph, that the mountain symbolizes the possibility of achievement. When mountaineers are asked why they climb a mountain, they invariably answer, "Because it's there," and they climb in order to reach the summit. So too with writers. Hemingway has often said that he writes because he wants to be the best. Nor is the symbolism of the mountain in "Snows" tacked on. The presence of the epigraph, like Kilimanjaro, looms over the story and the African plain where Harry dies.

11. In a context of self-deceit and bad faith, says Ibañez, the hyena symbolizes self-destruction ("Ethics of Writing" 105). See also Breuer, who says that Hemingway portrays death alternately as a whore, a bitch, and a hyena (245). Nakjavani notes that Hemingway referred to fame as a diseased whore, death's little sister, and that Hemingway wished that he, like Sartre, had refused the Nobel Prize in literature because now he was contaminated ("The Prose of Life" 142).

12. In a letter to William Faulkner from the Finca Vigía on July 23, 1947, Hemingway wrote that when writing, the best strategy was to write against dead writers, starting with Turgenev, then Maupassant, then Stendhal, and finally Dostoevsky (*Selected Letters* 624).

13. In the letter to Faulkner, Hemingway wrote that Flaubert was their most respected and honored master (*Selected Letters* 624). *Madame Bovary, L'éducation sentimentale,* and *Trois contes* ("Un cœur simple" is one of the stories) are listed in Michael Reynolds, *Hemingway's Reading* 124–25.

14. In "Vivienne de Watteville," Lewis says that "The title hangs over the entire story, just as Kilimanjaro dominates the real African landscape" (103).

15. Letter of September 16, 1853.

16. Gordimer says that "The 'Snows of Kilimanjaro' is one of the greatest short stories ever written. . . . It is the creative apogee of the painful, fearful exploration of the meaning of death" (94).

17. In a letter to John M. Howell, Richard Reusch writes: "When I went up in September, 1926, for the first time, I found the leopard curled up and dead on the ice a few feet below the Leopard Point. On the glacier nearby I found a frozen mountain goat. Apparently the leopard followed the goat, trying to catch it. A snow storm developed, accompanied by a heavy fog. According to the habit of the leopards, he curled up to keep himself warm and to wait for the fog to disappear. The goat pursued by him, went to the Ratzel glacier and froze there, some 300 feet away from the leopard" (99). Richard Reusch published an article in 1928 entitled "Mt. Kilimanjaro and Its Ascent." It was reprinted in *Tanganyika Notes and Records* 64 (1965).

18. In *Qu'est-ce que la littérature?* Sartre says that the world and the people who inhabit it are known by their acts. All human endeavor can be reduced to one single enterprise: to make *history* (265).

6. CAMUS AND SARTRE

1. For a comprehensive study of the ideological and personal clash between the two former friends, see Germaine Brée, *Camus and Sartre: Crisis and Commitment.*

2. Brée states that "in 1970 passers-by might encounter Sartre and Simone de Beauvoir on street corners distributing the barred Maoist-student paper, *La Cause du peuple—J'accuse;* and skeptical Parisians derived passing and rather affectionate diversion from the image of a short, tubby, elderly man of considerable renown with a ravaged face, hoisted on a barrel, surrounded by a group of student 'enragés'—extreme Maoist revolutionaries—at the exit of the large automobile works in the suburbs of Paris, exhorting the generally indifferent passing workmen to join the students who punctuated his appeal with the cry of 'Revolution!'" (see *Camus and Sartre* 2).

3. See the *Hemingway Review* 7 (1988), which has reprinted thirty of Hemingway's war dispatches to NANA.

4. Hemingway's text, with an introduction by William Braasch Watson, is reprinted in the *Hemingway Review* 7 (1988): 114–18. Hemingway likes the image of the intestine. In *Green Hills of Africa* he describes the classic hyena, which, when shot while running, would circle, snapping and biting at itself, pulling out the intestines and eating them with relish (37–38).

5. "The history of all hitherto existing society is the history of class struggles: freeman and slave, patrician and plebeian, lord and serf, guild-master and journeyman—in a word, oppressor and oppressed—stood in constant opposition to one another, carried on an uninterrupted, now hidden, now open fight, a fight that each time ended, either in a revolutionary reconstitution of society at large or in the common ruin of the contending classes" (Marx and Engels 81).

6. In the 1950s, Sartre allied himself with the Marxist-Leninist worldview and its revolutionary doctrine because he believed that dialectical materialism would move mankind toward freedom and the classless society.

7. MALRAUX, SPAIN, *L'ESPOIR*, AND *FOR WHOM THE BELL TOLLS*

1. See Martine de Courcel, who says that by late 1936, the Spanish civil war had ceased to be an affair for amateurs. The Russian air force had taken over the Republican command and General Smuskievich imposed upon Malraux and his team the heavy hand of Soviet bureaucracy (43). See also William Braasch Watson, who says that the Loyalist cause was defeated on March 31, 1939, one month after Hemingway began writing *For Whom the Bell Tolls* ("Hemingway's Attacks" 115).

2. See an address given by Malraux at the International Association of Writers for the Defense of Culture in London, June 1936. "I have always been impressed by the inability of the fascist arts to represent anything except the clash of man

against man. . . . Fascist civilization tends, in its last stage, to the total militarization of the nation. And fascist art, where it exists, tends to the estheticization of war. Now the enemy of the soldier is another soldier, is a man. Whereas, from liberalism all the way to communism, man's adversary is not man, but the earth. It is in the conflict with the earth, in the exaltation of man's victory over *things*, that there has developed one of the West's strongest traditions, from *Robinson Crusoe* to the Soviet film" ("Three Speeches" 36).

3. See Victor Brombert, "Malraux." See also "André Malraux" in Henri Peyre, *French Novelists of Today* 210–43.

4. See also *Malraux par lui-même*, as quoted by Picon: "In my eyes, the modern novel is a privileged means for expressing what is tragic in man, and not an elucidation of the individual" (66).

5. Malraux's novels contain few women. The military conflicts and political struggles that his works describe are peopled almost exclusively by men. *Man's Fate*, the English title of his most famous novel, and the men in it, as in *Man's Hope* (the English title of *L'espoir*), struggle against oppression and death, and they confront their destiny together, but they do so without women. Also, it is important to remember that in the context of the 1930s, and in accordance with Webster's first definition, the word "man" denotes a human being, whether male or female.

6. Because Malraux's endeavor is to lay bare the meaning of metaphysical destiny, "his achievement as a novelist need not conform to the literary and humanist norms of the well-ordered narrative, although he expresses his intentions via a story and an adventure quite concretely situated in a particular historical reality. Even as he 'relates' a moment in the life of one of his characters, Malraux does not *feel* it as a 'humanist' novelist would, for the action presented is not viewed in its restricted human context, but is made to vibrate with the meaning it possesses when confronting eternity" (Albérès 47).

7. See Bickford Sylvester: "While both writers were fascinated by romantic mysticism and by epiphanies climaxing violent action, Malraux found an outlet for his romantic zeal in political communion with others (as *Days of Wrath/Le temps du mépris*, especially, attests). Conversely, the American romantic individualist, Hemingway, rejected not only collectivism, but for the most part politics in any form. Malraux believed that man—social man—and especially the artist, could inspire other men and women to improve their lot. Despite Malraux's pragmatism, and even skepticism, he was a reformer; he believed that the inspiring artist could move mankind to at least marginal collective progress" (32–33).

8. In 1954, Gallimard reported that 130,000 copies of *L'espoir* had been sold since its publication in 1937, compared with 200,000 copies of the French translation of *For Whom the Bell Tolls*. The French critics believed that in this novel Hemingway had achieved the highest expression of his maturity as an artist. See Thelma M. Smith and Ward L. Miner 109. Despite the favorable reaction of the French press, Camus asserted that *For Whom the Bell Tolls* was the book of a child compared with *L'espoir* (49).

8. THE STONES OF VENICE, TIME, AND REMEMBRANCE

1. In "Hemingway as Artist in *Across the River and into the Trees:* A Revaluation," W. Craig Turner says that Hemingway incorporated more allusions into this work than into any of his other books (187). See also Donald R. Noble, *Hemingway: A Revaluation;* Peter Lisca, "The Structure"; Charles M. Oliver, "Hemingway's Study"; George Monteiro, "Hemingway's Colonel"; and James H. Meredith, "The Rapido River."

9. PRIDE

1. Originally published in *Les Temps Modernes* 6 (1951): 1537–41.

2. In a letter to Bernard Berenson sent from the Finca Vigía, Cuba, January 24, 1953, Hemingway wrote that *Si le grain ne meurt* was a good book, as were some of the others. "But I always felt about him the way some stupid people felt about cats. He made me feel the same way Alice Toklas did" (*Selected Letters* 802).

3. In his *Journal* Gide notes that *A Farewell to Arms* was a remarkable book (222).

4. For a discussion of Gide's dialogue with his Catholic opponents, see Stoltzfus, *Gide's Eagles* 73–125.

5. Roger Asselineau, in *Ernest Hemingway,* notes that Santiago's struggle with the marlin and the sharks reminds us of Greek tragedy in which the protagonist is defeated by forces that transcend him, and that the gods are punishing him for his pride (50). On one hand, this punishment, as it is with Oedipus, may be a physical defeat, but on the other, it is a metaphysical triumph that demonstrates the dignity of man asserting his power against overwhelming odds.

6. For a comprehensive discussion of the pagan and Christian themes in *The Old Man and the Sea,* see Ben Stoltzfus, *Gide and Hemingway: Rebels against God.*

7. In addition to the classical tradition of ancient Greece, which Gide used to structure such works as *Le Prométhée mal enchaîné* (*Prometheus Misbound*), *Oedipe,* and *Thésée* (*Theseus*), he also borrowed from the Judeo-Christian tradition. Many works, such as *Saül, Le retour de l'enfant prodigue* (*The Return of the Prodigal Son*), and *La porte étroite* (*Strait Is the Gate*), reveal an intimate knowledge of the Old and New Testaments, at least as intimate as Hemingway's, if not more so.

CONCLUSION

1. Although Camus always denied that he was an existentialist, both he and Sartre believed that the world was absurd, and an absurd world is one without a priori purpose. The fundamental difference in thinking between the two men was that Sartre believed that because God is dead everything is allowed, whereas Camus believed that although all things are theoretically possible, not all actions are acceptable. See *L'homme révolté* 413–32.

2. See *Green Hills of Africa,* in which Hemingway exalts the hunt and the pleasures of killing cleanly (272); see also *Death in the Afternoon,* where, says Hemingway, killing cleanly has been one of the great enjoyments of a part of the human race (232).

3. "Bullfighting is the only art in which the artist is in danger of death" (*Death* 91).

4. In *S/Z* Roland Barthes opposes the two terms "readerly" and "writerly" in order to call attention to the difference between denotation and connotation (4–5). The fourth and fifth dimensions to which Hemingway alludes are activated by the resonance and ambiguity of words and meanings whose connotations transcend denotation, that is, the one-on-one relationship of the signifier to the signified. See also Barthes, *Roland Barthes* 67.

5. Flaubert capitalizes the *A* of "Art" in order to give the word a heightened religious connotation.

6. Neither Robert Jordan's commitment to the Republican cause in *For Whom the Bell Tolls* nor Philip Rawlings's similar commitment in *The Fifth Column* compare in scope with *L'homme révolté,* Camus' extended meditation on the historical, metaphysical, and sociopolitical implications of the absurd.

7. In *Death in the Afternoon* Hemingway says that death is the supreme remedy for all misfortunes (104).

Bibliography

Aaron, Raymond. *L'opium des intellectuels.* Paris: Calmann-Lévy, 1955.

Albérès, R. M. "André Malraux and the 'Abridged Abyss.'" Trans. Kevin Neilson. *Yale French Studies* 18 (1957): 45–54.

Alden, Douglas W. "Proust and the Flaubert Controversy." *Madame Bovary and the Critics.* Ed. B. F. Bart. New York: New York University Press, 1966. 65–72.

Ansermoz-Dubois, Félix. *L'interprétation française de la littérature américaine d'entre-deux-guerres.* Lausanne: Concorde, 1944.

Apollinaire, Guillaume. *Alcools.* Paris: Gallimard, 1920.

———. *Calligrammes.* Paris: Gallimard, 1925.

———. "Les mamelles de Tirésias." *Oeuvres poétiques.* Paris: Gallimard, Pléiade, 1956. 1864–913.

Artaud, Antonin. "Le théâtre de la cruauté." *Le théâtre et son double.* Paris: Gallimard, 1964. 129–52.

Asselineau, Roger. *Ernest Hemingway.* Paris: Seghers, 1972.

———. "French Reactions to Hemingway's Works between the Two World Wars." *The Literary Reputation of Hemingway in Europe.* Ed. Roger Asselineau. New York: New York University Press, 1965. 39–72.

———. "Hemingway's Reputation in France since His Death in 1961." Special European issue of *Hemingway Review* 11 (Summer 1992): 75–80.

Atherton, John. "The Itinerary of the Postcard: Minimal Strategies in *The Sun Also Rises.*" *ELH* 53 (1986): 199–218.

Axelos, Kostas. *Vers la pensée planétaire.* Paris: Minuit, 1964.

Baker, Carlos. *Ernest Hemingway: Critiques of Four Major Novels.* Ed. Carlos Baker. New York: Scribner, 1962.

———. *Ernest Hemingway: A Life Story.* New York: Scribner, 1969.

———, ed. *Ernest Hemingway: Selected Letters, 1917–1961.* New York: Scribner, 1981.

———. *Hemingway: The Writer as Artist.* Princeton, NJ: Princeton University Press, 1970.

———. "Two African Stories." *Hemingway: A Collection of Critical Essays.* Ed. Robert P. Weeks. Englewood Cliffs, NJ: Prentice Hall, 1962. 118–26.

Baker, Jean-Claude, and Chris Chase. *Josephine: The Hungry Heart.* New York: Random House, 1993.

Barthes, Roland. *By Roland Barthes.* Trans. Richard Howard. New York: Hill and Wang, 1977.

———. "The Death of the Author." *Modern Criticism and Theory.* Ed. David Lodge. New York: Longman, 1988. 167–72.

———. *Le plaisir du texte.* Paris: Seuil, 1973.

———. *Roland Barthes.* Paris: Seuil, 1975.

———. *S/Z.* Trans. Richard Miller. New York: Hill and Wang, 1974.

Baudelaire, Charles. *Les fleurs du mal.* Paris: Gallimard, 1961.

Baym, Max I. "Franco-American Literary Relations." *Dictionary of French Literature.* Ed. Sidney D. Braun. New York: Philosophical Library, 1958. 130–37.

Baym, Nina. "Actually, I Felt Sorry for the Lion." Benson 112–20.

Beach, Sylvia. *Shakespeare and Company.* New York: Harcourt, Brace, 1956.

Beauvoir, Simone de. *La force de l'âge.* Paris: Gallimard, 1960.

———. *The Prime of Life.* Trans. Peter Green. New York: Lawrence Books, 1962.

Beck, Roger. *Planetary Gods and Planetary Orders of the Mysteries of Mithras.* Etudes préliminaires aux religions orientales dans l'empire romain 9. Leiden: E. J. Brill. 1988.

Beck, Warren. "The Shorter Happy Life of Mrs. Macomber." *Modern Fiction Studies* 1 (1955): 28–37.

Beemer, Lawrence. "Mule Variations: Pack Animals as Symbolism in Hemingway and Faulkner." Paper given at the Tenth International Hemingway Conference. Stresa, Italy, July 4, 2002.

Benson, Jackson J. *Hemingway: The Writer's Art of Self-Defense.* Minneapolis: University of Minnesota Press, 1969.

———, ed. *New Critical Approaches to the Short Stories of Ernest Hemingway.* Durham, NC: Duke University Press, 1990.

Berman, Ron. "Recurrence in Hemingway and Cézanne." *Hemingway Review* 23 (2004): 21–36.

Blanchot, Maurice. *Arrêt de mort.* Paris: Gallimard, 1977.

Botticelli, Sandro. *The Birth of Venus.* Uffizi Gallery, Florence.

Bradbury, Malcolm. *Dangerous Pilgrimages.* London: Penguin, 1995.

Braudel, Fernand. *The Perspective of the World.* Trans. Siân Reynolds. Berkeley: University of California Press, 1992.

Bredendick, Nancy. "'¿Qué tal, hombre, qué tal?': How Paratexts Narrow the Gap between Reader and Text in *Death in the Afternoon.*" Mandel 205–34.

Brée, Germaine. *Camus.* New Brunswick, NJ: Rutgers University Press, 1959.

———. *Camus and Sartre: Crisis and Commitment.* New York: Dell, 1972.

———. *Twentieth-Century French Literature.* Trans. Louise Guiney. Chicago: University of Chicago Press, 1983.

Brée, Germaine, and Margaret Guiton. "Return to Man: André Malraux—Maker of Myths." *The French Novel: From Gide to Camus.* New York: Harcourt, Brace, 1962. 180–93.

Breit, Harvey. "Talk with Mr. Hemingway." *New York Times Book Review,* Sept. 17, 1950: 14.

Brenner, Gerry. *Concealments in Hemingway's Works.* Columbus: Ohio State University Press, 1983.

Breuer, Horst. "Hemingway's 'Francis Macomber' in Pirandellian and Freudian Perspectives." *Studies in American Fiction* 31 (2003): 233–49.

Brodin, Pierre. *Les écrivains américains de l'entre-deux-guerres.* Paris: Horizons de France, 1946.

Brogan, Jacqueline Vaught. "Hemingway's *In Our Time:* A Cubist Anatomy." *Hemingway Review* 17 (1998): 31–46.

Brombert, Victor. "Malraux: Passion and Intellect." *Yale French Studies* 18 (1957): 63–76.

———. *The Novels of Flaubert.* Princeton, NJ: Princeton University Press, 1966.

Bruccoli, Matthew J., ed. *Conversations with Ernest Hemingway.* Jackson: University Press of Mississippi, 1986.

Bruneau, Jean. "Existentialism and the American Novel." *Yale French Studies* 1 (1948): 66–72.

Bryer, Jackson. *The Heart of Artemis.* New York: Harcourt, Brace, 1962.

Burnett, Whit, ed. *This Is My Best.* New York: Dial, 1942.

Camus, Albert. *Caligula.* In *Théâtre, récits, nouvelles* 3–108.

———. *Essais.* Paris: Gallimard, Pléiade, 1965.

———. *L'état de siège.* In *Théâtre, récits, nouvelles* 181–300.

———. *L'étranger.* In *Théâtre, récits, nouvelles* 1121–1210.

———. *L'homme révolté.* In *Essais* 407–709.

———. *Les justes.* In *Théâtre, récits, nouvelles* 301–93.

———. *Le malentendu.* In *Théâtre, récits, nouvelles* 109–80.

———. *Le mythe de Sisyphe.* In *Essais* 89–211.

———. *The Myth of Sisyphus.* Trans. Justin O'Brien. New York: Knopf, 1955.

———. "Noces." In *Essais* 51–88.

———. *La peste.* In *Théâtre, récits, nouvelles* 1211–472.

———. "Réflexions sur la guillotine." In *Essais* 1019–64.

———. *The Stranger.* Trans. Matthew Ward. New York: Knopf, 1988.

———. *Théâtre, récits, nouvelles.* Paris: Gallimard, Pléiade, 1962.

Casanova, Pascale. *The World Republic of Letters.* Trans. M. B. deBevoise. Cambridge, MA: Harvard University Press, 2004.

Catalano, Susan M. "Henpecked to Heroism: Placing Rip Van Winkle and Francis Macomber in the American Renegade Tradition." *Hemingway Review* 17 (1998): 111–17.

Cendrars, Blaise. *L'or: La merveilleuse histoire du Général Johann August Suter. Oeuvres completes.* Vol. 2. Paris: Denoël, 1960. 109–225.

———. "Le Panama ou les aventures de mes sept oncles." *Oeuvres complètes.* Vol. 1. Paris: Denoël, 1960. 34–49.

———. *Prose du Transsibérien et de la petite Jehanne de France.* Paris: Denoël, 1913.

———. *Le Transsibérien.* Paris: Seghers, 1957.

Cestre, Charles. "Ernest Hemingway: *Torrents of Spring.*" *La Revue Anglo-Améri-caine,* Aug. 1933: 574–75.

———. Review of *In Our Time. La Revue Anglo-Américaine,* April 1933: 372.

Chinard, Gilbert. *L'Amérique et le rêve exotique dans la littérature française.* Par-is: Droz, 1934.

Cocteau, Jean. *Les mariés de la Tour Eiffel.* Paris: Gallimard, 1923.

Cohen, Milton A. *Hemingway's Laboratory: The Paris in our time.* Tuscaloosa: University of Alabama Press, 2005.

Coindreau, Maurice. *Aperçus de littérature américaine.* Paris: Gallimard, 1946.

———. "Ernest Hemingway: *To Have and Have Not.*" *La Nouvelle Revue Fran-çaise* 26 (1938): 501–4.

———. "William Faulkner in France." *Yale French Studies* 10 (1952): 85–91.

Coover, Robert. *Spanking the Maid.* New York: Grove, 1982.

Courcel, Martine de. *Malraux: Life and Work.* New York: Harcourt, 1976.

Cowley, Malcolm. *A Second Flowering: Works and Days of the Lost Generation.* London: André Deutsch, 1973.

Cuisenier, André. *L'art de Jules Romains.* Paris: Flammarion, 1948.

———. *Jules Romains et l'unanimisme.* Paris: Flammarion, 1935.

Cumont, Franz. *Textes et monuments figurés relatifs aux mystères de Mithra,* 2 vols. Brussels: H. Lamertin, 1896, 1899.

Danby-Smith, Valerie. "Reminiscences of Hemingway." *Saturday Review,* May 9, 1964: 30–31, 57.

Davidson, Arnold E. "The Ambivalent End of Francis Macomber's Short Happy Life." *Hemingway Notes* 2 (1972): 14–16.

DeFalco, Joseph. *The Hero in Hemingway's Short Stories.* Pittsburgh: University of Pittsburgh Press, 1963.

Debray-Genette, Raymonde, ed. *Flaubert.* Paris: Didier, 1970.

Derrida, Jacques. *La dissémination.* Paris: Seuil, 1972.

———. *L'écriture et la différence.* Paris: Seuil, 1967.

———. *Of Grammatology.* Trans. Gayatri Chakravorty Spivak. Baltimore: Johns Hopkins University Press, 1974.

———. *The Post Card: From Socrates to Freud and Beyond.* Trans. Alan Bass. Chicago: University of Chicago Press, 1987.

Desternes, Jean. "Que pensez-vous de la littératre américaine?" *Combat,* Jan. 17, 1947: 2.

Dillingham, William B. "Hemingway and Death." *Emory University Quarterly* 19 (1963): 95–102.

Dos Passos, John. *The Best Times.* New York: New American Library, 1966.

Dragunoiu, Dana. "Hemingway's Debt to Stendhal's *Armance* in *The Sun Also Rises.*" *Modern Fiction Studies* 46 (2000): 868–92.

Drieu La Rochelle, Pierre-Eugène. Foreword. *L'adieu aux armes.* Paris: Galli-mard, 1932.

Duhamel, Georges. *Civilisation, 1914–1917.* Paris: Mercure, 1925.

———. *Scènes de la vie future.* Paris: Mercure, 1930.

Durkheim, Emile. *Les règles de la méthode sociologique.* Paris: Alcan, 1927.

Dussinger, Gloria R. "'The Snows of Kilimanjaro': Harry's Second Chance." Howell 158–61.

Eby, Carl P. *Hemingway's Fetishism: Psychoanalysis and the Mirror of Manhood.* Albany: State University of New York Press, 1998.

Eddins, Dwight. "Of Rocks and Marlin: The Existentialist Agon in Camus's *The Myth of Sisyphus* and Hemingway's *The Old Man and the Sea.*" *Hemingway Review* 21 (2001): 68–77.

Eliot, T. S. *Selected Essays, 1917–1932.* New York: Harcourt, 1932.

Empson, William. *Seven Types of Ambiguity.* New York: Meridian, 1958.

Evans, Oliver. "'The Snows of Kilimanjaro': A Revaluation." Howell 150–57.

Fantina, Richard. "Hemingway's Masochism, Sodomy, and the Dominant Woman." *Hemingway Review* 23 (2003): 84–105.

Federman, Raymond. *Double or Nothing.* Chicago: Swallow, 1971.

Felman, Shoshana. "Beyond Oedipus: The Specimen Story of Psychoanalysis." *Lacan and Narration: The Psychoanalytic Difference in Narrative Theory.* Ed. Robert Con Davis. Baltimore: Johns Hopkins University Press, 1983. 1021–53.

———. "On Reading Poetry: Reflexions on the Limits and Possibilities of Psychoanalytic Approaches." Muller and Richardson 133–56.

Flaubert, Gustave. "Un cœur simple." *Trois contes.* Paris: Garnier, 1956. 1–73.

———. *Correspondance.* Vol. 2. Paris: Gallimard, Pléiade, 1980.

———. *Madame Bovary.* Paris: Garnier, 1960.

Fleming, Robert E. "Communism vs. Community in *For Whom the Bell Tolls.*" *North Dakota Quarterly* 60 (1992): 144–50.

Frank, Joseph. "Spatial Form in Modern Literature." *Criticism: The Foundations of Modern Literary Judgment.* Ed. Mark Schorer, J. Miles, and G. McKenzie. Berkeley: University of California Press, 1958. 379–92.

Freud, Sigmund. *Beyond the Pleasure Principle.* Vol. 18 in *The Standard Edition of the Complete Psychological Works.* Trans. James Strachey. London: Hogarth, 1953.

———. *The Interpretation of Dreams.* Vol. 4 in *The Standard Edition of the Complete Psychological Works.* Trans. James Strachey. London: Hogarth, 1953.

Frohock, W. M. "Violence and Discipline." *Ernest Hemingway: The Man and His Work.* Ed. John K. M. McCaffery. Cleveland: World, 1950. 262–91.

Gaillard, Theodore L., Jr. "Hemingway's Debt to Cézanne: New Perspectives." *Twentieth Century Literature* 45 (1999): 65–78.

Gajdusek, Robert E. *Hemingway's Paris.* New York: Scribner, 1978.

Garet, Jean-Louis. *Un écrivain dans le siècle: Henry de Montherlant.* Paris: Ecrivains, 1999.

Garrick, John. "Two Bulls Locked Horn in Horn in Fight: The Rivalry of Hemingway and Malraux in Spain." *North Dakota Quarterly* 60 (1992): 8–18.

Gide, André. *Corydon.* Paris: Gallimard, 1924.

———. *Les faux-monnayeurs.* In *Romans, récits et soties* 931–1248.

———. *Incidences.* Paris: Gallimard, 1924.

———. *L'immoraliste.* In *Romans, récits et soties* 365–472.

———. *Journal, 1939–1949.* Paris: Gallimard, Pléiade, 1954.

———. *Le mariage du ciel et de l'enfer.* Paris: Corti, 1965.

———. *Les nourritures terrestres.* In *Romans, récits et soties* 152–248.

———. *Oedipe. Théâtre.* Paris: Gallimard, 1942. 249–303.

———. *Romans, récits et soties. Oeuvres lyriques.* Paris: Gallimard, Pléiade, 1958.

———. "Le voyage d'Urien." In *Romans, récits et soties* 13–68.

Ginsberg, Robert. *The Critique of War: Contemporary Philosophical Explorations.* Chicago: Regnery, 1969.

Giono, Jean. *Le chant du monde.* Paris: Gallimard, 1934.

Gordimer, Nadine. "Hemingway's Expatriates." *Transition* 80 (1999): 86–99.

Gordon, Caroline, and Allen Tate. "'The Snows of Kilimanjaro': Commentary." *The House of Fiction: An Anthology of the Short Story.* New York: Scribner, 1950. 419–23.

Greco, Anne. "Margot Macomber: 'Bitch Goddess' Exonerated." *Fitzgerald/Hemingway Annual, 1972.* Ed. Matthew J. Bruccoli and C. E. Frazer Clark Jr. Dayton, OH: NCR Microcard Editions, 1973. 273–80.

Griffith, Alison. "Mithraism." *Exploring Ancient World Cultures.* http://eawc.evansville.edu/essays/mithraism.htm.

Halliday, E. M. "Hemingway's Ambiguity: Symbolism and Irony." *Hemingway: A Collection of Critical Essays.* Ed. Robert P. Weeks. Englewood Cliffs, NJ: Prentice Hall, 1962. 52–71.

Halverson, John. "Christian Resonance in *The Old Man and the Sea.*" *English Language Notes* 2 (1956): 50–54.

Harris, Susan K. "Vicious Binaries: Gender and Authorial Paranoia in Dreiser's 'Second Choice,' Howells' 'Editha,' and Hemingway's 'The Short Happy Life of Francis Macomber.'" *College Literature* 20 (1993): 70–83.

Hartman, Geoffrey H. "The Taming of History." *Yale French Studies* 18 (1957): 114–28.

Hemingway, Ernest. *Across the River and into the Trees.* New York: Scribner, 1950.

———. *L'adieu aux armes.* Trans. Maurice Coindreau. Paris: Gallimard, 1932.

———. "Cinquante mille dollars." Trans. Ott de Weymer. *La Nouvelle Revue Française* 29 (1927): 161–91.

———. *Cinquante mille dollars.* Trans. Ott de Weymer. Paris: Gallimard, 1928.

———. "A Clean, Well-Lighted Place." *The Short Stories of Ernest Hemingway* 379–83.

———. *The Complete Short Stories of Ernest Hemingway.* The Finca Vigía Edition. New York: Scribner, 1987.

———. *The Dangerous Summer.* New York: Scribner, 1960.

———. *Death in the Afternoon.* New York: Scribner, 1932.

———. *Dix indiens.* Trans. Marcel Duhamel. Paris: Gallimard, 1946.

———. *En avoir ou pas.* Trans. Marcel Duhamel. Paris: Gallimard, 1945.

———. *A Farewell to Arms.* New York: Scribner, 1929.

———. "Fascism Is a Lie." *New Masses,* June 22, 1937: 4.

———. *The Fifth Column and Four Stories of the Spanish Civil War.* New York: Scribner, 1969.

———. *For Whom the Bell Tolls.* New York: Scribner, 1940.

———. "The Franco-German Situation." *Dateline: Toronto.* New York: Scribner, 1985. 260.

———. *The Garden of Eden.* New York: Scribner, 1986.

———. *Green Hills of Africa.* New York: Scribner, 1935.

———. *Hemingway: Nouvelles complètes.* Ed. Antoine Jacottet. Paris: Gallimard, 1999.

———. "L'heure triomphale de Francis Macomber." Trans. Marcel Duhamel. *Carrefour,* Feb. 9, 1949; Feb. 16, 1949; Feb. 23, 1949; March 2, 1949; March 9, 1949.

———. "Humanity Will Not Forgive This." *Pravda,* Aug. 1938: 4.

———. *in our time.* Paris: Three Mountains Press, 1924.

———. *In Our Time.* New York: Scribner, 1925.

———. "L'invincible." Trans. Georges Duplaix. *Le Navire d'Argent* 2 (1926): 161–94.

———. *Islands in the Stream.* New York: Scribner, 1970.

———. *Men without Women.* New York: Scribner, 1927.

———. *Mort dans l'après-midi.* Trans. René Daumal. Paris: Gallimard, 1938.

———. *A Moveable Feast.* New York: Scribner, 1964.

———. *Les neiges du Kilimandjaro et autres nouvelles.* Trans. Marcel Duhamel. Paris: Gallimard, 1957.

———. *The Old Man and the Sea.* New York: Scribner, 1952.

———. *Pour qui sonne le glas.* Trans. Denise van Moppès. Paris: Gallimard, 1950.

———. "Propre et bien éclairé." Trans. Marcel Duhamel. *Solstice,* June 1946: 143–48.

———. *Selected Letters, 1917–1961.* Ed. Carlos Baker. New York: Scribner, 1981.

———. "The Short Happy Life of Francis Macomber." *The Short Stories of Ernest Hemingway* 1–37.

———. *The Short Stories of Ernest Hemingway.* New York: Scribner, 1953.

———. "The Snows of Kilimanjaro." *The Short Stories of Ernest Hemingway* 52–77.

———. *Le soleil se lève aussi.* Trans. Maurice Coindreau. Paris: Gallimard, 1933.

———. *The Sun Also Rises.* New York: Scribner, 1926.

———. *To Have and Have Not.* New York: Scribner, 1937.

———. *The Torrents of Spring.* New York: Scribner, 1926.

———. *True at First Light.* New York: Scribner, 1999.

———. *Under Kilimanjaro.* Ed. Robert W. Lewis and Robert E. Fleming. Kent, OH: Kent State University Press, 2005.

———. *Les vertes collines d'Afrique.* Trans. Jeanine Delpech. Paris: Gallimard, 1937.

———. *Le vieil homme et la mer.* Trans. Jean Dutour. Paris: Gallimard, 1952.

Hicks, Granville. "Twenty Years of Hemingway." *New Republic,* Oct. 23, 1944: 524, 526.

Hily-Mane, Geneviève. *Ernest Hemingway in France, 1926–1994: A Comprehensive Bibliography.* Reims: CIRLEP, 1995.

Hinkle, James. "What's Funny in *The Sun Also Rises*." *Ernest Hemingway: Six Decades of Criticism*. Ed. Linda W. Wagner. East Lansing: Michigan State University Press, 1987. 77–92.

Hoffman, Steven K. "Nada and the Clean, Well-Lighted Place: The Unity of Hemingway's Short Fiction." Benson 172–91.

Hoog, Armand. "Malraux, Möllberg and Frobenices." *Yale French Studies* 18 (1957): 87–96.

———. "The Romantic Spirit and the American 'Elsewhere.'" *Yale French Studies* 10 (1952): 14–28.

Howell, John H., ed. *Hemingway's African Stories: The Stories, Their Sources, Their Critics*. New York: Scribner, 1969.

Hubert, Renée Riese, and Judd D. Hubert. "Masson's and Mallarmé's *Un coup de dés*: An Esthetic Comparison." *Nineteenth-Century French Studies* 18 (1990): 508–23.

Hutton, Virgil. "The Short Happy Life of Macomber." *University Review* [Kansas City] 30 (1964): 253–63.

Ibañez, Beatriz Penas. "Hemingway's Ethics of Writing: The Ironic Semantics of 'Whiteness' in 'The Snows of Kilimanjaro.'" *North Dakota Quarterly* 70 (2003): 94–118.

———. "'Very Sad but Very Fine': *Death in the Afternoon*'s Imagist Interpretation of the Bullfight-Text." Mandel 143–64.

Jakobson, Roman. *Fundamentals of Language*. The Hague: Mouton, 1956.

James, Jamie. "The 'Solitary Volcano.'" *Los Angeles Times Book Review*, Jan. 6, 2008: R2.

Jobst, Jack, and W. J. Williamson. "Hemingway and Maupassant: More Light on 'The Light of the World.'" *Hemingway Review* 13 (1994): 52–61.

Jones, Robert B. "Mimesis and Metafiction in Hemingway's *The Garden of Eden*." *Hemingway Review* 7 (1987): 2–13.

Josephs, Allen. "Hemingway's Spanish Sensibility." *The Cambridge Companion to Hemingway*. Ed. Scott Donaldson. New York: Cambridge University Press, 1996. 221–42.

Justice, Hilary K. "'Prejudiced through Experience': *Death in the Afternoon* and the Problem of Authorship." Mandel 237–56.

Kennedy, J. Gerald. *Imagining Paris: Exile Writing and American Identity*. New Haven, CT: Yale University Press, 1993.

Kennedy, J. Gerald, and Jackson Bryer, eds. *French Connections: Hemingway and Fitzgerald Abroad*. New York: St. Martin's Press, 1998.

Kenner, Hugh. "Ezra Pound and the Light of France." *Yale French Studies* 10 (1952): 54–64.

Killinger, John. *Hemingway and the Dead Gods: A Study in Existentialism*. [Lexington]: University of Kentucky Press, 1960.

Krieger, Murray. *Words about Words about Words: Theory Criticism and the Literary Text*. Baltimore: Johns Hopkins University Press, 1988.

Lacan, Jacques. *Ecrits: A Selection.* Trans. Alan Sheridan. New York: Norton, 1977.

———. *Ecrits I.* Paris: Seuil, 1966.

———. *Le Séminaire: Livre II. Le moi dans la théorie de Freud et dans la technique de la psychanalyse.* Ed. Jacques-Alain Miller. Paris: Seuil, 1978.

———. "Seminar on 'The Purloined Letter.'" Trans. Jeffrey Mehlman. Muller and Richardson. Baltimore: Johns Hopkins University Press, 1988. 28–54.

Lacasse, Rodolphe. *Hemingway et Malraux: Destins de l'homme.* Montreal: Cosmos, 1972.

Lacouture, Jean. *André Malraux.* Trans. Alan Sheridan. New York: Pantheon, 1975.

Larbaud, Valery. *Ce vice impuni, la lecture: Domains anglais.* Paris: Gallimard, 1925.

———. "Paris de France." *Jaune, bleu, blanc.* Paris: Gallimard, 1927. 7–30.

Lathan, Aaron. "A Farewell to Machismo." *New York Times Magazine,* Oct. 16, 1977: 52–55, 80–82.

Lawson, Carolina Donadio. "Hemingway, Stendhal, and War." *Hemingway Notes* 6 (1981): 28–33.

Le Bon, Gustave. *Psychologie des foules.* Paris: Presses Universitaires de France, 1939.

Lehan, Richard. *A Dangerous Crossing: French Literary Existentialism and the Modern American Novel.* Carbondale: Southern Illinois University Press, 1973.

Levet, Henry J.-M. "Cartes postales." *Poèmes.* Paris: La Maison des amis des livres, 1921. 69–79.

Levin, Harry. *Refractions: Essays in Comparative Literature.* London: Oxford University Press, 1966.

Lewis, Robert W., ed. *Hemingway in Italy and Other Essays.* New York: Praeger, 1990.

———. "Hemingway, Malraux and the Warrior-Writer." *North Dakota Quarterly* 60 (1992): 58–71.

———. "Vivienne de Watteville, Hemingway's Companion on Kilimanjaro." Howell 101–9.

Lisca, Peter. "The Structure of Hemingway's *Across the River and into the Trees.*" *Modern Fiction Studies* 12 (1966): 232–50.

Listoe, Daniel. "Writing toward Death: The Stylistic Necessities of the Last Journey of Ernest Hemingway." *North Dakota Quarterly* 64 (1997): 89–95.

Llona, Victor. "The Sun Also Rose for Ernest Hemingway." *Fitzgerald/Hemingway Annual, 1972.* Ed. Matthew J. Bruccoli and C. E. Frazer Clark Jr. Dayton, OH: NCR Microcard Editions, 1973. 159–71.

MacLeish, Archibald. *A Continuing Journey.* Boston: Houghton Mifflin, 1968.

Madsen, Axel. *Malraux: A Biography.* New York: Morrow, 1976.

Magny, Claude-Edmonde. *L'âge du roman américain.* Paris: Seuil, 1948.

Malherbe, Henry. *La flame au poing.* Paris: Albin Michel, 1917.

Mallarmé, Stéphane. *Poésies.* Paris: Gallimard, 1952.

———. *Un coup de dés jamais n'abolira le hasard.* Paris: Gallimard, 1914.

———. *Un coup de dés jamais n'abolira le hasard.* Paris: Amateurs du Livre et de l'estampe moderne, 1961. Lithographs by André Masson.

Malraux, André. *La condition humaine*. Paris: Gallimard, 1933.

———. *Les conquérants*. Paris: Grasset, 1928.

———. *Days of Wrath*. Trans. Haakon M. Chevalier. New York: Random House, 1939.

———. *L'espoir*. Paris: Gallimard, 1937.

———. *Man's Fate*. Trans. Haakon M. Chevalier. New York: Modern Library, 1934.

———. *Man's Hope*. Trans. Stuart Gilbert and Alastair MacDonald. New York: Random House, 1938.

———. *Les noyers de l'Altenburg*. Paris: Gallimard, 1948.

———. "A Preface for Faulkner's *Sanctuary*." *Yale French Studies* 10 (1952): 92–94. Anonymously translated and reprinted from *La Nouvelle Revue Française* 41 (1933): 744–47.

———. *Le temps du mépris*. Paris: Gallimard, 1935.

———. "Three Speeches: Our Cultural Heritage." Trans. Kenneth Douglas. *Yale French Studies* 18 (1957): 27–38.

———. *La voie royale*. Paris: Grasset, 1930.

———. *The Voices of Silence*. Trans. Stuart Gilbert. New York: Doubleday, 1953.

———. *Les voix du silence*. Paris: Gallimard, Pléiade, 1951.

Mandel, Miriam B., ed. *A Companion to Hemingway's* Death in the Afternoon. Rochester, NY: Camden House, 2004.

Marion, Denis. "Ernest Hemingway, *L'adieu aux armes*." *La Nouvelle Revue Française* 41 (1933): 632–33.

Marx, Karl, and Friedrich Engels. "The Communist Manifesto." *On Revolution*. Vol. 1 of *The Karl Marx Library*. Ed. and trans. S. K. Padover. New York: McGraw-Hill, 1971. 79–107.

Maurois, André. *A la recherche de Marcel Proust*. Paris: Hachette, 1949.

Mayoux, Jean-Jacques. "Ernest Hemingway: *To Have and Have Not*." *Etudes anglaises* 2 (1938): 194–95.

Meredith, James H. "The Rapido River and the Hürtgen Forest in *Across the River and into the Trees*." *Hemingway Review* 134 (1994): 60–66.

Messent, Peter. "'The Real Thing'? Representing the Bullfight and Spain in *Death in the Afternoon*." Mandel 123–41.

Meyers, Jeffrey. *Hemingway: A Biography*. New York: Harper, 1983.

Michaud, Régis. *Panorama de la littérature américaine contemporaine*. Paris: Kra, 1928.

Michaux, Henri. "Lieux lointains." *Mercure de France*, no. 1109 (1956): 52.

Miller, Paul W. "Hemingway vs. Stendhal, or Papa's Last Fight with a Dead Writer." *Hemingway Review* 19 (1999): 127–40.

Moddelmog, Debra A. *Reading Desire: In Pursuit of Ernest Hemingway*. Ithaca, NY: Cornell University Press, 1999.

Monnier, Adrienne. *Rue de l'Odéon*. Paris: Albin Michel, 1960.

Monteiro, George. "Hemingway's Colonel." *Hemingway Review* 5 (1985): 40–45.

Montgomery, Marion. "The Leopard and the Hyena: Symbol and Meaning in 'The Snows of Kilimanjaro.'" Howell 145–49.

Montherlant, Henry de. *Les bestiaires*. Paris: Gallimard, 1954.

———. *The Bullfighters*. Trans. Edwin Giles Rich. New York: Dial, 1927.

———. *Chant funèbre pour les morts de Verdun*. Paris: Grasset, 1924.

———. *Le chaos et la nuit*. In *Romans* 852–1047.

———. *Le maître de Santiago*. Paris: Gallimard, 1947.

———. *Les olympiques*. Paris: Grasset, 1938.

———. *Le reine morte*. Paris: Gallimard, 1948.

———. *Romans*. Ed. Michel Raimond. Vol. 2. Paris: Gallimard, Pléiade, 1982.

———. *La rose de sable*. In *Romans* 1–428.

Morgan, Kathleen, and Luis A. Losada. "Tracking the Wounded Buffalo: Authorial Knowledge and the Shooting of Francis Macomber." *Hemingway Review* 11 (1991): 25–30.

Muller, John P., and William J. Richardson, eds. *The Purloined Poe: Lacan, Derrida, and Psychoanalytic Reading*. Baltimore: Johns Hopkins University Press, 1988.

Nakjavani, Erik. "The Aesthetics of the Visible and the Invisible: Hemingway and Cézanne." *Hemingway Review* 2 (1986): 2–11.

———. "Knowledge as Power: Robert Jordan as an Intellectual Hero." *Hemingway Review* 7 (1988): 131–46.

———. "The Prose of Life: Lived Experience in the Fiction of Hemingway, Sartre and Beauvoir." *North Dakota Quarterly* 70 (2003): 140–65.

Nietzsche, Friederich Wilhelm. *Thus Spoke Zarathustra: A Book for All and No One*. Trans. Marianne Cowan. Chicago: Regnery, 1957.

Noble, Donald R., ed. *Hemingway: A Revaluation*. Troy, NY: Whitson, 1983.

Oldsey, Bernard. "Hemingway's Beginnings and Endings." *College Literature* 7 (1980): 213–38.

———. *Hemingway's Hidden Craft: The Writing of* A Farewell to Arms. University Park: Pennsylvania State University Press, 1979.

Oliver, Charles M. *Ernest Hemingway A to Z: The Essential Reference to the Life and Work*. New York: Facts on File, 1999.

———. "Hemingway's Study of Impending Death: *Across the River and into the Trees*." Lewis 143–52.

Olson, Robert G. *An Introduction to Existentialism*. New York: Dover, 1962.

Perruchot, Henri. *Montherlant*. Paris: Gallimard, 1959.

Peyre, Henri. *French Novelists of Today*. New York: Oxford University Press, 1967.

Picon, Gaëtan. *Malraux par lui-même*. Paris: Seuil, 1955.

Plimpton, George. "Ernest Hemingway: The Art of Fiction XXI." *Paris Review* 18 (1958): 84.

Pound, Ezra. *ABC of Reading*. New York: New Directions, 1960.

Prévost, Jean. Foreword. *Le soleil se lève aussi*. Paris: Gallimard, 1933. 7–11.

Proust, Marcel. *A la recherche du temps perdu*. 3 vols. Paris: Gallimard, Pléiade, 1954.

———. "A propos du style de Flaubert." *Flaubert*. Ed. Raymonde Debray-Genette. Paris: Didier, 1970. 46–55.

Ragland-Sullivan, Ellie. "The Magnetism between Reader and Text: Prolegomena to a Lacanian Poetics." *Poetics* 13 (1984): 381–406.

Renan, Ernst. *Marc-Aurèle et la fin du monde antique*. Paris: Calmann Lévy, 1882.

Reusch, Richard. "Mt. Kilimanjaro and Its Ascent." Howell 99.

Reynolds, Michael. *Hemingway: The Final Years*. New York: Norton, 1999.

———. *Hemingway: The 1930s*. New York: Norton, 1997.

———. *Hemingway: The Paris Years*. New York: Norton, 1989.

———. *Hemingway's First War: The Making of* A Farewell to Arms. Princeton, NJ: Princeton University Press, 1976.

———. *Hemingway's Reading, 1910–1940: An Inventory*. Princeton, NJ: Princeton University Press, 1981.

———. The Sun Also Rises: *A Novel of the Twenties*. Boston: G. K. Hall, 1988.

———. *The Young Hemingway*. New York: Blackwell, 1986.

Robbe-Grillet, Alain. *Glissements progressifs du plaisir*. Paris: Minuit, 1974.

Romains, Jules. *Le bourg régénéré*. Paris: Vanier, 1906.

———. *Les hommes de bonne volonté*. 27 vols. Paris: Flammarion, 1932–1946.

———. *Knock*. Paris: Gallimard, 1924.

———. *Manuel de déification*. Paris: Sansot, 1910.

———. *Puissances de Paris*. Paris: Gallimard, 1919.

———. *Verdun*. Paris: Flammarion, 1938.

———. *La vie unanime*. Paris: L'Abbaye, 1908.

Ross, Ishbel. *The Expatriates*. New York: Crowell, 1970.

San Juan, E., Jr. "Ideological Form, Symbolic Exchange, Textual Production: A Symptomatic Reading of *For Whom the Bell Tolls*." *North Dakota Quarterly* 60 (1992): 119–43.

Sartre, Jean-Paul. "American Novelists in French Eyes." *Atlantic Monthly* 178 (1946): 114–18.

———. *Being and Nothingness: An Essay on Phenomenological Ontology*. Trans. Hazel E. Barnes. New York: Philosophical Library, 1956.

———. *The Chips Are Down*. Trans. Louise Varèse. London: Rider, 1951.

———. *Le diable et le bon Dieu*. Paris: Gallimard, 1951.

———. *L'être et le néant*. Paris: Gallimard, 1943.

———. *L'existentialisme est un humanisme*. Paris: Nagel, 1952.

———. *The Family Idiot*. Trans. Carol Cosman. Chicago: University of Chicago Press, 1981.

———. *Huis clos*. In *Théâtre* 111–68.

———. *L'idiot de la famille: Gustave Flaubert de 1821 à 1857*. Paris: Gallimard, 1970.

———. *Les jeux sont faits*. Paris: Nagel, 1946.

———. "The Living Gide." *Situations*. Trans. Benita Eisler. New York: Braziller, 1965. 50–53.

———. *La mort dans l'âme*. Paris: Gallimard, 1949.

———. *Morts sans sepulture*. In *Théâtre* 169–251.

———. *Les mouches*. In *Théâtre* 7–109.

———. *Le mur*. Paris: Gallimard, 1939.

————. *Nausea*. Trans. Lloyd Alexander. New York: New Directions, 1964.

————. *La nausée*. Paris: Gallimard, 1938.

————. *On Cuba*. Trans. anonymous. New York: Ballantine, 1961.

————. *Qu'est-ce que la littérature?* In *Situations II*. Paris: Gallimard, 1948. 55–330.

————. *Théâtre*. Paris: Gallimard, 1947.

————. *The Wall (Intimacy) and Other Stories*. Trans. Lloyd Alexander. New York: New Directions, 1948.

————. *What Is Literature?* Trans. Bernard Frechtman. New York: Harper, 1965.

Saussure, Ferdinand de. *Cours de linguistique générale*. 3rd ed. Paris: Payot, 1967.

Schmigalle, Gunther. "Seven Ambiguities in Ernest Hemingway's *For Whom the Bell Tolls*." *North Dakota Quarterly* 60 (1992): 72–82.

Schwartz, Nina. "Discourse in *The Sun Also Rises*: A Cock and Bull Story." *Criticism: A Quarterly for Literature and the Arts* 26 (1984): 49–69.

Shattuck, Roger. *The Banquet Years*. New York: Doubleday, 1961.

Simon, Jean. *Le roman américain au xxème siècle*. Paris: Boivin, 1950.

Sipriot, Pierre, ed. *Album Montherlant*. Paris: Gallimard, Pléiade, 1979.

Smetana, Josette. *La philosophie de l'action chez Saint-Exupéry et Hemingway*. Paris: La Marjolaine, 1965.

Smith, Paul, ed. *A Reader's Guide to the Short Stories of Ernest Hemingway*. Boston: Hall, 1989.

Smith, Thelma M., and Ward L. Miner. *Transatlantic Migration: The Contemporary American Novel in France*. Durham, NC: Duke University Press, 1955.

Sokoloff, Alice Hunt. *Hadley: The First Mrs. Hemingway*. New York: Dodd, Mead, 1973.

Sontag, Susan. *Against Interpretation*. New York: Doubleday, 1986.

Sophocles. *Oedipus at Colonus*. Trans. Robert Fitzgerald. Vol. 3 of *Greek Tragedies*. Ed. David Grene and Richard Lattimore. Chicago: University of Chicago Press, 1960. 107–87.

Spilka, Mark. *Hemingway's Quarrel with Androgyny*. Lincoln: University of Nebraska Press, 1990.

Stanton, Edward F. *Hemingway and Spain: A Pursuit*. Seattle: University of Washington Press, 1989.

Stein, Gertrude. *The Autobiography of Alice B. Toklas*. New York: Random House, 1933.

————. *The Making of Americans*. New York: Harcourt, 1934.

————. *Paris France*. New York: Scribner, 1940.

Stephens, Robert O. "Hemingway and Stendhal: The Matrix of *A Farewell to Arms*." *PMLA* 88 (1973): 271–80.

Stoltzfus, Ben. "Georges Chennevière and Les Fêtes du Peuple." *Comparative Literature* 28 (1976): 343–62.

————. *Georges Chennevière et l'unanimisme*. Paris: Minard, 1965.

————. *Gide and Hemingway: Rebels against God*. Port Washington, NY: Kennikat, 1978.

———. *Gide's Eagles*. Carbondale: Southern Illinois University Press, 1969.

———. "John Dos Passos and the French." *Comparative Literature* 2 (1963): 146–63.

Stoneback, H. R. "Hemingway and the Camargue: Van Gogh's Bedroom, the 'Gypsy' Pilgrimage, Saint-Louis, the Holy Marys, *Mirèio*, Mistral, Mithra, and Montherlant." *North Dakota Quarterly* 66 (1999): 164–95.

———. "Lovers' Sonnets Turn'd to Holy Psalms: The Soul's Song of Providence, the Scandal of Suffering, and Love in *A Farewell to Arms*." *Hemingway Review* 9 (1989): 33–76.

———. *Reading Hemingway's* The Sun Also Rises: *Glossary and Commentary*. Kent, OH: Kent State University Press, 2007.

Sugiyama, Michelle Scalise. "What's Love Got to Do with It? An Evolutionary Analysis of 'The Short Happy Life of Francis Macomber.'" *Hemingway Review* 15 (1996): 15–32.

Svoboda, Frederic Joseph. *Hemingway and* The Sun Also Rises: *The Crafting of a Style*. Lawrence: University Press of Kansas, 1983.

Swerdlow, Noel. "Review Article: On the Cosmical Mysteries of Mithras." *Classical Philology* 86 (1991): 48–63.

Sylvester, Bickford. "The Writer as *l'homme engagé*: Persona as Literary Device in Hemingway and Malraux." *North Dakota Quarterly* 60 (1992): 19–39.

Thornberry, Robert S. "Ideology and the Pragmatic Narrative: *L'espoir* Revisited." *North Dakota Quarterly* 60 (1992): 225–36.

Töpffer, Rodolphe. Unpublished notes. 1834–1836.

Turnell, Martin. "Madame Bovary." *Flaubert: A Collection of Critical Essays*. Ed. Raymond Giraud. Englewood Cliffs, NJ: Prentice Hall, 1964. 97–111.

Turner, W. Craig. "Hemingway as Artist in *Across the River and into the Trees*: A Revaluation." Noble 187–204.

Ulansey, David. *The Origins of the Mithraic Mysteries*. New York: Oxford University Press, 1989.

Valéry, Paul. *Charmes*. Paris: Gallimard, 1922.

———. "La liberté de l'esprit." *Oeuvres*. Ed. Jean Hytier. Vol. 2. Paris: Gallimard, 1960. 1077–99.

———. "La tentation de (saint) Flaubert." *Variété*. Vol. 5. Paris: Gallimard, 1944.

Vaughn, Elizabeth D. "*In Our Time* as Self-Begetting Fiction." *Modern Fiction Studies* 35 (1989): 707–16.

Verlaine, Paul. *Oeuvres complètes de Paul Verlaine*. Vol. 1. Paris: Le club du meilleur livre, 1959.

Vermeer van Delft, Jan. *View of Delft*. About 1662. Mauritshuis, The Hague.

Vondrak, Amy. "'The Sequence of Motion and Fact': Cubist Collage and Filmic Montage in *Death in the Afternoon*." Mandel 257–79.

Watson, James Gray. "'A Sound Basis of Union': Structural and Thematic Balance in 'The Short Happy Life of Francis Macomber.'" *Fitzgerald/Hemingway Annual, 1974*. Ed. Matthew J. Bruccoli and C. E. Frazer Clark Jr. Dayton, OH: NCR Microcard Editions, 1975. 215–28.

Watson, William Braasch. "Hemingway's Attacks on the Soviets and the Communists in *For Whom the Bell Tolls.*" *North Dakota Quarterly* 60 (1992): 103–18.

———. Introduction to Hemingway's "Humanity Will Not Forgive This." *Hemingway Review* 7 (1988): 114–18.

———, ed. "War Dispatches to NANA (North-Atlantic Newspaper Alliance)." *Hemingway Review* 7 (1988): 114–18.

Watts, Emily Stipes. *Ernest Hemingway and the Arts.* Urbana: University of Illinois Press, 1971.

Waugh, Patricia. *Metafiction: The Theory and Practice of Self-Conscious Fiction.* New York: Methuen, 1984.

Weeks, Robert P., ed. *Hemingway: A Collection of Critical Essays.* Englewood Cliffs, NJ: Prentice Hall, 1962.

Wickes, George. "The Right Place at the Right Time." Kennedy and Bryer 3–14.

Wilkinson, David. *Malraux: An Essay in Political Criticism.* Cambridge, MA: Harvard University Press, 1967.

Wood, James. "The Man behind Bovary." *New York Times Book Review,* April 16, 2006: 1, 10–11.

Young, Philip. *Ernest Hemingway.* New York: Rinehart, 1952.

Index

Fictional characters are alphabetized by first name.

musicality of, 31, 33, 35; objective correlatives in, 31, 34; objectivity of, xxii,
98–99, 119; plot and story line in, 22;
Pound's influence on, 3, 162n3; proleptic
images in, xxiii, xxvii, 35, 138, 159; as
prose of ecstasy, 65–66, 76; as prose poetry, 43; Proust's compared to, 130, 132,
134–35; recurring images in, 22, 26–27;
rejecting psychological analysis, xxii,
86; repetition in, 21–22, 26, 31–33, 35, 37,
40, 45–46, 52–53, 133, 138, 159; repetition
of "damn" and "hell," 50, 52; repetition
of "lovely" in, 31–35; rhetorical devices
in generating meaning, 56–57; sense
of loss in, xxi; sense of the absurd in,
xxi; shifting images in, 135; "The Short
Happy Life of Francis Macomber" as
characteristic of, 81; short sentences
in, xxii; similarity to Flaubert's, 35,
97; simultaneity in, 40, 53, 133; Stein's
influence on, 3–4, 16, 21–22; symmetry

in, 134; use of objective and subjective
simultaneously, 32; verbal clusters, 53;
in *For Whom the Bell Tolls*, 113–14; word
play in, 33–34, 38, 40, 45–48, 54. *See also*
Iceberg technique of writing
Writing style, Malraux's, 114, 119, 125; shifting images in, 120, 123
Writing styles: cablese, 16–17; Gide's, 9–11,
145, 159; in *L'espoir* vs. *For Whom the
Bell Tolls*, 118–20, 125; literariness of, 47;
musicality and polyphony of, 42–43;
psychological analysis in, xxi, 4, 119;
readers filling in levels of written and
unwritten text, 41–42; simultaneity and
juxtaposition in, 18–19, 42–43, 114, 118

Young, Philip, 82

Zhou Enlai, 105
Zola, Emile, xvii, xxiii–xxiv
"Zone" (Apollinaire), 19